Reflecting Where the Action Is

The selected works of John Elliott

John Elliott

Routledge
Taylor & Francis Group

LONDON AND NEW YORK

First published 2007
by Routledge
2 Park Square, Milton Park, Abingdon, Oxon OX14 4RN

Simultaneously published in the USA and Canada
by Routledge
270 Madison Ave, New York, NY 10016

*Routledge is an imprint of the Taylor & Francis Group,
an informa business*

© 2007 John Elliott

Typeset in Sabon and Futura by
Newgen Imaging Systems (P) Ltd, Chennai, India
Printed and bound in Great Britain by
The Cromwell Press, Trowbridge, Wiltshire

British Library Cataloguing in Publication Data
A catalogue record for this book is available
from the British Library

Library of Congress Cataloging in Publication Data
A catalog record for this book has been requested

ISBN10: 0–415–36935–5 (hbk)
ISBN10: 0–415–36993–2 (pbk)
ISBN10: 0–203–02958–5 (ebk)

ISBN13: 978–0–415–36935–0 (hbk)
ISBN13: 978–0–415–36993–0 (pbk)
ISBN13: 978–0–203–02958–9 (ebk)

For Christine

CONTENTS

ACKNOWLEDGEMENTS

Many of the ideas explored in this selection of papers emerged in the course of conversations. I have been fortunate to have spent most of my professional life in what I can only describe as 'conversational communities'. The conversations I participated in while a teacher at Senacre School during the 1960s, about how to transform the quality of life in classrooms for our students, had an enduring influence on my thinking and practice as an academic in the field of education. In particular, I owe a great deal to the school's visionary headteacher, Norman Evans, who became a life-long friend. I am also indebted to John Hipkin, Pamela and Peter Judge, Michael Head and other members of a talented professional community of teachers at Senacre and beyond.

On leaving Senacre, I had the good fortune to become a member of Lawrence Stenhouse's team, working initially with him on the Humanities Curriculum Project and then as one of his staff at the Centre for Applied Research in Education which he founded at the University of East Anglia in 1970. The design of the Ford Teaching project was heavily influenced by a conversation with Lawrence over a drink in the university staff club. Stenhouse, once described by a former colleague, David Jenkins, as "a chess player in a world of draughts," has had an enduring influence on my thinking about education and educational research, as will be evident to the reader of these chapters. I like to think that we complimented one another. He showered me with creative ideas. Sometimes I was able to show him how they shaped up in practice.

I am grateful to Barry MacDonald for the encouragement he gave me on HCP and at CARE to develop my own ideas, often via critiques of my colleagues' work including his own. Barry, however busy, was always willing to give me time for conversation. My interest in conceptualising action research as a democratic process of knowledge construction was stimulated and informed by Barry's attempt to cast programme evaluation in democratic form. Other HCP and CARE people, including collaborating teachers, have contributed to my thinking about the issues explored in these chapters, particularly Clem Adelman, Dave Ebbutt, Stephen Kemmis, Saville Kushner, Beverly Labbett, Maggie MacLure, Nigel Norris, Jean Rudduck, Helen Simons, Bridget Somekh, Ian Stronach, Brian Wakeman and Rob Walker.

Stenhouse regarded the Humanities Project as the first philosophically-based curriculum development. His design acknowledged the work of Richard Peters on 'the concept of education' and he encouraged me to study the philosophy of education under Peters at the University of London Institute of Education while working on HCP. Peters took a great interest in the project, and contributed to my thinking about the relationship between educational aims and processes and their implications for educational research. A number of Cambridge-based philosophers of education from the 'Peters' stable' saw HCP as a rich source of ideas worthy of philosophical inquiry, and maintained an enduring dialogue with Stenhouse and his team. I joined the group as a kind of 'bridging agent'. Its members included David Bridges, Richard Pring, and Hugh Sockett and, with other philosophers of education such as Wilf Carr and Joe Dunne, we came to share a philosophical agenda which was concerned to radically reconceptualise the theory–practice relationship in the educational field. This agenda and the conversations it gave rise to have significantly influenced this selection from the totality of my work. I could have given greater priority to my published research reports or contributions to the debates about educational research methods. I chose not to, and am tempted to blame my wife Christine for this. When I asked her what I should include in this volume, without hesitation she replied "your think-pieces." I immediately understood what she meant and must confess to feeling pleased with her response. The outcome of my conversations over the years with David Bridges, Wilf Carr, Richard Pring and Hugh Sockett has been to view the action research I engaged in with colleagues and teachers as a form of practical philosophy. Since this view of action research is regarded by many as a somewhat idiosyncratic one, I felt that it was important to select chapters in which I locate it in established traditions of philosophical and social thought. However, I have tried to keep my writing anchored in a continuous involvement over the years in a series of concrete action research projects I have engaged in with teachers, as well as in post-graduate Masters and Doctoral Degree programmes designed to support teachers as action researchers.

My eight-year 'break' from CARE at the Cambridge Institute of Education provided me with a gateway into work with schools across six Local Education Authorities, and resulted in an informal regional networked learning community of schools and teachers. I am grateful to all those LEA advisers, Teachers' Centre Wardens, Headteachers and Teachers who taught me to remain optimistic about the potential of action research to effect worthwhile change in classrooms and schools in spite of an increasingly centralised policy context. They are too numerous to mention. I would, however, like to acknowledge a great debt to colleagues at the Cambridge Institute who collaborated with me to develop and sustain action research at the grassroots of the educational system. I am particularly in debt to Jennifer Nias and Marion Dadds, with whom I launched a successful CARE MA based in Cambridge. Our conversations in team meetings about how to practically manage and facilitate course-based action research at Masters level freed me from any tendency towards methodological dogmatism, as did conversations with sociologist, the late Rex Gibson. Marion articulated a view of action research as a form of 'passionate inquiry'. Although I supervised her doctoral research some 20 years ago, I have only recently realised the significance of her work, as will be evident in the final chapter in this volume. Rex kept a critical but not unsympathetic eye on the advocacy of action research at the CIE. He taught me not to dismiss too summarily certain traditions and canons of sociological inquiry. His humorous deconstructions of methodological dogma in all areas of educational research and indeed of academic culture in general during the 1980s are remembered by many today. As a new member of staff at CIE, I will never forget Rex's contribution at a meeting with the University's Department of Education. It was aimed at getting us to share our research interests. When it came to Rex's turn he simply said "I am interested in why those of us who work in academic institutions grow a little greyer and greyer everyday."

CARE has been a node in an international network which, over the years, has provided a global context for conversations about linking theory and practice in education. In this context, my conversations with Mike Atkin, Katherine Chan, Angel Perez Gomez, David Grossman, Mary Louise Holly, Ernie House, Paul Morris, Joan Rué, Maria Saez, Lou Smith, Bob Stake, to name but a few, have often marked an extension of my thinking about what might legitimately vary across cultures in the way action research shapes up, and what to hold invariant.

I owe special debts to Christine O'Hanlon, my wife. She has read and used many of the chapters in this volume with her post-graduate and doctoral students, and provided me with valuable critiques and honest feedback over the years with respect to both the ideas I struggled to articulate and how well I succeeded. Christine also endured the sacrifice of much 'quality time' together during the months that I obsessively struggled to write the introduction to this volume. In the end it was far too long, and I depended on her to cut it down to size. I am grateful for the parsimonious character of her complaints. This book is dedicated to her.

Last but not least, I would like to register my gratitude to Maureen Parker, my secretary. Maureen has rectified my terrible punctuation for many years, and played a special role in liaising with journal editors and publishers on my behalf. She undertook, with her usual speed, efficiency and 'keep cool under pressure' attitude, the complex task of securing copyright permission for me to include the chapters selected. I am grateful for permission to include the following:

Chapter 1 A Curriculum for the Study of Human Affairs: The Contribution of Lawrence Stenhouse, *Journal of Curriculum Studies*, Vol. 15, No. 2, pp. 105–123, 1983. Copyright permission granted by Taylor & Francis.

Chapter 2 Developing Hypotheses about Classrooms from Teachers' Practical Constructs: An Account of the Work of the Ford Teaching Project, *Interchange*, Vol. 7, No. 2, pp. 2–22, OISE 1976–77. With kind permission of Springer Science and Business Media.

Chapter 3 Preparing Teachers for Classroom Accountability, *Education for Teaching*, pp. 49–71, Summer 1976. Copyright permission granted by the Journal Division of Taylor & Francis.

Chapter 4 Self-Evaluation and Teacher Competence, *Irish Educational Studies*, Proceedings of the Annual Conference of the Irish Educational Studies Association, 1994.

Chapter 5 Classroom Research: Science or Commonsense? *Understanding Classroom Life*, pp. 12–25 (eds) R. McAleese and D. Hamilton, NFER, 1978. Copyright permission granted by Prof. David Hamilton and Prof. Ray McAleese.

Chapter 6 Educational Theory, Practical Philosophy and Action Research, *British Journal of Educational Research*, Vol. XXXV, No. 2, pp. 149–169, June 1987. Copyright permission granted by Blackwell Publishing.

Chapter 7 Implications for Classroom Research for Professional Development, *World Yearbook of Education 1980, Professional Development of Teachers*, pp. 308–323 (ed.) E. Hoyle. Copyright permission granted by Taylor & Francis.

Chapter 8 Making Evidence-Based Practice Educational, *British Educational Research Journal*, Vol. 27, No. 5, pp. 555–574, 2001. Copyright permission granted by Taylor & Francis.

Chapter 9 Using Research to Improve Practice: The Notion of Evidence-Based Practice, pp. 264–290, *International Handbook on the Continuing Professional Development of Teachers* (eds) C. Day and J. Sachs, Open University Press: Maidenhead, 2004. This material is reproduced with the kind permission of the Open University Press/McGraw-Hill Publishing Company.

Chapter 10 Rethinking Pedagogy as the Aesthetic Ordering of Learning Experiences, Presented at the UK Philosophy of Education Annual Conference, New College, Oxford, April 2003.

Chapter 11 Doing Action Research – Doing Practical Philosophy. What the academy does with an antigonistic view of educational inquiry? *Prospero*, Vol. 6, Nos 3 and 4, 82–100.

Chapter 12 The Struggle to Redefine the Relationship between 'Knowledge' and 'Action' in the Academy: Some Reflections on Action Research, *Educar*, No. 34, 2004, pp. 11–26, Universitat Autònoma de Barcelona.

INTRODUCTION

The school-based curriculum development movement

The essays selected for inclusion in this volume span a period of over 30 years, from the early 1970s to the beginning of this century. The question they all address is: *How can teachers make life in their classrooms an educationally worthwhile experience for their students?* For me it is the central pedagogical question that teachers, educational managers and administrators and policy-makers need to address. The question assumes that the teacher is the primary agent of educational change. It can be reformulated in broader terms: *How can life in classrooms be made into an educationally worthwhile experience for students?* This question asks us to entertain the possibility that classrooms can be directly changed by 'agencies' which exist beyond the school and classroom.

The first chapter in this volume, 'A Curriculum for the Study of Human Affairs' (1983), opens with a retrospective account, written a decade and a half later, of how I and my colleagues teaching the humanities subjects tried to find curriculum answers to this question. I argue that we only partially succeeded in realising our aspiration to make the curriculum more meaningful for our students because we neglected the pedagogical conditions for bringing about educationally worthwhile curriculum change. We largely reproduced the old conditions and thereby distorted the curriculum we were attempting to offer our students.

We selected and organised curriculum content in new ways, according to cross-subject themes and topics, to make it more relevant to their lives. In doing so were aware that this implied a pedagogical shift in the way students were to be engaged with the content; more emphasis on inquiry and discussion and less on didactic instruction. What we failed to appreciate were the difficulties of accomplishing such a shift. We simply assumed that it would be easy to change our pedagogy to match our pedagogical aims, and lacked any understanding of the terms and conditions that shaped our established practice and which we unwittingly continued to reproduce.

Curriculum change, conceived as changing the conditions in classrooms which shape the learning experiences of students, involves not only changes in the selection and organisation of content but also in the ways that content is pedagogically mediated to students. In order to effect significant curriculum change at the classroom level teachers need to reflexively deconstruct and reconstruct the terms and conditions that shape their pedagogical practice. Ways of supporting teachers to do this systematically in a sustainable form were unavailable. The curriculum projects that proliferated during the 1960s and 1970s in England and Wales, under the auspices of the

Schools Council (a tri-partite partnership between central and local government and the teachers' unions) did not in general provide such support. Most of these projects espoused 'inquiry' and 'discovery' learning as pedagogical aims, but they assumed that the curriculum materials they produced, would provide teachers with sufficient support to realise these aims in practice. Many project teams became disillusioned when they discovered that teachers in practice failed to use the materials in ways that were consistent with the pedagogical aims of their projects. They tended to explain the problem in terms of teachers resisting and subverting curriculum change, and failed to acknowledge a need to help teachers reflect systematically about the terms and conditions that shaped their practice.

Curriculum development as a pedagogical experiment

The exception to this state of affairs was the Schools Council Humanities Curriculum Project (1967–1972) under the direction of Lawrence Stenhouse. I left my innovatory secondary modern school in 1967 to join the central team of this project and remained a member until its period of funding expired in 1972. The main body of 'A Curriculum for the Study of Human Affairs' (1983) is devoted to a consideration of Stenhouse's curriculum theory, as evidenced in the design of the HCP. The essay was prompted by the death of Stenhouse in 1982, and written at the end of the school-based curriculum development movement in the UK, some 10 years after the Schools Council ceased to fund the HCP and was itself being closed and replaced by a government controlled curriculum agency. Centralised government intervention on curriculum matters was fast encroaching, in the wake of a school-based curriculum development movement that was widely regarded as a failure.

I see the HCP as an answer to the central pedagogical question I posed at the beginning of this introduction. HCP placed pedagogy rather than content at the centre of the curriculum development problem. The curriculum problem, as manifested in widespread learner disaffection, still persists in the UK and indeed more globally, because pedagogy has been consistently decentred in curriculum discourse. The *standards-driven* reforms that emanated from the UK and USA from the late 1980s, and found widespread global niches, have been based on an instrumental and objectivist rationality. This rationality separates ends and means in education and prescribes that the former should drive the latter. Politically it has legitimated the development of an elaborate technology of surveillance and control – target setting, performance indicators, league tables, external and internal quality audit, performance management and standardised assessment – to increase the power of the state to shape teaching and learning in schools and other educational institutions. Paradoxically we find liberal democratic states deploying non-democratic means to effect educational reform.

In designing the HCP Stenhouse was perfectly aware that at least one manifestation of an instrumental and objectivist rationality was looming on the educational horizon in the form of 'planning by objectives'. He produced some of the finest critiques of this approach to curriculum design, and argued that it distorted the nature of knowledge and what constituted a worthwhile educational process in a democratic society.[1]

Stenhouse defined the Humanities as the study of values and developed a framework for organising curriculum content around social situations and human acts that raised controversial issues in society. He then proposed that teachers should enable students to engage with the content in a form that *developed their understanding of social situations and acts and the value issues they raised.* However, he went further by spelling out the pedagogical implications of this aim in the form of a set of 'principles of procedure'. The latter specified the conditions teachers needed to establish in their classrooms to enable students to develop their understanding. For example, he argued that this aim implied a process of learning through discussion rather than instruction. It is a process in which the teacher refrains from using her authority position to promote her own views, protects the expression of divergent views, and accepts responsibility for quality and standards in the discussion by asking students to reflect about their own views and those of others in the light of evidence. These principles left space for teacher's to judge how best to apply them in their particular classroom situation. They provided both a practical orientation for teaching, as opposed to a tight prescription, and a focus for teacher research.

In 'A Curriculum for the Study of Human Affairs' I call the procedural principles that Stenhouse specified for the HCP, a 'praxiology', inasmuch as it constitutes a practical expression of an educational aim. Such a praxiology is very different from a technology of teaching grounded in an instrumental and objectivist rationality that separates educational aims from the pedagogical means of bringing them about.

I try in this essay to show how Stenhouse's idea of 'social understanding' as a pedagogical aim does not separate its development from interpretation and judgement. 'Understanding a social situation' is not a matter of getting students to look at the facts about it from the standpoint of an impartial spectator in which they cast aside their own evaluative perspectives. It is always possible to offer competing descriptions of situations and events because all description is framed by an evaluative point of view. Such descriptions constitute different interpretations of the evaluative significance of a situation or event for the way people ought to live.

The HCP asked teachers to provide students with access to competing descriptions of a social situation or event, not in order to demonstrate what constitutes a true understanding, but as a basis for a free and open discussion about the value issues it raised. In this context students were challenged to view the situation from evaluative standpoints other than their own and in doing so to clarify, reflect about, and possibly modify their own value position. Underpinning the praxiology of HCP was the idea that students developed their understanding of social situations and acts through reflective conversations that enabled them to modify, as opposed to detaching themselves from their biases.

Reflecting now on Stenhouse's praxiology, I would argue that the HCP was in effect asking teachers to entertain a democratic conception of rationality as an educational and pedagogical aim. As such it was challenging the objectivist theory of knowledge that underpinned conventional pedagogy. In my essay on Stenhouse, I argue that this view of the development of 'understanding' bears a marked resemblance to Gadamer's interpretative hermeneutics. I will examine Gadamer's hermeneutics at a later point, when discussing the relationship between educational action research and the so-called foundation disciplines of education.

In asking teachers to implement a curriculum proposal Stenhouse did not want them to do this uncritically. He asked them to see themselves as engaged in an experiment for the purpose of testing the idea's that underpinned the proposal. Teachers were cast in the role of co-researchers, working alongside educational and curriculum theorists to test the value of their ideas for improving the quality of teaching and learning in classrooms. Viewed in this light the pedagogical question referred to earlier also becomes a research question. Pedagogy is cast as a form of inquiry that mirrors the learning process for students. The HCP team came to recognise the project's experimental pedagogy as a form of action research.

The kind of action research that emerged from the HCP challenged, and still challenges, a view of educational research that serves the interests of an objectivist and instrumental rationality. This view assumes that the relationship between educational outcomes and processes is a contingent one, and that the task of educational research is to discover the most effective means of producing outcomes that can be defined in advance and quite independently of any reference to such means. It is a view that persists to this day and has become reinforced by policy-makers in their attempts to justify strong state intervention to shape students learning experiences in classrooms. Such intervention decentres the teacher as the primary agent of change.

Chapter 2, *'Developing Hypotheses about Classrooms from Teachers' Practical Constructs'* (1976/77), is an account of the first action research project I directed with teachers in the years that followed my engagement with the HCP. The Ford Teaching Project (1972–1974) was an attempt to redress a major implementation problem that curriculum development projects of the 1960s and 1970s encountered; namely, the failure of teachers to match their practice with the pedagogical aims espoused by many of these projects under the label of inquiry/discovery learning. The project was founded on the belief that many teachers sincerely wanted to re-shape the learning process in their classrooms as an inquiry/discovery process, but lacked sufficient support for establishing the appropriate pedagogical conditions.

The aspiration of the Ford Teaching Project was to involve teachers engaged in school-based curriculum development in developing a cross-curricular pedagogy through action research. The project shared many of the features that characterised the HCP. However, in working across the curriculum and school sectors (primary, middle and secondary) its aspiration to generate a shared pedagogy raised the issue of generalisation through action research even more starkly than the HCP. The problems of implementing a pedagogical aim might be expected to vary across contexts, as might the solutions to them. The range and variety of teaching contexts involved in Ford T was rather greater than that in the HCP. Nevertheless teachers found that in sharing case study evidence of their practice and discussing it together they could identify with many of the problems experienced by their peers and thereby support each other in developing and testing solutions to them. By the end of the project they had evolved a sufficient amount of 'overlapping consensus'[2] to be able to list quite systematically some general hypotheses about problems and solutions for other teachers to test through action research. Ford T challenged the assumption of many policy-makers and educational researchers that one cannot generalise across case data because it cannot be statistically aggregated. This assumption still prevails to a high degree.

Holding teachers to account

One solution to the problem of educational change that emerged from the mid-1970s onwards was the teacher accountability movement. I started to examine what the idea of 'the teacher as a researcher' implied for helping teachers to become more account-able for their practice in classrooms. Chapter 3, *'Preparing Teachers for Classroom Accountability'* (1976), is one of my first attempts to do this. Drawing on my experi-ence of the HCP and Ford T and the ideas of philosophers like Rawls, evaluation the-orists like House and Stake, and curriculum theorists like Schwab and Stenhouse, I try to develop a pluralistic and democratic model of accountability that is grounded in collaborative action research carried out by teachers. I argue that this model could be used by teachers to support reflective conversations about their classroom practice with a diversity of educational stakeholders. Action research has a form of accountability built into it, expressed as a willingness on the part of teachers to open up their practice to scrutiny and discussion by others – each other, students, their parents and other interested parties – in order to take their views into account in developing their professional practice.

In developing the model I explore what teachers as educators in a democratic society can legitimately be held to account for, and critique the assumptions about this that underpin the dominant utilitarian model that had emerged in the USA, and was being rapidly transported into the UK. It was a period of intense disillusionment with the work of teachers in classrooms and their ability to effect worthwhile educational change. Underpinning the utilitarian model I argue is an objectivist and instrumentalist rationality that imposes an unfair and anti-educational view of the teachers role and responsibilities in a democratic society. Chapter 3 was an attempt to present an alternative vision of accountability that is consistent with the idea of teachers as self-evaluating agents of change. However, it is the utilitarian model that remains operationally dominant today.

Making teachers more accountable became a device for 'driving up standards' defined as standardisable and measurable learning outputs. Teacher performance in classrooms was to be externally evaluated in terms of its instrumental effectiveness in producing state mandated outputs. In this accountability scenario teachers are viewed as technical functionaries responsible for the delivery of a standards agenda they have little say about. It leaves little space for a view of teachers as the primary agents of pedagogical change.

Chapter 4, '*Self-Evaluation and Teacher Competence*' (1994), is an attempt to explain why teachers in schools failed to respond to an invitation to engage in a form of self-evaluation that appeared to safeguard their professional autonomy in the classroom. I cite two factors as being especially significant. These are the cultural and the competence factors.

Self-evaluation appears, from a standpoint outside the occupational culture of teachers, to be highly compatible with this culture, inasmuch as it is a culture that prizes the freedom of teachers to exercise their own professional judgement. However, those on the inside of the culture often experience proposals for self-evaluation to constitute a threat to their professional autonomy. I draw on a paper by Helen Simons to explain this. She argued that teachers understanding of professional autonomy is framed by the central values which shape their culture; namely, privacy, territoriality and hierarchy. Professional autonomy is largely understood as the right of teachers to teach as they desire in the privacy of their own classroom under the protection of an administrative hierarchy. Formal self-evaluation from this cultural perspective constitutes a breach of privacy, territorial possession and the administrative protection of these conditions. These values I argue constitute the conditions that enable teachers to exercise a high degree of pedagogical control over the processing of large amounts of information by students in classrooms. By destabilising those conditions self-evaluation threatens this control, and I would now argue does so to an even greater degree than many forms of external evaluation.

Another factor, which explains why the self-evaluation movement fell on stony ground, is that it did not have any strategies for developing teachers' capabilities as self-evaluators. Many at the time simply presumed that self-evaluation was something teachers did naturally on the basis of an introspective and individualistic process of reflection informed by questions on a checklist. The accountability context merely required teachers to formalise what they did informally.

In Chapter 4, I argue against the notion that self-evaluation is largely an individualistic and introspective process, and for the view that it involves a teacher becoming discursively self-aware of what (s)he is doing through reflecting with others about his or her practice. In order to engage in such a process teachers need to be capable of describing what they are doing in language both to themselves and others. I suggest that there are techniques of data gathering that enhance this capability. For example, a teacher becomes capable of answering the question "Do I ask children leading questions?" through gathering observational data and eliciting student interpretations of their questions. Teacher research develops self-evaluation capabilities that are constitutive of a democratic form of accountability.

Paradigms of educational research

The emergence of the idea of action research into the academic domains of educational research, educational theory and teacher education was and still is accompanied by considerable controversy. It became part of a continuing ideological warfare that is sometimes called 'the battle of the paradigms'. I have sometimes been viewed as a promoter of paradigm conflict and Chapter 5, *'Classroom Research: Science or Commonsense'* (1978), might be regarded as an early example of this? In it I draw a distinction between 'Educational Research' and 'Research on Education'. Research can be described as educational if its primary aim is the practical one of realising educational values in action. This implies that it constructs knowledge in the action context of teachers, and when it involves outsiders, in collaboration with them. 'Educational research' therefore is a form of action research, and may involve external researchers collaborating with teachers to construct knowledge. I depict research that dissociates the construction of knowledge from the action context of teachers as 'research on education', and tended to assume at the time of writing that such research is largely shaped through the academic disciplines.

Looking afresh at *'Classroom Research: Science or Commonsense'*, I can see that I was particularly concerned to distinguish educational research from a form of research that is cast in the form of a positivistic science. The advocates of such a science hold that there are not different kinds of knowledge, since all genuine knowledge is based on sense experience and concerned with the description and explanation of empirical facts. Facts are about a world governed by the laws of cause and effect. It is the task of research to build our knowledge of them in every area of experience, including our experience of the social world. From the standpoint of positivism, science provides us with knowledge that is beyond speculation and it therefore constitutes a sure and certain foundation on which to build a modern society. I still hold with my distinction between 'educational research' and 'research on education', but since the mid-1980s have tended to draw it ways that do not necessarily exclude all forms of inquiry within the specialised disciplines from the former category.

Issues about the contribution of the disciplines to the development of educational practice is the subject of Chapter 6 *'Educational Theory, Practical Philosophy and Action Research'* (1987). This essay revisits many of the themes explored nearly a decade earlier in *'Classroom Research: Science or Commonsense?'* It does so in a context where the rationalist conception of the relationship between educational theory and practice that had dominated Teacher Education for over a decade – particularly in the UK – no longer prevailed. I try to set what is at issue about the contribution of the disciplines to the development of educational practice in the wider context of Gadamer's Interpretative Hermeneutics. According to Gadamer developing our understanding of a practical situation is not a matter of discerning meaning that exists 'out there', as an objective property, waiting to be discovered. Looked at from his perspective a teacher's understanding of her classroom situation is inevitably biased by her historically conditioned beliefs and values. Nevertheless, her understanding can evolve and develop in what Gadamer calls 'the play of conversation' with others (imaginary or real) around the object of her understanding (her practical situation). In this way new possibilities for action in the situation are opened up.

In '*Classroom Research: Science or Commonsense?*' it is the objectivist presumption that centrally defines the boundary between 'educational research' and 'research on education'. Later in Chapter 6 I form the view that inasmuch as discipline-based researchers, within the field of education, develop the questions they address, and validate the answers they arrive at, by engaging with the 'play of conversation' surrounding situations that arise in the context of practice, then they may also be regarded as engaged in 'educational research'. The problem here is that such research depends on certain conditions operating in the context of use; namely, the engagement of teachers in reflexively self-critical practice. It may not be enough for specialist researchers to simply consult teachers and survey their opinions. The quality of the questions developed as a focus for inquiry, and the usefulness of the answers, will depend on the quality of teachers' thinking in the context of their practice. Good disciplines-based research in education and practitioner inquiry are mutually dependent processes.

In Chapter 7 '*Implications of Classroom Research for Professional Development*' (1980) I again return to themes initially addressed in '*Classroom Research: Science or Commonsense*'. The context is the growth of teacher effectiveness research. I argue that such research, cast in the form of the process-product paradigm, embodies assumptions about teaching as an activity that neglects the way educational values are constituted in the pedagogical relationship between teachers and students. It tends to conceptualise this relationship as a power-coercive one, and implies that learning is a passive and compliant process.

I claim that, inasmuch as research is 'educational' it must support the development of educative action by teachers in their classrooms. I go on to argue that this task cannot be accomplished independently of establishing a dialogue with teachers about their pedagogical aims, the practical problems they experience in realising them, and strategies for solving them. Such dialogue in itself constitutes a process of professional development for the teachers involved. Hence, in aiming to establish an educative pedagogical relationship between teachers and learners educational research also constitutes a process of teacher professional development. I argue that this contrasts with the view, implicit in much teacher effectiveness research, that the construction of knowledge about what makes an effective teacher is a quite separate process to learning to become one.

Conceptions of teaching as an evidence-based profession

'*Implications of Classroom Research for Professional Development*' was published in 1980, but raises issues about the relationship between research and teaching that I take up again two decades later in the context of a policy discourse that is promoting the idea of 'teaching as an evidence-based profession'. Chapter 8 '*Making Evidence-Based Practice Educational*' (2001) is a critique of the ideas of David Hargreaves, the most influential promoter of the idea of 'evidence-based teaching' in the UK.

Hargreaves has done much to re-shape research priorities in education by arguing that qualitative research had limited utility for maximising desired learning outcomes in schools inasmuch as it is not a source of 'actionable knowledge'. He defines such knowledge as "decisive and conclusive evidence that if teachers do X rather than Y in their professional practice, there will be a significant and enduring improvement of outcome." Hargreaves is very clear about the kind of evidence this knowledge consists of. It takes the form of statistically based generalisations based on data from experimental and random controlled trials. This conception of 'actionable knowledge' has proved attractive to policy-makers in their anxiety to find ways of 'driving-up standards' in classrooms and schools.

In my critique of Hargreaves, I draw on MacIntyre's argument that many social scientists desire to position themselves favourably in the policy arena, and do so by presenting their science as capable of making the policy-makers dream of power come true. Whilst they may mutually acknowledge as academics that exceptions to their generalisations make little difference to whether they remain in the corpus of 'knowledge' within their discipline, as people who wish to establish that discipline's credibility on the political stage they feel the need to present its findings as having the status of causal laws with the power to accurately predict the consequences of human behaviour. The apparent contradictions in Hargreaves' views about the status of evidence from experimental and random controlled trials might well be explained I argue in these terms.

At the heart of my response to Hargreaves is an attempt to construct an alternative account of evidence-based teaching, drawing on the work of Lawrence Stenhouse and Richard Peters. Both pointed out that in educational discourse the term 'aims' is often used to refer to values that are internal to the process of education as opposed to the extrinsic purposes and functions it may also serve. I argue for making evidence-based practice more 'educational' by engaging teachers in gathering evidence about the extent to which their interventions in particular classroom situations enables or constrains students' participation in an educationally worthwhile learning process. Although such evidence will be gathered in particular concrete situations as case evidence, it is always possible for teachers to identify types of intervention which either constrain or enable the development of a worthwhile form of learning across their different classroom contexts. Such 'generalisations' can then provide hypotheses for other teachers to explore in their particular classroom settings. If some conclude that there is no evidence that a generalisation of this kind holds in their case, then this need not under-mine its value as a guide to discerning the practically significant features of classroom situations. Even the elimination of certain possibilities helps to clarify understanding.

Chapter 9, '*Using Research to Improve Practice: The Notion of Evidence-Based Practice*' (2004), is largely an exploration of teachers' perspectives on what counts as relevant and credible evidence to inform teaching in situations where significant num-ber of students appear to be manifestly disaffected from learning. In 1997 the UK Teacher Training Agency (TTA) funded four pilot research consortia – consisting of a partnership between schools, a higher education institution and a local education authority – to promote teachers engagement with research at the level of the class-room. The restructuring of educational research to focus on teaching and learning was an important part of the TTA agenda in setting up the Consortia. I was the leader of the research team in a Norwich-based Consortium (NASC) that focused on disaffection from learning.

In Chapter 9, I argue that the initiative embodied two different conceptions of 'evidence-based teaching', each sustained in tension with the other via inter-personal networks of affiliation that cut across organisational boundaries between a quasi-government agency, the school system and academic institutions. The concluding section depicts how the NASC programme in particular operated with a different conception of evidence-based teaching to one shaped by 'standards-driven' educational reform. Whereas the latter views useful evidence as a source of rules for rationally ordering learning experiences to produce standardised and measurable learning outcomes, NASC teachers in the main viewed evidence as useful if it made them more aware of the sheer complexity of the situations they face in their classrooms, and of the task of creating a meaningful learning environment that caters for individual differences in their learners. Rather than providing a basis for rationally organising learning experiences, the evidence they gathered through action research served as a basis for aesthetically ordering them. Such an ordering involves creating a harmonious learning environment that fully acknowledges complexity and caters for the diverse needs and abilities of individual students. It calls for artistry in teaching.

In Chapter 10, '*Rethinking Pedagogy as the Aesthetic Ordering of Learning Experiences*' (2002), I further develop the distinction between two conceptions of pedagogy, as either a rational or an aesthetic ordering of learning experiences and link it to another distinction I have been developing, between a reductionist 'standards-driven' conception of change and a 'pedagogically-driven' conception grounded in the discernment of complexity. I draw on the Confucian concept of modelling in a teaching and learning context to depict an aesthetically ordered learning process that is characterised by a *harmonisation*, as opposed to a *standardisation*, of learning experiences. Such a process I argue can accommodate both the authority of the teacher and the autonomy of the learner, whereas one that involves standardisation cannot. Confucius's thinking about teaching and learning has a number of points of contact with that of Dewey, Stenhouse and Peters. In particular all three conceptualise an educational space for self-creation on the part of learners, compared with a view of teaching and learning as a process in which the mind of the teacher is simply reproduced in the learner.

Resolving the dualism of 'theory and practice'

In '*Educational Theory, Practical Philosophy, and Action Research*' (Chapter 6) I explore what is at issue between Gadamer and Habermas because at the time of writing Carr and Kemmis had developed an influential account of action research based on Habermas's ideas. They called it the 'critical' action research paradigm and contrasted it with the 'practical' and 'technical' action research paradigms. This categorisation was based on Harbermas's idea that knowledge was constituted by different kinds of human interests. Carr and Kemmis used Habermas to construct a bridge between educational theory and practice and for a time I was attracted to the idea of 'critical action research'. Eventually I found myself rejecting their construction to argue that the 'critical' is an inherent dimension of 'the practical'. I found myself agreeing with Gadamer in this respect. Gadamer argued that Habermas has created an unreal opposition between reflection and tradition. Traditions are dynamic and changing in response to internal critique rather than the kind of static and unchanging entities Habermas depicts. Gadamer admits that within practical/hermeneutic discourse the critique of pre-judgements is limited and partial, but that this is true also for critical theorems. The latter do not escape the finite conditions and the particularity of reflection, which characterise all human inquiry. If this is so then Harbermas's attempt to ground critical theorems in rational foundations for determining their truth, his consensus theory, collapses. Open and free dialogue no longer has to be justified as a process for determining the truth of theories.

Chapter 11 '*Doing Action Research – Doing Practical Philosophy*' (2000) addresses critiques of action research from rather different standpoints; one by Hammersley from a rather conventional view of the relationship between theory and practice and the other from a post-modern deconstructionist perspective by MacLure. However, both deny that action research can constitute a unity of theory and practice. In response to these critiques I construct an account of educational action research and the unity of theory and practice from a standpoint that both Hammersley and MacLure fail to acknowledge; namely, a view of moral inquiry that MacIntyre calls 'tradition'.

From the standpoint of tradition I argue that there are no secure and certain foundations, transcending time and circumstance, in which to ground universal conceptions of the human good. There are therefore no fixed standards of reasoning for determining what ends are worth pursuing through social practices, like education. Standards of reasoning are inevitably historically situated, and become embedded in the traditions that shape our social practices. However, this need not imply the death of 'theory' I suggest. Educational action research, which involves teachers sharing their practical insights into how to realise their educational values in concrete teaching situations, can yield useful summaries of their insights and judgements in the form of universal 'rules of thumb' to guide reflection in and on action. The action hypotheses developed in the contexts of the HCP and Ford Teaching Project can be regarded as having this form and function. Even if many academics would deny the status of 'theory' to such 'rule of thumb' hypotheses I would suggest that according to them such a status would be quite consistent with commonsense and everyday usage.

The resistance within academic institutions to acknowledging a form of inquiry that unifies theory and practice is the focus of the final chapter in this selection. In *'The Struggle to Redefine the Relationship between "Knowledge" and "Action" in the Academy'* (2004) I address the radical challenge that post-structuralist and post-modern thinkers have posed to an academic culture that has been shaped by the distinctions that underpin Descartes' *Cogito*; between subject and object, appearance and reality, mind and body, theory and practice. One question I explore is whether there is still a meaningful use of the terms 'theorising' and 'theory' once the Cartesian picture of the mind has failed to withstand the critiques of both philosophical pragmatists and post-structuralist/post-modern thinkers. In reading this, and other chapters in this volume, readers will be aware that I want to conclude that there is. Whether my arguments convince they alone can decide.

My account of action research implies that teachers through their research can exercise some kind of rational control over their activities. Since it excludes the idea that teachers are empowered to effect change by applying theory to their practices, it is easy for traditional educational researchers and post-structuralist/modernist thinkers alike to assume that I am simply portraying action research as a form of non-theoretical and instrumental rationality concerned with making technical refinements to their practices.

I develop an alternative reading of action research in Chapter 12, and in doing so draw heavily on Hannah Arendt's classification of human activity in *The Human Condition* and John MacMurray's philosophical portrayal of *The Self as Agent*, which I regard as a much neglected work that broadly falls within the tradition of philosophical pragmatism. By drawing on these two texts I attempt to reinstate the idea of the 'autonomous self' in different terms to those expressed by Descartes' *Cogito*, and use it as a basis for further developing my account of action research as a unification of theory and practice.

Concluding remarks

The essays in this book develop an account of educational action research as a unity of theory and practice. In the main they draw on a pragmatic philosophical tradition that finds an intelligible use for the term 'theory' that does not depend on a purely intellectual mode of reflection. From the standpoint of pragmatism "To argue for a certain theory – is to argue about what we should do."[3] All theories, the pragmatist would argue, are tools for dealing with the practical circumstances of life, regardless of whether this is acknowledged by their creators. The fact that some command a measure of universal assent does not mean that they mirror some reality, which exists beyond the particularities of contingent existence, only that human beings discern similarities as well as differences in their practical circumstances. This is why educational action research can aspire to develop educational theory that is capable of commanding a high measure of universal assent amongst educators. To deny this is to treat such research as non-theoretical and small-scale practical inquiries carried out by individual teachers and lacking in generalisability. It is to collude with a research culture that still resists the view that worthwhile educational change can only in the final analysis be effected through the agency of teachers working together as professional learning communities.

Notes

1   See Stenhouse, L. (1975) *An Introduction to Curriculum Research and Development*, London: Heineman, Chs 5–7.
2   See Rawls, J. (1993) *Political Liberalism*, New York: Columbia University Press, pp. 150–172 (1996 Edition).
3   Rorty, R. (1999) in *Philosophy and Social Hope*, London: Penguin Books, p. xxv.

PART 1

CURRICULUM DEVELOPMENT AS A PEDAGOGICAL EXPERIMENT

CHAPTER 1

A CURRICULUM FOR THE STUDY OF HUMAN AFFAIRS
The contribution of Lawrence Stenhouse

Journal of Curriculum Studies, Vol. 15, No. 2, pp. 105–123, 1983

The humanities in the innovatory secondary modern school

In the early 1960s I was teaching religious studies in an English secondary modern school; a type of school which admitted all those pupils who failed the entrance test into grammar schools.[1] At first, secondary modern schools offered a diluted, watered-down version of the grammar school curriculum plus an additional diet of practical subjects such as wood and metalwork, needlecraft and cookery, rural studies etc. By the time I began teaching in one, the alienation of the pupils was becoming increasingly clear to the majority of teachers. Some responded by adopting evermore repressive measures of control. Some secondary modern schools became little more than concentration camps in which to contain, rather than educate, the vast majority of the nation's children. As one senior teacher instructed me when I was a student teacher 'Your job is to keep the lid on the garbage can'. Other teachers responded to the alienation they faced daily by asking the question, 'What does it mean to educate these pupils?' The answers they generated created the 'innovatory secondary modern school'. I taught in one and it was a formative experience.

The key ideas underlying the curricular reforms we introduced into the secondary modern school were those of 'relevance' and 'responsible judgement'. The curriculum area on which we embarked became known as 'the humanities': that group of subjects which carried such labels as english, history, geography and religious studies. All of these subjects dealt with some aspect of human experience and activity but tended to be presented didactically as discrete bodies of inert factual information; the products of work in academic disciplines, unrelated to the lived experience of those required to memorize and recall them in classrooms. It was the organization and transmission of knowledge about human affairs in traditional academic categories that we began to challenge for the sake of 'relevance' and 'responsible judgement'. We tried to reorganize knowledge about human affairs in categories which expressed human experience as it was lived or anticipated by the pupils themselves; for example, 'The family', 'Industry and work', 'Relations between the sexes', 'Law and order', 'Poverty', etc. Such a reconceptualization of curriculum content arose out of a concern to make curriculum content relevant to 'the lives of pupils' here and now. But this implied a corresponding shift in pedagogy to allow the pupils to exercise their own judgement with respect to the significance (for the way they lived their lives) of the information presented.

We embarked on an attempt to move away from an instruction-based towards a discussion-based classroom. Information was no longer to be transmitted as a body of inert facts, but as a conveyor of personal meaning – as something to be interpreted, evaluated, and personally appropriated in the light of the experience of the pupils. This, at least, was the aspiration.

In my school, at least, this reconceptualization of curriculum content and the pedagogy appropriate to it began within the traditional academic timetable. But gradually specialist subject teachers realized they were handling the same topics in similar ways; largely because the pupils began to complain they were doing the same things under different subject labels. As a result we gradually began to abandon the traditional practice of teaching different subjects in separate time-units and by implication started to undermine the idea of the teacher as an expert on a specialist body of knowledge. Topic-centred team-teaching organized in substantial blocks of time under the general label of 'the humanities', co-ordinated by someone called 'head of humanities', became the order of the day in the innovatory secondary modern school during the latter half of the 1960s.

However, the curricular reforms initiated within the innovatory secondary modern school by no means constituted an undistorted realization of the aspirations teachers expressed in terms of ideas like 'relevance' and 'responsible judgement'. Teachers found it difficult in practice to leave the security of seeing themselves as subject experts. Even within the organizational framework of topic-centred team-teaching a pattern of 'key lessons', differentiated along subject lines, evolved. Typically a topic might last for four or five weeks, and each week's time allocation would be devoted to looking at the topic from the point of view of a particular subject. For example, I remember one school taking the topic 'communication'. It went something like this: the work for week 1 was initiated by a key lesson in which the historian talked about the development of communication systems through the ages. It was the geographer's turn for the key lesson in week 2 and it focused on present transportation systems in the UK. In week 3 an English literature specialist talked about 'inter-personal communication in contemporary literature'. Then in week 4 the religious studies teacher explained how God communicated with human beings through the medium of angels. On each week the 'key lesson' was succeeded by 'discussion' and 'follow-up work' in small groups. All too often the 'discussion' took the form of teacher question – pupil answer – teacher question – pupil answer etc. Rather than constituting a free and open exchange of ideas about the moral, social or political significance of the information transmitted in the 'key lesson' it functioned as an exercise in establishing the teacher's understanding of the significance of the facts in the minds of the pupils. 'Follow-up' written work played a similar role.

Little attention was given to the logical inter-relationships between the various bodies of knowledge presented or to how they were to be integrated psychologically within the lived experience of the pupils. It was just assumed that, given the 'relevance' of the content, the pupils would be able to make the psychological connections with their own experience for themselves. And of course many didn't; remaining in their previous state of boredom and alienation.

In some schools the attempt to link existing factual knowledge with the lived experience of pupils was abandoned altogether. 'Discussion' in the classroom was conceived as a 'debate' about human issues grounded solely in the existing experience of pupils. The more 'heated' the argument, the better the discussion – from the teacher's point of view. It indicated that the pupils were 'involved', 'motivated' and no longer bored, and therefore signalled some kind of progress. But, like the 'key lesson' approach, it failed to address the central problem of how pupils could extend their understanding of their 'lived experience'. All too often in my experience such discussions went round in circles; each pupil merely affirming in the face of opposition their existing interpretations of experience. Teachers provided little which might throw new light on the experience of each pupil and thereby move their 'understanding' forwards. Although the teachers who adopted this approach left the security of their 'subject expertise' they resorted to a familiar pattern of human inter-change in both academic and everyday life, namely, that of a point-scoring argument, the purpose of which is to undermine the position of those one disagrees with rather than reflect about one's own.

The innovations within the humanities curriculum of the English secondary modern school were, in my view, distorted by a failure on the part of teachers to realize an adequate theory of understanding in the teaching of human affairs. Our practice, if not our aspirations, remained trapped in an 'objectivist' theory of understanding. While it allowed us to organize knowledge content in topic categories and find some room for 'discussion' in classrooms, it also left room for the teacher to operate in the comfortable securities of the subject expert and the didactic pedagogy this status implies.

The theory was as follows: one understands a human act or situation when one knows the relevant facts about it. It is only after it has been so *understood* that one is in a position to *interpret* its moral, social, or political significance correctly. The latter 'insights' can then be applied by pupils to extend their insights into their own experience, and thereby serve as a basis for responsible judgements about how they ought to conduct their lives. Understanding, interpretation, and application to experience (judgement) are thus conceived as quite distinct cognitive processes, but linked in a logically necessary pedagogical sequence.

This theory shaped classroom practice as follows. First, pupils were instructed in the facts, and only then allowed to 'discuss' their moral, social, or political significance. If time then permitted they were allowed to explore the implications of the 'insights' they gained to their own lives.

How could teachers of the humanities in the innovatory secondary modern school of the 1960s have made a better job of their attempt to translate their aspirations into practice? Well, for a start they could have had better support from educational theorists and philosophers who spent a considerable amount of intellectual energy sniping from academia. Many of their criticisms of emerging practice – 'sloppy thinking on the part of teachers', 'the lack of intellectual discipline and rigour which the new curricula provided for pupils' – were often quite valid. But what the theorists consistently failed to do was to indicate to teachers how the theories of knowledge and education they employed in criticism could be translated into a form of practice from which pupils in secondary modern schools would benefit. In other words, the theorists failed to offer teachers a translation of their theories into a form of practice which indicated how the problem of pupil alienation from the traditional humanities subjects might be solved.

What the humanities teachers of the 1960s needed were practical procedures which addressed the problem of how to make established knowledge in the human field relevant to the life experiences of pupils in terms of a novel theory of understanding; that is, one which significantly differed from the theory informing established practice. I will call such a procedural expression of ideas a *praxiology*. The function of a praxiology is to mediate between ideas and attempts to actualize them in practice. By shaping ideas in a practical form it not only assists the realization of ideas in practice, but also allows them to be tested and modified in the light of practice. A praxiology supports the art of translating ideas into action without restricting the practitioner's judgement about how this is best done.

Most humanities teachers in English secondary schools had to wait until the early 1970s before such a praxiology was available to them. It came in the form of the Schools Council/Nuffield Foundation Humanities Project, directed by Lawrence Stenhouse. I was fortunate enough to have been a member of the team which helped Stenhouse on this enterprise from 1967 to 1972. What emerged was a curriculum conceived as a praxiology (although Stenhouse to my knowledge did not call it such). Since this was, and still is, a rather novel conception of what a curriculum is, I want to digress a little in the next section and explore its rationale and implications more fully before moving on to look at the Humanities Project as an example.

Curricula as praxiologies

Via the Humanities Project, Lawrence Stenhouse introduced a radically different theory of knowledge to teachers of the humanities, which challenged them to view understanding, interpretation, and application in personal judgement as a unified process. His views were first fully articulated in abstract form in *Culture and Education* (1967).[2] To my knowledge, few teachers read the book. Retrospectively, Stenhouse may have been more disappointed about its impact on professional educational theorists than teachers. For he believed that educational theories only fostered the professional development of teachers when they were given practical shape in the form of a curriculum teachers could use in their classrooms. He wrote:

> all educational thinkers...should pay teachers the respect of translating their ideas into curriculum. And that means enough contact with classroom reality or enough consultancy with teachers to discipline all ideas by the problems of practice.
>
> Only in curricular form can ideas be tested by teachers. Curricula are hypothetical procedures testable only in classrooms. All educational ideas must find expression in curricula before we can tell whether they are day dreams or contributions to practice. Many educational ideas are not found wanting, because they cannot be found at all.
>
> If someone comes along asking you to adopt an idea or strive after an objective; political maturity or basic literacy, ask him to go away and come back with a curriculum or give you a sabbatical to do so for him.[3]

Taking his own advice Stenhouse shaped the theories articulated in *Culture and Education* into the practical form of the Humanities Project.

What Stenhouse offered teachers of the humanities was 'a curriculum' conceived as a set of hypothetical classroom procedures they could *experiment* with as a basis for the reflective translation of educational ideas into educational action. From this conception of a curriculum Stenhouse derived his now famous idea of the 'teacher as a researcher'. If curriculum is the medium through which educational ideas are tested and developed then teachers must be viewed as having a central role in theory generation. Their reflections about the problems of implementing the theories embodied in curricula should, Stenhouse argued, lie at the heart of all curriculum research.

According to Stenhouse, the 'research' role of the teacher isn't merely concerned with the development of theories about methods conceived instrumentally as technical rules for bringing about preconceived learning outcomes. He not only rejected the traditional view that a curriculum was simply a syllabus – a list of content to be covered – but also mounted a penetrating critique[4] of the now popular idea that it is a 'rational plan' of content and methods conceived in terms of their instrumentality for bringing about preconceived knowledge in the learner. Stenhouse's ideas of a curriculum and of the teacher as a researcher are grounded in a radically different theory of the educational process to the technological model which underlies the notion of a 'rational curriculum plan'. For him education was not a process of social engineering in which ends and means could be clarified independently of each other. He was very much influenced by R. S. Peters's view that our ideas about educational ends refer not so much to quantifiable products of an educational process as to qualities to be realized in, and constituted by, the process itself.[5] Conceptions of educational ends refer to ideals, values, and principles, to be realized *in* the way teachers proceed to relate pupils to the content of education and not to the extrinsic outcomes of this process. *Educational* ends constitute intrinsic criteria for judging what is to count as a worthwhile *educational process*.

This distinction between an educational and a technological process reflects Aristotle's distinction between *praxis* and *poiesis*.[6] The latter refers to a set of operational procedures for producing quantifiable consequences which can be clearly specified in advance, whereas the former refers to the realization of an ideal way of life; to the actualization of certain ethical qualities *in* the way people conduct their lives with others. *Praxis* is a matter of actualizing our ideals and values in an appropriate form of action, and it is always an unfinished enterprise requiring continuous self-reflection and analysis. Moreover, it implies that means cannot be reflected upon independently from ends. By reflecting about the extent to which we have actualized our ideals *in* action we not only develop new understandings of *how* to act, but also deepen our understanding of the ideals themselves.

More than any other contemporary educational theorist, Stenhouse grasped the pedagogical significance of viewing education as a form of *praxis* rather than a technological process. He understood that good teaching was an art rather than the mastery of techniques. In art he argued:

> Idea and action are fused in practice. Self-improvement comes in escaping from the idea that the way to virtuosity is the imitation of others – pastiche – to the realisation that it is the fusion of idea and action in one's own performance to the point where each can be 'justified' in the sense that it is fully expressive of the other. So the idea is tuned to the form of the art and the form used to express the idea.
>
> Thus in art ideas are tested in form by practice. Exploration and interpretation lead to revision and adjustment of idea and of practice. If my words are inadequate, look at the sketchbook of a good artist, a play in rehearsal, a jazz quartet working together. That, I am arguing, is what good teaching is like. It is not like routine engineering or routine management.
>
> The process of developing the art of the artist is always associated with change in ideas and practice. An artist becomes stereotyped or derelict when he ceases to develop. There is no mastery, always aspiration. And the aspiration is about ideas – content – as well as about performance – execution of ideas.[3]

By viewing curricula as praxiologies – as hypothetical strategies for realizing ideas in practice – Stenhouse posited them as both expressions and objects of practical judgement. As expressions of other people's practical judgements – educational theorists for example – they are a source of ideas. Every attempt by a teacher to translate a curriculum into action involves asking the question 'What is the meaning or point of doing this?' In this way the teacher is forced to grapple with the ideas underlying the judgements which shape the curriculum. But this does not imply that teachers are thereby compelled to passively accept the ideas which confront them. By rendering the practical judgements which shape curricula problematic, Stenhouse made them objects for personal critique by teachers.

Curricula foster improvements in educational practice not because they compel teachers to implement their underlying ideas but because they create a framework within which teachers can extend their own ideas by bringing them into a dialectical relationship with other people's. The insights or understandings which emerge and get translated into action 'go beyond' not only teachers' previous ideas but also those they confront in the curriculum. Curricula for Stenhouse were the media through which teachers developed their own insights and learned to translate them into practice. But the understandings and skills so developed always involve 'going beyond' the curriculum. Hence, curricula need to be continuously revised in the light of teachers' judgements. As I shall show later, this view of professional learning expresses the same theory of understanding that Stenhouse applied to *education* generally.

The Humanities Project is best understood as the medium through which Lawrence Stenhouse conducted a dialogue with the teaching profession. Today, 10 years after the project team disbanded, some people are keen to point to evidence – for example, from the Schools Council's *Impact and Take-up* research published in (1978) – that the Stenhouse materials and teaching strategies as he conceived them are rarely used in secondary schools. At best they see this as a sign that an interesting, and even novel, educational innovation failed to 'take' on a large scale in schools. But this constitutes a serious misunderstanding of Stenhouse's conception of the role of the educational theorist as a curriculum developer. For him the success of his dialogue rested not so much on whether teachers are still using his curriculum, as on the extent to which those that did have deepened their own insights into the nature of education, teaching, learning and knowledge, and with them the capacity to translate them into forms of action within their classrooms.

Writing about the fashionable idea which he himself helped to generate – no curriculum development without teacher development – Stenhouse warned:

> that does not mean, as it often seems to be interpreted to mean, that we must train teachers in order to produce a world fit for curricula to live in. It means that by virtue of their meaningfulness curricula are not simply instructional means to improve teaching but are expressions of ideas to improve teachers. Of course, they have a day-to-day instructional utility: cathedrals must keep the rain out. But the students benefit from curricula not so much because they change day-to-day instruction as because they improve teachers.[3]

Towards a vernacular humanism: the humanities project

The problem Stenhouse addressed through the Humanities Curriculum Project 'rang bells' with a number of us teaching the humanities in the innovatory secondary modern school. He took it from the Schools Council Working Paper No. 2 on *Raising the School Leaving Age*:

> The problem is to give every man some access to a complex cultural inheritance, some hold on his personal life and on his relationships with the various communities to which he belongs, some extension of his understanding of, and sensitivity towards other human beings. The aim is to forward understanding, discrimination and judgement in the human field – it will involve reliable factual knowledge, where this is appropriate, direct experience, imaginative experience, some appreciation of the dilemmas of the human condition, of the rough hewn nature of many of our institutions, and some rational thought about them.[7]

Reviewing this passage later in a paper entitled 'Towards a vernacular humanism' (to my knowledge unpublished), Stenhouse remarked that 'I still find this a moving statement of an aspiration towards a humanistic education for all'. And it was a humanistic aspiration not simply because it emphasized the study of human affairs, but because it restated the importance of individual judgement as against rule by authority in the conduct of life. A humanistic education was concerned with the emancipation of the individual. And for Stenhouse it rested 'upon the passionate belief that the virtue of humanity is diminished in man when judgement is overruled by authority'. He defined the 'most civilised state' as the one whose 'citizens are successfully trusted with the responsibility of judgement'.

Stenhouse wanted to extend the type of education he had received in a school for the elite – Manchester Grammar School – to all. In that school he claimed his teachers had presented knowledge as intrinsically problematic and invited their pupils to question and judge it. Looking at the educational system as a whole he wrote: 'we are still two nations, because we produce through education a majority ruled by knowledge, not served by it, an intellectual, moral and spiritual proletariat, characterised by instrumental competencies rather than autonomous powers'. (From 'Towards a vernacular humanism'.) He saw the majority of schools operating with an arid scholastic view of knowledge, conceiving it 'as a matter of law rather than speculation, of assertion rather than enquiry, and of style'. So, given a commission by the Schools Council to construct a humanities curriculum for adolescent pupils of average and below-average academic ability, most of whom were still housed in secondary modern schools, he set about helping teachers to become 'the instrument of a redistribution of the means of autonomy and judgement'.

His point of departure was to define the humanities as the study of human issues which were of universal concern within society to pupils and to their parents and teachers. They constituted human acts and social situations which are empirically controversial in our society, for example abortion, divorce, the roles of men and women in society, streaming by ability in schools, war and pacifism, nuclear weapon production etc. In addition, they are areas of experience where society acknowledges the right of individuals to disagree and exercise their own judgement.

The project redefined the subject-matter of the humanities in terms of its relevance to areas of human experience in which pupils would be expected to exercise judgement. It then specified a general aim to orientate the teaching of humanities so defined: to develop an understanding of social situations and human acts and of the controversial value issues which they raise.

I can remember being rather puzzled as to precisely what this formulation of Stenhouse's meant. He not only resisted the 'rational planning' procedure of operationally defining general aims in terms of measurable learning outcomes, but also politely ignored my attempts to sharpen the concept of 'understanding' through philosophical analysis. However, he did submit the idea to a type of analysis which was at the time quite unique in the field of curriculum development. Drawing on R.S. Peters's claim that educational aims imply process rather than outcome criteria, he proceeded to analyse the idea of 'understanding' into principles of classroom procedure. In other words, from a general aim he generated what I have called a praxiology. But let him describe this process:

> To abandon the support of behavioural objectives is to take on the task of finding some other means of translating aims into practice. We attempted to analyse the implications of our aim by deriving from it a specification of use of materials and a teaching strategy consistent with the pursuit of the aim. In other words we concentrated on logical consistency between classroom process and aim, rather than between predetermined terminal behaviours and aim.[8]

Given this basic view that general aims in education imply the kind of classroom conditions which are necessary for their realization, Stenhouse felt little need for sophisticated philosophical analyses conducted from the armchair. Greater clarity about the project's general aim, he argued, would emerge from teachers' attempts to translate its principles of procedure into action. The argument exactly mirrored Aristotle's view that in *praxis*, as opposed to instrumental action, ends cannot be reflected upon independently from means.

The procedural principles that emerged constituted a 'theory of understanding' rendered in the form of a praxiology for teachers of the humanities. It was something which, in my view, teachers had needed for some time, but it was not widely accessible until after the initial trial phase of the project in schools. The project's official handbook asserts the following principles:

1   that controversial issues should be handled in the classroom with adolescents;
2   that the teacher accepts the need to submit his teaching in controversial areas to the criterion of neutrality at this stage of education, i.e. that he regards it as part of his responsibility not to promote his own view;
3   that the mode of enquiry in controversial areas should have discussion, rather than instruction, as its core;
4   that the discussion should protect divergence of view among participants, rather than attempt to achieve consensus;
5   that the teacher as chairman of the discussion should have responsibility for quality and standards in learning.[9]

These *principles* are not so specific as to tell teachers what to do. In other words they are not *rules*. Exactly how they are to be translated into classroom action remains an open question. They leave room for practical deliberation and reflection by teachers. This is a point I shall return to later.

For Stenhouse these principles, which he summarized as the 'demand that the teacher should be neutral on the issues under discussion but committed to certain procedural values' – *in* authority but not *an* authority – meant that it was not possible for the teacher to be a source of information 'in his own person' since this way of transmitting information 'will inevitably be coloured or at least limited by his own views'. Yet, he argued, to expect students (as pupils were significantly called in the project) 'to be the sole source of information in a discussion group of adolescents seems unwise'. So he solved this problem by conceptualizing relevant information as *material evidence*. The project produced packs of materials on such themes as 'War and society', 'The family', 'Relations between the sexes', 'Education', 'Poverty', 'People and work', 'Living in cities', and 'Law and order', which were revised and commercially published after the trial phase (1967–1970) by Heinemann Education Ltd. The 'evidence' was produced in the form of multi-media materials including print, photographs, tape-recordings, and film. It consisted of 'factual' material drawn from the behavioural sciences and history, as well as experiential material drawn from the arts – poetry, literature, song, music, paintings etc.

For Stenhouse, this material constituted *evidence of human ideas*, which were relevant to the discussion of human issues. Even the 'factual' statements drawn from the social sciences and history were to be treated as such. They were not to be treated simply as evidence of social facts, but as evidence of the theories and values which entered into people's interpretations of the social facts. This was a position Stenhouse held about facts in general; it was not merely related to those of the social studies. It runs throughout his argument in *Culture and Education*, and is the basis of his general conception of knowledge as intrinsically problematic. If facts are not just inert 'things out there' to be passively observed but dynamic interpretations of the world in the light of people's theories and values, then they are objects for discussion and judgement.

Stenhouse's position is very much in tune with that of the great philosopher of science, Karl Popper. In his intellectual autobiography *Unended Quest* (1974), Popper makes a distinction between World 1 – of things and objects, World 2 – of subjective experiences like thought processes, and World 3 – the ideas and theories which constitute the content of experience and thought. He writes:

> It is clear that everybody interested in science must be interested in World 3 objects. A physical scientist, to start with, may be interested mainly in World 1 objects – say, crystals and X-rays. But very soon he must realize how much depends on our interpretation of the facts, that is, on our theories, and so on World 3 objects.[10]

Popper's distinctions give us a better grasp of Stenhouse's view of how information generally should be handled in classrooms; as evidence of World 3 and not simply of World 1 objects. He called this third realm 'Culture'.

And so teachers of the humanities had the important role of mediating 'culture' to students, and this meant treating the material evidence or information in which it was embedded as open to discussion and individual judgement in classrooms. Their task was to introduce this evidence in terms of its relevance to the issue being discussed, and in accordance with the principles of procedure laid down. The pedagogic style was to be responsive to the views being expressed by students. 'Evidence' was to be 'fed into the process' and not used to predetermine it. This approach demanded great skill, because it involved a radical departure from the traditional procedure of presenting information merely as evidence of facts about the world of objects and things. It also involved a radical shift from the traditional role of the teacher as *an* authority, who by transmitting information via his or her own person endorsed its status as fact.

This conception of classroom information as providing access to the realm of culture was difficult for pupils as well as teachers to translate into action.

One of my major tasks as a member of the project team was to help teachers reflect about the implementation problems in the classroom. I remember being called into a school where the pupils were failing to discuss 'evidence' the teacher was putting before them. The teachers wondered whether 'the reading level' required by the material wasn't too high. This was a common complaint which often resulted in teachers carrying out a comprehension exercise 'before the pupils were able to discuss'. I observed a lesson in this school and true enough the students remained silent when faced with the evidence. After the lesson I interviewed them. The conversation went something like this:

J.E.   You didn't say very much?
St.   No, we don't like the readings.
J.E.   Why not?
St.   We disagree with them.
J.E.   Fine, why don't you say what it is you disagree with, in the classroom?
St.   The teacher wouldn't like it.
J.E.   Why not?
St.   The teacher agrees with them.
J.E.   How do you know?
St.   He wouldn't have given them to us if he disagreed with them, would he?

What the teachers had failed to clarify to the students was the different conception of classroom knowledge they were now attempting to operate with. Role change on the part of the teacher depends upon a corresponding change on the part of students. This can only be accomplished by clarifying and discussing the new expectations with students. And this in turn rests upon teachers grasping the theories of schooling students have developed from years of classroom experience, and which enter into and prejudice their interpretations of the 'new situation'.

The implementation of the project's innovatory procedures for handling information in classrooms ultimately rested on teachers' research into the ways students interpreted and responded to their actions in the classroom. In helping teachers in the trial schools to do this – through tape-recording their lessons, interviewing their students, and then analysing this data – the now extensive 'teachers as researchers' movement was born (see Nixon[11]).

During the trial phase of the project, members of the central team and teachers collaboratively gathered, shared, and analysed classroom data. From this process some common understandings were developed about the problems of translating the projects principles for handling evidence into action. At the dissemination phase these 'insights' were offered as hypotheses for teachers to test in relation to data drawn from their own classrooms. In order to avoid any suggestion of prescription they were posed as a series of questions for teachers adopting the project to answer.

Points to bear in mind when playing back and analysing tapes of discussions:

1   To what extent do you interrupt pupils while they are speaking? Why and to what effect?
2   Do you press individuals to take up moral positions? If so, what is the effect on the individual concerned?
3   Reflective discussion can often be slow-paced and contain sustained silences. What proportion of these silences are interrupted by you? Is your interruption ever simply a matter of breaking under the strain rather than a real contribution

to the task of the group? If the teacher gives way under the strain of silences and inevitably comes in to talk, the students can use silence as a weapon to make him take over the task they should face as a group.

4 Are you consistent and reliable in chairmanship? Are all the students treated with equal respect, and are all views, including those with which you sympathise, critically examined?

5 Do you habitually rephrase and repeat students' contributions? If so, what is the effect of this?

6 Do you press towards consensus? For example, 'Do we all agree?' If so, what is the effect of this type of question? Compare this with the effect of: 'What do other people think?' 'Does anyone disagree with that?' 'Can anyone see another possible view or interpretation?'

7 To what extent do you confirm? Do you for example, say: 'Yes' or 'No' or 'An interesting point' or 'Well done' or 'That's interesting'? What is the effect of this on the group? Is there any trace of students looking for rewards to you rather than to the task?

8 To what extent do you ask questions to which you think you know the answer? What is the effect of such questions on the group? What is the effect of questions to which you do not know the answer?

9 What prompts you to provide the group with a piece of evidence? Was the piece of evidence in practice helpful? If so, why? If not, why not?

10 Are you neutral on controversial issues? Do you disclose generalised moral judgements? For example, do you make it apparent that you think war is justified or not justified or that you think comprehensive schools are better – or worse – than grammar schools? Are values implicit in the question you ask? Are they implied in the words, gestures or tone of voice with which you follow a student's statement? Are you careful to maintain balance in clarifying or summarising a position or point of view? Are you scrupulous not to feed into the discussion evidence intended to push the group towards a view you yourself hold? Do you draw attention by questions to certain parts or aspects of a piece of evidence which seem to support a viewpoint with which you agree? Do you always encourage minority opinions?

11 Do you attempt to transmit through eliciting questions your own interpretation of the meaning of a piece of evidence such as a poem or a picture?[9]

In the first section of this chapter I argued that what innovatory teachers of the humanities lacked in the 1960s was a theory of understanding articulated as a praxiology. This is precisely what the Humanities Project provided them with for the 1970s. And during its trial phase a number of teachers proved that, given opportunity and support for reflective analysis, they could use it to improve the match between their aspirations and practice. The project in my view proved that, although it was difficult, teachers could develop a pedagogy which went some way towards realizing their dreams.

For the rest of this section on the Humanities Project I want to 'abstract' the theory of understanding embedded in its praxiology for handling evidence in classrooms.

I will begin with the principle that *discussion* rather than *instruction* should be the core activity in the classroom.

The project didn't see discussion as the only classroom activity. Creative and essay writing, drama, expressive art etc., all had a function as outcomes from, and inputs into, discussion. As such they constituted the students' creation of additional evidence to be looked at. The packs of materials produced by the project were only conceived as a *foundation collection* to get the process under- way. But then it was expected that the need for additional evidence, either created or discovered by the students through their own 'research', would be generated from the discussion group. Thus discussion was conceived as the core activity which co-ordinated and fostered a more general process of inquiry into an issue. Such an inquiry could last for weeks. This principle of discussion as the core activ- ity highlighted the failure of previous attempts to make discussion anything more than peripheral to instruction in classrooms.

The principle flows from Stenhouse's conception of the 'knowledge' to be trans- mitted by teachers as intrinsically problematic. As such it invites individual judge- ments and promotes an exchange of views. In attempting to translate this principle into action teachers are confronted with a radically different view of classroom learning to the one they have traditionally operated with. The established theory was that information had to be understood before it was judged; hence, the prob- lem trial-school teachers had in resisting comprehension exercises when students responded to evidence with silence. But by conceptualizing information as evidence for discussion, Stenhouse rejected the established theory and reinstated judgement. This assumed that understanding cannot be achieved independently of judgement. It is only by evoking students' judgements – in effect their prejudices – that they develop an understanding of human acts and situations.

This view is very similar to Gadamer's theory of interpretation (hermeneutics).[12] He argues that every act of interpretation, whether it be of a linguistic text or some other human act, involves bringing our fore-conceptions or prejudgements to bear on the evidence. This is a condition, not a barrier, to understanding, because we can only grasp meanings which derive from other people's experience in terms of the meanings we give to our own. There is no such thing as a bias-free interpreta- tion. The danger lies in the workings of unconscious bias, since this prevents us from being open to other people's meanings. However, once we become aware of our prejudices we can control them to establish a dialectical relationship with the evidence. The meanings which emerge as a result lie neither objectively in the evi- dence nor subjectively in the prejudgements brought to bear on it. They emerge from within the dialectical process itself. Thus the development of understanding is a working-out of, and extension of, one's prejudices in relation to evidence of other people's meanings. In explaining his mentor, Heidegger's theory of under- standing, Gadamer writes:

> The process...is that every revision of the fore-project is capable of projecting before itself a new project of meaning, that rival projects can emerge side by side until it becomes clearer what the unity of meaning is, that interpretation begins with fore-conceptions that are replaced by more suitable ones. This constant process of new projection is the movement of understanding and inter- pretation. A person who is trying to understand is exposed to distraction from fore-meanings that are not borne out by the things themselves. The working- out of appropriate projects, anticipatory in nature, to be confirmed 'by the things' themselves, is the constant task of understanding. The only 'objectivity' here is the confirmation of a fore-meaning in its being worked out.[12]

Within the Humanities project it is the teacher's transmission of evidence as 'problematic knowledge' which enables students to make their prejudices explicit and thereby become aware of them. But this kind of transmission also allows a variety of prejudgements to emerge. And so the process of knowledge transmission is such that, in Gadamer's words, 'rival projects can emerge side by side'. The importance of alternative viewpoints emerging from the confrontation with evidence is underlined by the principles that the teacher should *protect divergence of view* and *refrain from using his or her authority position to promote their own views*. The former principle should not be confused, as we often had to point out, with 'promoting divergence'. The point of 'protecting divergence' is to allow the full range of existing unconscious biases to emerge, and not to manipulate biases into existence for the sake of divergence. And this is obviously inconsistent with the teacher who uses his or her authority position to promote their own views. Such a strategy inevitably imposes a constraint on the conscious expression of biases when they contradict the teacher's own.

Many teachers have interpreted the principle of procedural neutrality as the teacher not presenting his own views to the class, and Stenhouse himself tended to promote this interpretation. However, I would argue that if a teacher gave his own views, having made it clear that they should be treated as equally problematic to those expressed by students, and subsequently handled the discussion impartially, then his conduct would have been procedurally neutral. Since in practice it is so difficult for students to disassociate a teacher's authority position from his 'personal knowledge', neutrality will normally involve refraining from expressing his or her views in person; at least in the early stages of the work with students.

Now the teacher's role in introducing evidence is not simply to stimulate rival judgements, but also to *discipline the discussion* which emerges as a result. Hence, the principle that as chairman the teacher is *responsible for quality and standards in learning*. After the initial stage of eliciting, divergent views had successfully emerged in trial-school classrooms (where teachers were advised to work with half-classes), the project team noticed a tendency for the discussion to take the form of a hot and heated argument in which each student merely 'dug in' and defended his or her views by attempting to undermine other people's. Although teachers often perceived this as an indicator for a 'good discussion', since the pupils appeared 'involved', the project team felt it indicated little development of understanding. Such development seemed to imply a degree of openness towards having one's judgements modified. We began as a result to draw a distinction between *argumentative* and *reflective discussion*.

The significance of the emergence of alternative views is that it gives each individual an opportunity to look at an issue from a variety of perspectives and therefore adopt a more open attitude towards his or her own judgements. Teachers can help each student in this respect by ensuring that they *listen to* the words in which other students express their views, and attempt through asking questions to grasp something of other ways of looking at a situation; of the criteria and standards others employ for evaluating it. By ensuring that students listen to, and ask questions of each other, teachers exercise responsibility for the quality and standards of learning, because this kind of reflective discussion establishes the dialectic of meanings through which understanding – what Gadamer describes as 'the unity of meaning' – is developed.

But, as Stenhouse realized, teachers not only exercised this responsibility by getting students to listen and ask questions of each other's views. In order to provide conditions for developing understanding of an issue, they needed to widen the discussion by introducing relevant evidence from our rich cultural inheritance.

And here, too, the procedure is one of establishing a dialectical process between evidence and individual judgement by ensuring that students listen to, and ask questions of, the evidence.

I hope I have done sufficient to indicate something of the theory of understanding embedded in the Humanities Project's pedagogical procedures for handling information in classrooms. It is a theory which posits understanding, interpretation, and judgement as different aspects of a unified learning process. In the project's handbook for teachers, Stenhouse wrote: 'The insight into a situation offered by evidence can be grasped only by the exercise of judgement in its interpretation'.[8] In order to understand facts about a human act or situation we need to interpret them (including facts about human artifacts like works of art) in terms of the theories and ideas which underlie their construction. But we cannot do this without bringing our prejudgements about these acts and situations to bear in our interpretations. By becoming aware of our own prejudgements we become more open to the meanings the facts express. Out of the dialectical process which emerges our understanding of the facts is extended, and our judgement of the act or situation to which they refer modified. It is *in*, not as a result of, the development of understanding that the capacity for responsible judgement is extended.

Within the praxiology of the Humanities Project, Stenhouse embedded a theory of understanding which coherently demonstrated how information about human acts and situations could be made 'relevant' to the 'responsible judgement' of individuals. In *Culture and Education* he summarized his position as follows:

> We are faced with the fact that we interact with the past through an immense store of written records and works of art. These stored ideas allow us to bring 'the best that has been thought and said' into a dialogue with our contemporary culture. Interaction with the past is an element in our own cultural development; and it is of course a major role of the educational system to keep going this conversation of past with present.

Although there are many teachers in the UK today who would claim that the Humanities Project helped them to radically improve their professional practice, the winds of political change were blowing through secondary education in the early 1970s. The growth towards comprehensive schools speeded up considerably. It was politically justified by the claim that they could do as good a job as the grammar schools, and for a wider range of the population. The criterion of success was taken from the grammar school; namely, pupil pass rates in public examinations. David Hargreaves has recently argued that: 'Leading members of the Labour Party, from Hugh Gaitskell to Harold Wilson, proclaimed to the public that the comprehensive schools would be "grammar schools for all" '.[13] And so, according to Hargreaves, through the growth of comprehensive reorganization and people's attempts to legitimate it in terms of a grammar school education for all, secondary education in Britain became 'grammarized'. He points out that this led to the death of the innovatory aspirations of many teachers in secondary modern schools. The emphasis increasingly during the 1970s was on maximizing every pupil's chances of examination success. 'Subjects' came back and with them a concept of knowledge as a body of inert factual information to be recalled and comprehended, but rarely problematic enough to discuss.

[. . .]

References

1 Evans, N. *Curriculum Change in Secondary Schools, 1957–2004*, Wobourn Series (London, Routledge, 2005).
2 Stenhouse, L. *Culture and Education* (Nelson & Sons, London, 1967).
3 Stenhouse, L. Curriculum research and the art of the teacher. *Curriculum*, 1 (Spring 1980).
4 Stenhouse, L. Some limitations of the use of objectives in curriculum research and planning. *Pedagogica Europaea*, 6 (1970), pp. 73–83.
5 Peters, R.S. *Authority, Responsibility and Education* (George Allen and Unwin, London, 1963).
6 Aristotle *Ethics Books 3 and 6* (Penguin, Harmondsworth).
7 The Schools Council *Raising the School Leaving Age*, Working Paper No. 2 (HMSO, London, 1965).
8 Stenhouse, L. The Humanities Curriculum Project: the rationale. *Theory into Practice*, 10 (1970).
9 Stenhouse, L. *The Humanities Project: An Introduction* (Heinemann Educational Books, London, 1970).
10 Popper, K.R. *Unended Quest: an Intellectual Autobiography* (Collins/Fontana, Glasgow, 1976).
11 Nixon, J. (ed.) *A Teacher's Guide to Action Research* (Grant McIntyre, London, 1981).
12 Gadamer, Hans-Georg *Truth and Method* (Sheed and Ward Stagbooks, London, 1975), pp. 236–237.
13 Hargreaves, D. *The Challenge For the Comprehensive School* (Routledge & Kegan Paul, London, 1982).

CHAPTER 2

DEVELOPING HYPOTHESES ABOUT CLASSROOMS FROM TEACHERS' PRACTICAL CONSTRUCTS

An account of the work of the Ford Teaching Project

Interchange, Vol. 7, No. 2, pp. 2–22, OISE 1976–77

The context of the project[1]

The Ford Teaching Project was an attempt to involve 40 teachers in the East Anglian region of the United Kingdom in a programme of action research into the problems of implementing inquiry/discovery approaches in classrooms. The project developed out of a concern that the curriculum reform movement, sponsored by the Nuffield Foundation and the Schools Council in the UK, had largely failed at the level of classroom implementation. On the basis of the model of research, development, and diffusion, ideas were poured into the system. Many became distorted in the process of dissemination. Teachers in the target audience, sceptical of the possibilities of implementing the reformers' ideas in their classrooms, negotiated what they were prepared to accept. Another problem was that even those teachers who consciously embraced the radical nature of the innovations offered were not aware if these ideas actually guided their practice. The theories one consciously subscribes to are not necessarily those that unconsciously guide practice. Curriculum reformers are confronted either with the cynics, who refuse "to dream" and subsequently try to transform their ideas to fit their own reality, or with the dreamers, who idealize their practice to fit their dreams.

The fundamental problem of curriculum reform lies in the clash between the theories of the reformers and those implicit, often unconsciously, in the practice of teachers. Reformers fail to realize that fundamental changes in classroom practice can be brought about only if teachers become conscious of the latter theories and are able to reflect critically about them. Reformers' attempts to advocate their own theories may also reflect a lack of self-criticism, for they could present them in an experimental form as ideas to be tested and evaluated by the teachers themselves. Teachers would then be encouraged to reflect about the theories implicit in their own practices and cease to regard them as self-evident. The curriculum reform movement has largely missed an opportunity to involve teachers in the process of theory development.

Perhaps the notable exception among curriculum reformers in the UK is Lawrence Stenhouse (Stenhouse *et al.*, 1970), the Director of the Schools Council Humanities Project. Stenhouse sees curriculum development as the business of getting teachers to test the feasibility of a curriculum proposal in practice. Concerned with helping them handle controversial issues with adolescents in the classroom, his team defined a set of teaching principles for discussion-based inquiry aimed at an understanding of the issues. These included the infamous criteria of "procedural neutrality" and "protecting divergence." The team asked teachers to explore the problem of implementing these principles in practice. A considerable amount of their resources went into helping teachers collect and analyse data about their own classroom situations.

It was out of my involvement in this work, as a member of Stenhouse's team, that the idea of the Teaching Project (eventually sponsored in 1973 by the Ford Foundation) arose. It became clear that many of the problems of implementing discussion-based inquiry approaches were caused by teachers' habitual and unconscious behaviour patterns. For example, students' failure to discuss ideas could be explained in terms of teachers' tendencies to invite consensus, reinforce some views rather than others, and promote their own views. It was only by becoming aware of these patterns and reflecting about the theories implicit in them that teachers were able to modify their behaviour. These theories, once conscious, furnished reasons for refraining from performing under these descriptions and thereby generated new practical theories, e.g., about ways of protecting divergence in discussion. Such theories were implicit in teachers' conscious attempts to change their behaviour patterns in the light of the project's principles of procedure.

It also became clear that many of the salient patterns referred to could be generalized across classrooms, subject areas, and schools. Teachers involved in the project were drawn from different subject areas and exhibited similar behaviour patterns. It was this observation that suggested that the reasons for the general failure of teachers to implement the inquiry/discovery approaches advocated by the majority of curriculum development projects might be highly generalizable, even across student age levels. It suggested the possibility of teachers getting together across classrooms, schools, age levels, and curricula, to develop collaboratively a practical theory of inquiry/discovery teaching.

The organizational framework of the project

Forty teachers from 12 schools were invited to join the project. They were supported by a central team of three: two full-time researchers – Clem Adelman and myself – and a secretary, Tina Reay, who was also responsible for co-ordinating liaison between schools and between schools and ourselves. In addition, two local authority advisers to schools were nominated by the local regional authorities to help us support the work of teachers in their area on a part-time basis.

The teachers were grouped in school teams, as members of which it was hoped they would meet frequently to discuss teaching problems and share ideas about methods of collecting data. The teams were interdisciplinary in the sense that members were drawn from different curriculum areas. They also came from different kinds of schools, i.e., junior (7–11), middle (8–12 or 9–13), and secondary schools (11 or 13+). Arrangements were made at teachers centres for twice-a-term inter-school meetings between two to four teams. During the four terms the project lasted in schools, all the teachers were also brought together for three residential four-day conferences – at the beginning, halfway through, and at the end of the period (1973–1974). These arrangements were intended to supply teachers with opportunities for lateral communication across established educational boundaries, which tend to be guarded by those above them in the educational hierarchy. House (1974) argued that, since lateral communication between teachers increases rewards from peers and feeds professional ambition, it threatens hierarchical control over teachers' access to ideas and has political implications for increasing their professional autonomy. It was our view that lateral communication about classroom problems increases teacher autonomy because it supports critical reflection about practice and thereby gives teachers greater control over their own behaviour. The provision of such opportunities for sharing ideas reflected our aspiration to involve a group of teachers in the development of a theory about their own practice – in this case of inquiry/discovery teaching – that subsequently other teachers might have access to as support for their continuing reflection about classroom problems.

The project's design as classroom action research

Those curriculum reformers in the UK who have expressed concern with the failure of the research, development, and diffusion model to secure implementation have tended to offer a problem-solving approach as a possible solution to fostering innovation at the classroom level. MacDonald and Walker (1976) defined the main features of this approach as follows:

> In the Problem-solver perspective the receiver . . . initiates the process of change by identifying an area of concern or by sensing a need for change. Once the problem area is identified, the receiver undertakes to alter the situation either through his own efforts, or by recruiting suitable outside assistance . . . the receiver in the P-S model is actively involved in finding an innovation to solve his own problem. . . . The relationship between sender and receiver is one of collaboration.

The essential features of the problem-solving approach are (1) its focus on practical problems defined by practitioners, and (2) collaboration between outsiders and practitioners, who in dialogue seek solutions to the practitioners' problem. Initially these reflected the basic elements of our project's design, with one exception. Our design was concerned with generalization. We wanted teachers not only to monitor their own problems and develop practical hypotheses about how they arose and could be resolved, but also to explore the extent to which these problems and hypotheses could be generalized to other teachers' classrooms. In this connection we were attracted by Rappaport's (1970) definition of action research as something that "aims to contribute both to the practical concerns of people in an immediate problematic situation and to the goals of social science by joint collaboration within a mutually acceptable ethical framework." We consequently came to prefer *action research* rather than *problem-solving* as a description of our design.

However, on later reflection, Rappaport's view of action research appears to be distorted by his interests as a social scientist. We were concerned with the development of a general theory, but we preferred to describe it as a *practical* rather than a social science theory. Practical theories have evaluative implications for the question "what ought to be done?", and if "a social science theory" implies something that is value-neutral, then this would not reflect our aspirations. In our view action research involves theorizing about practical problems in particular situations and exploring the extent to which these practical theories are generalizable. Implicit in our design is a distinction between *practical* and *theoretical* theories.

In the early part of 1973 we recruited teachers who experienced some dissonance between their practice and their aspirations to implement inquiry/discovery approaches. At this time we were not interested in the no-problems people. From our positions as university researchers, it was difficult to get access to the teachers we wanted. We had to work our way down the hierarchy from local authority administrators to head teachers before gaining access to groups of teachers. By the time we met groups of "interested" teachers it was difficult to determine how the project had been communicated to them and whether or not their motives for joining stemmed from a genuine desire to reflect about their classroom problems. The difficulties this situation presented for us become clear if I explain our attempts to put across the idea of collaborative action research to the teachers who assembled for our launching-off conference during the Easter 1973 vacation.

Rather naively, we assumed the teachers were all anxious to get working on some systematic reflection on their classroom problems. We outlined the main purpose of the conference as "the negotiation of research tasks, roles, procedures, and methods," and had produced a document to serve as the basis for discussion.[2] The idea was to revise the document as a result of discussion and distribute it as an agreed contract between teachers and ourselves. A brief summary of the document is as follows:

A. Action-research tasks

1   To identify and diagnose in particular situations the problems that arise from attempts to implement inquiry/discovery approaches effectively, and to explore the extent to which problems and diagnostic hypotheses can be generalized.
2   To develop and test practical hypotheses about how the teaching problems identified might be resolved, and to explore the extent to which they could be generally applied.
3   To clarify the aims, values, and principles implicit in inquiry/discovery approaches by reflecting about the values implicit in the problems identified.

B. Roles

Responsibility for the action-research tasks to be shared between teachers and the central team working with them. The central team would also take some responsibility for circulating the reports of school teams to other schools.

C. Methods of data collection

1. *Teacher field-notes*. Keeping field-notes is essentially a method of reporting observations of, and reflections about, classroom problems and the teachers' own reactions to them. They should be written as soon as possible after a lesson and, if possible, draw on impressionistic jottings made during a lesson. The greater the time lapse the more difficult it becomes to accurately reconstruct problems and responses and retain conscious awareness of one's thinking about them at the time.

2. *Pupil diaries*. Since the practical problems of teaching are those that arise in the teachers' relationship to their students, the latter are in a good position to identify and diagnose them. However, getting honest feedback from students is difficult. One possible solution is to ask students towards the end of sessions to produce in writing their own accounts of the lesson, and to give them control over teacher access to the accounts. Even if teachers never gain complete access, students might draw on these diaries when discussing classroom problems with them. The fact that they have reflected about them prior to discussion may increase their capacity to report their views honestly.

3. Teacher-student discussion. Teacher field-notes and student diaries might be used as resources in discussions where teachers and students share their accounts of lessons. These could be tape-recorded for further study.

4. Tape-recording. Teacher field-notes cannot capture what the teacher was unaware of at the time. Tape-recordings can. They can provide teachers with valuable data about their own and their students' behaviour, and thereby help them to become aware of both their own actions and students' responses to them. Tape-recordings of classroom events can be useful sources of evidence against which to check teachers' and students' retrospective accounts of lessons.

5. Case studies. At the end of the last term of the research, teachers might produce a case study of problems and strategies with a particular class of students during that term. The study would be based on data collected by the methods and techniques just outlined.

D. Reporting procedures

At the end of each term each co-ordinator of a school team would send the central team a report on team meetings within the school. The report would cite common problems and hypotheses identified by the team.

E. Ethics of research

Since the action research would involve other teachers' and central team members' having access to data from a teacher's classroom, some agreement had to be reached about *who* has rights of control over *what* data. The following procedural principles were suggested:

1   Individual teachers ought to control both the extent to and the conditions under which other teachers have access to data from their classrooms.
2   Head teachers ought to control the extent to which classroom data from their school are accessible to outsiders and the conditions under which access is given.
3   Individual teachers ought to control the central team's access to both their classrooms and private interview situations with students.
4   Classroom data gathered by the project's central team ought to be made accessible to the teachers concerned, except data over which students have rights of control, i.e., student accounts of classroom problems and teaching strategies.
5   Students interviewed by the central team ought to control the extent to which others, including their teachers, have access to their accounts.

The teachers' general reaction to the document was that they didn't have time to carry out the tasks in the ways suggested. We realized that such scepticism is often well founded. Schools have not on the whole institutionalized support for reflective teaching. Teachers embark on innovations without the time and opportunity required for resolving the classroom problems they pose.

We spent a considerable part of our initial discussions with head teachers trying to negotiate institutional support for the work of school teams, e.g., for opportunities to meet together in school time. Interested head teachers at the time said they "would see what could be done," but many, as we discovered later, did very little. Perhaps, in this initial stage, we should have concentrated more on the selection of schools than on the recruitment of teachers within them. There is probably a strong correlation between the opportunities an institution allows for practical reflection and the ability of the teachers who work in it to be aware of gaps between aspirations and practice. In retrospect it was clear that the two school teams who made the greatest initial progress on the tasks outlined were those with the most opportunities for discussion and reflection in their schools.

Many teachers at the conference felt not only that they didn't have time to reflect about problems but also that there was little point in doing so. These teachers had little sense of their practice not matching their dreams. They assumed they were already practising inquiry/discovery teaching quite successfully. Later we learned that some teachers were involved simply because participation in projects enhances career prospects, and, as they were already "doing inquiry/discovery," involvement might bring rewards with a minimum of effort. There was another, smaller group of teachers who appeared to lack any commitment to inquiry/discovery approaches at all. Again, we later discovered that these had come because their head teachers had intimated, "If you want to get a good reference, you don't say no."

Our attempts to "negotiate" teacher participation in action research resulted in a rather reserved acceptance of our document in principle, with some suggested alterations. At the time, our ignorance of why teachers had come prevented us from appreciating the unreality of our attempts. During the first term of the project in schools, it became clear that, in the majority of cases, action research was simply not getting off the ground. Regular team meetings materialized in only two schools. A small minority of teachers used field-notes, tape-recorded their lessons, and discussed classroom problems with students. The majority asked students to keep diaries, but reported little evidence of any deeper thinking beyond "it was a bit boring," or "the lesson was all right." Feed-back from schools was sparse. About two-thirds of the teachers appeared to believe they had few problems in implementing inquiry/discovery approaches successfully. We had agreed to go into schools to work with teachers once problems began to emerge, but telephone inquiries during the first half of the term were met with the typical reply, "Everything seems to be going well," implying, "Don't call us, we'll call you."

This experience of trying to involve teachers in action research led to further developments in the project's design. We faced a situation where two-thirds of the teachers who had joined the project appeared to have little interest in doing action research or opportunities within their schools to cultivate such interests. We therefore had to draw a firm distinction between those teachers who are ready to reflect more deeply about their practice because they at least sense gaps between it and their aspirations, and those who are not ready because they have no sense of any such gap existing. After the first conference it became clear that our problem was how to motivate the majority of teachers to adopt a reflective stance, since the action research approach presupposes readiness to reflect. And even those dozen or so teachers who were properly motivated found pressures of time and work load overriding their commitment to the enterprise.

In the light of these considerations we defined a second-order action-research role for ourselves, namely, to develop practical hypotheses relevant to the question, "How can one make teachers begin to reflect about their practice?" It was in this context that the idea of the *self-monitoring teacher* began to crystallize as the key concept. Self-monitoring is the process by which one becomes aware of one's situation and one's own role as an agent in it. Awareness is, in the language of Dewey, the end-in-view of the self-monitoring agent. However, self-monitoring, although a necessary condition of awareness, is by no means sufficient. It expresses an objective attitude towards situation and self and indicates that certain subjective obstacles to awareness have been overcome, e.g., bias and prejudice. As Hamlyn (1972) argued, "objectivity" does not imply the achievement of "truth." It remains possible for a person who gives an objective account of a situation to honestly misdescribe some aspects at the same time, perhaps because of the complexity, ambiguity, or insufficiency of the evidence.

The concept of self-monitoring clarified for us what was involved in practical reflection. In its light one can make a clear distinction between (1) teachers who are adopting an objective stance to their practice but require support in collecting and analysing more sufficient data as a basis for constructing accurate accounts; (2) teachers who are not adopting an objective stance but, inasmuch as they feel their situation to be problematic, are ready to do so; (3) teachers who are neither ready nor able to adopt an objective stance to their practice. We now think that at the beginning of the project only one of the 40 teachers was self-monitoring to any significant extent. Another 12 probably had some genuine sense of their teaching being problematic. Two-thirds of the teachers fell into the third category. At the end of the project we estimated that 25 teachers had made some progress at self-monitoring. (Eight teachers dropped out during the first term.)

Teachers' theories of teaching

The negotiation of tasks, roles, procedures, and methods was not the only aim we set ourselves at the launching-off conference. We wanted the teachers to begin to explore typical problems. Realizing that they would initially be very defensive about citing their problems in front of people they hardly knew, we prepared excerpts of lessons from transcripts, videotapes, tape-recordings, and slides for them to discuss. We hoped that this material, taken from the lessons of teachers not involved in the project, would enable them to talk about typical classroom problems without drawing too much attention to their own practice.

The discussions of transcripts and recordings were marked by apparent communication difficulties. Different teachers appeared to use different terms to mean the same or different things, or to use the same terms but to disagree in their application. We felt that if teachers were subsequently going to share ideas they would have to develop a common language for talking about classrooms together.[3] After the conference we listened to the recordings of the discussions to try to clarify the communication difficulties, and found that a number of terms tended to be used again and again in teachers' judgements about teaching situations. The most frequently recurring terms, other than "discovery" and "inquiry," were formal, informal; structured, unstructured; framework; teacher-directed; self-directed (child); guided; open-ended; dependent (child), independent (child); subject-centred, child-centred.

We invited teachers to discuss the meanings of these terms at team and regional meetings and to report back. We also went into schools and discussed them with teachers. We discovered that although teachers might be using different terms they were often doing so to label the same things. A surprising degree of consensus appeared to exist about which dimensions of meaning are significant in appraisals of teaching situations. Three main dimensions emerged:

1. *Formal–informal; dependent–independent.* The terms formal–informal were used to pick out the degree of intellectual dependence–independence of students on the teacher's authority position.

2. *Structured–unstructured; subject-centred–child-centred.* Structured was inter-changeable with framework, but more widely used than the latter. Structured–unstructured could be interchanged with subject-centred–child-centred. Both these sets of terms referred to the teachers' aims and were used to describe the degree to which they were concerned with getting students to achieve preconceived knowledge outcomes. The more the teacher's aims are concerned with getting preconceived knowledge outcomes, the more structured or subject-centred the teaching; the more they are concerned with the *process* rather than the *products* of learning, with how the student is to learn rather than with what, then the more unstructured or child-centred the teaching.

3. *Directed–guided–open-ended.* These three terms picked out points along a single dimension and referred to the methods by which teachers try to implement their aims. The teachers' methods tend to be directive when they prescribe in advance for students how a learning activity is to be performed. They are guided when they are responsive to problems perceived by students in performing learning activities, e.g., by asking questions, making suggestions, or introducing ideas in response to task problems cited by students. Open-ended methods are negative in character, being solely concerned with refraining from imposing constraints on students' abilities to direct their own learning. The directed–guided–open-ended dimension picked out the degree of control the teacher tries to exert over the learning activities of the student.

To facilitate communication between teachers about the three dimensions, we suggested that descriptions of teaching situations should be couched in the following terms only: formal–informal; structured–unstructured; directed–guided–open-ended. Discussions and interviews with teachers about the meanings of terms also clari-fied apparent disagreements about the application of terms. Teachers held different views about which meanings were compatible and incompatible with each other. Thus for some teachers an informal classroom was associated with unstructured teaching and seen to be incompatible with a structured approach. For others, there was no incompatibility between structured teaching and an informal classroom situation. These different views explained disagreements about whether a particu-lar classroom situation was to be classified as informal or formal. Similar problems arose with appraisals of the extent to which aims are structured rather than unstructured. Some teachers strongly associated open-ended strategies with the pur-suit of unstructured aims, while others believed guided methods were compatible with such aims.

It became clear that the ways these meanings were associated with each other in teachers' minds reflected their theories of inquiry/discovery teaching. Several associations were elicited, as shown in Figure 2.1. It should be obvious that the meanings identified were determined by the teachers' values. Significant meanings are made so by teachers' aspirations to foster and protect self-directed learning (independent reasoning) in classrooms. They pin-point variables that may affect students' abilities to direct their own learning. Thus the degree to which teachers intend preconceived knowledge outcomes may influence the control they attempt to exercise over students' thinking, which in turn may influence the extent to which the learning situation provides a context that protects (informal) and fosters self-direction. The outline in Figure 2.1 schematically represents the range of teach-ers' views about how pedagogically significant classroom variables interact with each other. It consequently reflects the different practical theories teachers brought to bear in analysis of the classroom data presented to them at the first conference. Many of the disagreements between teachers could be explained not just in terms

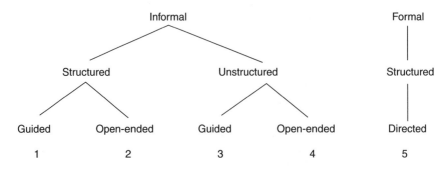

Figure 2.1 Interaction of inquiry/discovery teaching variables.

of terminological confusions – although these also abounded — but in terms of conflicting practical theories. Although there was general agreement about the effects of structured–directed approaches on the learning situation, there was disagreement about how a learning context that protected and fostered self-directed learning could be achieved. We discovered that a few teachers were sufficiently sophisticated to realize that different theories could be held in different contexts. These teachers tended to be aware of more than one pattern of meanings. However, a substantial number of teachers believed that an informal–structured–guided pattern could be realized in any classroom situation.

I now set out explicitly the theories implicit in each of the patterns of meaning shown in Figure 2.1:

1   *Informal–structured–guided.* A teacher can pursue preconceived knowledge outcomes by guiding students towards them without imposing constraints on their ability to direct their own learning.
2   *Informal–structured–open-ended.* A teacher can pursue preconceived knowledge outcomes *and* foster and protect self-directed learning by concentrating solely on removing constraints and refraining from any kind of positive intervention in the learning process.
3   *Informal–unstructured–guided.* A teacher can foster and protect self-directed learning *and* exercise positive influence on the learning process so long as this influence is not exerted to bring about preconceived knowledge outcomes.
4   *Informal–unstructured–open-ended.* A teacher cannot foster and protect self-directed learning *and* pursue preconceived knowledge outcomes *or* exercise positive influence on learning processes. Teaching strategies must be restricted to protecting students' self-direction.
5   *Formal–structured–directed.* A teacher fails to protect self-directed learning by pursuing preconceived knowledge outcomes in a way that is intended to make the student intellectually dependent on the teacher's authority position.

During the second term of the project we asked teachers to identify which of these theories guided their own practice and to test the extent to which the theory accurately described it. For example, a teacher who became aware of adopting a structured–guided approach would know that theory 1 was tending to guide practice. The teacher could then test the extent to which the theory was being realized by assessing whether or not the approach actually protected and fostered self-directed learning. If it didn't, then the teacher needed to generate a new theory. The schema outlined in Figure 2.1 was derived empirically and describes a number of theories that actually informed our teachers' practice. However, it does not represent the full range of patterns that could possibly be developed about the relationships between teachers' categories. By relating the categories in terms of all their logically possible combinations we eventually produced the typology of teaching patterns shown in Figure 2.2.

Not all of these 10 types could possibly guide practice in the sense of reflecting teaching patterns a teacher might want to realize. The typology reflects both unintended as well as intended outcomes of teaching. Types 3, 6, 7, 9, and 10 indicate gaps between aspirations and practice while types 1, 2, 4, 5, and 8 indicate intentional patterns. For example, in type 7, structured–guided signifies an attempt to protect self-directed learning while pursuing preconceived knowledge outcomes. However, the presence of the third aspect, formal, indicates that guidance fails to protect self-directed learning when teaching is structured.

We found that a large number of our teachers operated with the theory that it was possible to protect self-directed learning and pursue preconceived knowledge outcomes at the same time (type 2) if they adopted responsive (guided) rather than directive methods of teaching. However, on reflection many of them discovered that the structured–guided approach did not work. They became aware that such approaches unintentionally resulted in students remaining in a state of intellectual dependence on the teachers' authority position. As a result the theory implied by the formal–structured–guided association (type 7) began to inform their practice and became implicit in a more informal–unstructured approach in the classroom (types 4 and 5).

It is worth pointing out the implications of the patterns reflected in this typology. The value of self-directed learning is implied by both the formal–informal and the directed–guided–open-ended sets of categories. The former set picks out the extent to which self-directed learning is *actually* protected while the latter picks out whether or not the teacher is *trying* to protect self-direction. Both guided and open-ended indicate a desire not to intervene in ways that impose constraints on self-directed learning. If the type 2 pattern guides teachers' conception of their practice, it will have normative implications for them. The truth of the theory implies that they *ought* to adopt a structured–guided approach in their classroom. However, if they discover that the theory is false, and that the type 7 pattern tends to hold instead, then they develop a new theory. The fact that teachers' theories are not value-free and imply practical judgements about what ought to be done is what makes them practical theories. If teachers are not modifying their teaching behaviour over time, one has good grounds for assuming that they are not testing and developing theory.

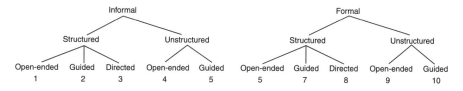

Figure 2.2 Typology of teaching patterns.

The categories generated from our discussions and interviews with teachers provided the basis for theory clarification, testing, and development in the project. They furnished a framework for discussions not only between teachers but also between teachers and ourselves. So many past attempts to produce theories of teaching have been fruitless in practice because researchers have refused to take into account the perspectives of practitioners and to build theory from this standpoint. Researchers tend to locate theory within the context of a value-free "theoretical" discipline. But if theory development is to have any practical significance for teachers, it must be rooted in those conceptualizations that arise out of their practical deliberations about what to do. And these conceptualizations will inevitably express an evaluative point of view. In our view there can be no value-free educational research, since what makes research "educational" is its contribution to the development of theories that have normative implications for those who are committed to education.

Criteria for testing practical theories of inquiry/discovery teaching

Both at the initial conference and in later discussions and interviews with teachers it was clear that they characterized inquiry/discovery teaching as an attempt to protect and foster self-direction in the learning situation. This aim was assumed to be conceptually related to inquiry/discovery approaches. In other words, it was not possible for teachers to adopt the approach without attempting to protect and foster self-direction. Our teachers disagreed about whether other ends, such as knowledge outcomes that are extrinsically related to these approaches, could be pursued at the same time. But what was agreed was that for the inquiry/discovery teacher, learning outcomes do not necessarily justify means. Whatever knowledge outcomes are pursued, the methods one adopts must satisfy the criteria of protecting and fostering students' ability to achieve this knowledge through their own powers of reason.

It is against these criteria that the inquiry/discovery teacher needs to test the sort of practical theories I have outlined. However, self-directed learning is a rather abstract idea and we thought we could help teachers test and develop theory if we could analyse it into more concrete criteria.

There has been a tendency for theorists to view educational aims as end-products of learning and to try to analyse abstract ideas into more specific behavioural objectives. However, in performing our analysis we were heavily influenced by the philosophical work of R.S. Peters on the nature of discourse about aims in education. His views were first articulated in a seminal paper published in 1963 entitled, "Must an Educator Have an Aim?" (Peters, 1968). He argued that it is important not to confuse two quite distinct ways of conceptualizing aims in education. Sometimes aims are appropriately conceived as products or end-states. It is here that the language of objectives is appropriate. At other times it is more appropriate to view aims as clusters of values and principles of procedure that not so much define the intended products of teaching and learning activities as the manner in which they are to be performed. As Peters said, "Values are involved in education not so much as goals or end-products, but as principles implicit in different manners of proceeding or producing."

We believed that self-directed learning should be conceived as a procedural aim of this kind, and that it would distort its nature as a process criterion to view it as an end-product or object of mastery by students. There is no end-state that can be labelled "self-directed" as opposed to "other-directed." People can be placed on a continuum but judgements are necessarily qualitative. Students can become more rather than less self-directed. But as a criterion it can never be fully realized. Objectives appropriately specify standards of mastery learning. Students can gain mastery in terms of knowledge and skills but they cannot gain mastery in self-direction. The standard is an infinitely receding one. The fostering and protection of self-direction then are criteria by which teachers can criticize their performance but they are never aspirations that can be fully realized. There is therefore necessarily an element of indeterminacy in practical theorizing about education procedures. Nevertheless, we were convinced that the quality of teachers' judgements could be enhanced by clarifying the values and principles implicit in the complex idea of self-directed learning.

It is perhaps no coincidence that the first person in the UK to launch a major attack on the objectives' model of practical theorizing was also the first person to operationalize Peters' views in a piece of practical curriculum development. I refer again to Stenhouse (1969), who wrote:

> We adopted a research plan based upon the specification of a procedure of teaching which should embody the values implied in the aim in a form which could be realised in the classroom. This means that the changes which we specify are not changes in terminal student behaviour but in the criteria to which teachers work in the classroom. These changes are defined by enunciating certain principles of procedure or criteria of criticism which are expressions of the aim. They are, if you like, specifications of a form of process.

Following Peters and Stenhouse, we set about the task of analysing the aims of our teachers into procedural values and principles. But we did so only after preliminary discussions with them about the values they believed to be embodied in their aims. These discussions served as orientation points for our analysis.

We suggested that the aims of "protecting and fostering self-directed learning" could be analysed into the following student "freedoms" (1) to identify and initiate their own areas of inquiry; (2) to express their own ideas and develop them into hypotheses; (3) to test their ideas and hypotheses against relevant evidence; (4) to discuss ideas, i.e., to defend their own ideas in the light of rational criteria, and to bring these criteria to bear on the ideas of others, including those of teachers. To exercise these freedoms, two sets of conditions are necessary. First, students must be free from external constraints on their ability to exercise the freedoms, i.e., they must be "free from" external constraints if they are to be "free to." Second, students must possess the necessary intellectual capacities to exercise the freedoms. For example, students may be free from constraints on the expression of certain ideas but be unable to express them because they lack the necessary concepts. The first set of conditions we called *extrinsic enabling conditions* and the second set *intrinsic enabling conditions*.

Teachers must proceed in the light of certain principles, which specify their role responsibilities for creating the conditions necessary for the realization of the aim. The distinction between the two enabling conditions makes it possible to analyse the principles into two clusters. The first cluster we called *negative principles* because they specify responsibilities for removing external constraints. The second cluster we called *positive principles* because they specify responsibilities for fostering the necessary intellectual capacities.

Negative principles: refrain from (1) preventing students from identifying and initiating their own areas of inquiry, (2) preventing students from expressing their own ideas and hypotheses, (3) restricting students' access to relevant evidence and drawing their own conclusions from it, (4) restricting students' access to discussion. Positive principles: (1) help students develop the capacity to identify and initiate their own areas of inquiry, (2) help students develop their own ideas into testable hypotheses, (3) help students evaluate evidence in the light of its relevance, truth, and sufficiency, (4) help students learn how to discuss.

It should be clear that the negative principles provide criteria for assessing the extent to which the teaching approach *protects* self-directed learning and thereby maintains an informal learning context. The positive principles provide criteria for assessing the extent to which the capacity for self-direction is being positively fostered by the teacher within informal learning contexts. According to our teachers, "informal" merely signifies independence from teacher-imposed constraints. It is a further question whether or not students are free to direct their own learning within the informal situation.

About halfway through the second term of our work with teachers, we circulated a document that included both the categories and theories we had derived from discussions with them and the criteria for testing theories we had analysed from their aims.[4] We hoped the document would provide some guidelines for self-monitoring in the classroom. However, we realized that it would be useful only for those teachers who had already begun to question their own practical theories. Fortunately, over the previous months we had begun to make some progress in helping teachers to do so.

Triangulation as a method of initiating self-monitoring

During the first term of the project the need to develop strategies to motivate the majority of our teachers to self-monitor in their practice became apparent. We finally decided on a more interventive approach than originally envisaged. Clem Adelman and I initiated a triangulation procedure in some teachers' classrooms, and then circulated full sets of data gathered in this way to all the other teachers in the project. Realizing that triangulation can be a threatening process, we selected only those teachers we believed to be ready to self-monitor in their practice in some depth, and hoped that they would also be prepared to let other teachers have access to the data gathered. We also hoped that in being prepared to give others access to their problems these teachers might motivate the rest to take a deeper look at what they were doing, albeit by the use of rather gentler methods than full-blown triangulation.

The idea of triangulation developed out of a combination of Adelman's interest in ethnomethodology, particularly the work of Cicourel and Garfinkel, and my own previous attempts in the Humanities Project to help teachers compare their own accounts of classroom discussion with those of their students. I had found teachers extremely reluctant in the main to elicit feed-back from students, and even those who tried were largely unable to elicit honest accounts. The intervention of an outsider for the latter group was essential to get the process going. It therefore came as no great surprise when we found teachers in the Ford Project were either not trying to elicit their students' accounts or trying unsuccessfully.

Triangulation involves gathering accounts of a teaching situation from three quite different points of view: those of the teacher, the students, and a participant observer.[5] Who gathers the accounts, how they are elicited, and who compares them depend largely on the context. The process of gathering accounts from three distinct standpoints has an epistemological justification. Each point of the triangle stands in a unique epistemological position with respect to access to relevant data about a teaching situation. The person in the best position to gain access via introspection to the intentions and aims in the situation is the teacher. The students are in the best position to explain how the teacher's actions influence the way they respond in the situation. The participant observer is in the best position to collect data about the observable features of the interaction between teacher and students. By comparing an account with the accounts from the two other standpoints, a person at one point of the triangle has an opportunity to test and perhaps revise it on the basis of more sufficient data.

Because the teachers we selected had been unsuccessful in eliciting honest feed-back from students, the participant observers (Clem Adelman and myself) took the initiative in collecting accounts. And, because we were primarily concerned with fostering self-monitoring in teachers, the accounts were primarily collected for the teacher to study. However, wherever possible we encouraged teachers to involve students in comparing the three sets of data. Triangulation can not only foster dialogue between an outside researcher and a teacher researcher, it can also foster three-way discussion and develop research potential in students.

Our technique involved having a post-lesson interview with the teacher before interviewing the students (interviews were recorded on tape). This interview enabled us to identify the kinds of data it was necessary to collect from students if the teacher was to have an opportunity to compare two accounts of the same event. It also enabled us to identify discrepancies between the teacher's account and our own, a situation that provided further criteria for eliciting relevant information from students.

The danger in interviewing the teacher first is that it leads to an over-structured interview with the students and prevents them from focussing on their concerns in a lesson. Nonetheless, we tried to interview students in a fairly unstructured way, only homing in on the events we had in mind after some account of them had been initiated by the students. If the students omitted any reference to them, we tended to mention them towards the end of the interview. Another danger is that the participant observer may over-structure the interview with the teacher, viewing the situation as an opportunity for testing his/her own accounts of events. Here again we tried to work from the teacher's own judgements about which features of the lesson were significant, introducing our own agenda when it matched the teacher's or was a natural development of it.

The value of interviewing the teacher first is that it is less threatening to the teacher, who tends to give an account more freely because there is no worry about how the interviewer's questions are influenced by what the students have said or whether the accounts are wildly discrepant.

The participant observers also exercised the initiative in negotiating the teacher's access to student accounts. We interviewed students only with the teacher's permission, and made it clear that teacher access would have to be negotiated with students. Prior to individual interviews with students, we told them as a group that we were after honest accounts and that, to ensure this, we would give them control over the teacher's access. On only two occasions did groups of students (we normally interviewed groups selected by the teachers) refuse to give teachers access but many groups demanded some reassurance from teachers that they would discuss their accounts with them and not react over-defensively to what was said.

The participant observers had a significant role to play in creating conditions of trust between teachers and students. Students generally feared their teacher's reaction. This situation accounted for their reluctance to give honest feed-back directly in the face-to-face situation. We found that a teacher who was able to conform to the conditions of access negotiated with students through us, and demonstrate an open attitude to their comments, was increasingly able to collect their accounts without our help. Once the teacher came to appreciate the value of triangulation, the participant observer could hand over to the teacher much of the initiative for the collection of accounts. As the project progressed we found that many of our teachers began to initiate triangulation procedures for themselves. They called us in, told us what to look for, and took the initiative in eliciting both our accounts and those of students, although on occasions they still asked us to interview students to check on their own progress in getting honest feed-back.

It was important for the participant observers in interview situations to refrain from introducing their own views in ways that inhibited the interviewee's freedom of response. Normally we gave the teacher access to our own account only after we had their own. Later, though, when teachers began to exercise more control over the triangulation process and were more open to other views, we were able to exchange views frankly with them in the post-lesson situation. The interview situation became transformed into one of discussion. We found that some teachers suspected that their students would tend to give us what we wanted to hear in our interviews with them. It was therefore important to interview in a way that demonstrated to the teachers that we were not manipulating students to give accounts that simply confirmed our own.

As participant observers we were anxious not to impose our own judgements on teachers. Teachers feel very threatened by persons they perceive as occupying evaluation roles, perhaps because much of the teacher evaluation currently practised gives teachers few rights of reply and is therefore perceived to be a somewhat punitive activity. Triangulation places the outsider in a different light, for it requires the person's appraisals of a situation to be placed in the context of other views, including those of the teacher. However, danger does exist when the outsider takes the initiative in collecting accounts. The sooner the teacher is able to take the initiative in this respect the better.

As well as observing, and in the initial stages interviewing, the participant observers recorded lessons. If the classroom was highly centralized, in the sense that it was possible to monitor everything that was going on at the same time, we used tape-recordings. If not, we adopted a tape and slide technique of recording developed by Adelman.[6] The teacher wore a radio-microphone, which picked up interchanges with students as the teacher moved around the classroom. The participant observer took photographs (pulsed onto the tape), which helped to place the recorded talk in a visual context. The attempt was to document visually to whom the teacher is talking, when the teacher moves from one place to another or from one student or group to another, when students leave or enter the group the teacher is talking to, and the nature of the task the teacher is talking to the students about. We didn't use video-tape recordings because the majority of our teachers didn't have play-back facilities. Since the main function of recording was to collect data to help teachers self-monitor in their practice, the recording medium had to be something the teachers could easily use.

The participant observers' tape-recordings were used in interview situations and by teachers when comparing accounts. In post-lesson interviews with teachers, we sometimes adopted the device of playing the tape-recording and allowing the teacher to stop it and comment as desired. This device helps the teacher to reconstruct classroom events. We also found it useful in interviewing with students. When accounts are being compared, recordings are useful as a basis for checking. For example, if a student argues that the teacher was always applying pressure by constantly saying, "Do you agree with that?", the teacher (or student, or both) can turn to the recording as evidence of how often the teacher actually said this sort of thing.

We tried as much as possible to self-monitor in our own conduct as participant observers and interviewers within the triangulation situation. We did so partly by encouraging teachers to give us feed-back about how they viewed our role. Here is how some teachers (Cooper and Ebbutt, 1974) reacted to triangulation material gathered by me:

> The arrival of the first transcripts of tapes made during lessons, and of subsequent discussions about those lessons between John Elliott and the pupils in the absence of the teacher was a very important moment, for this was the first time that the teachers had come face to face with facts and evidence about their own teaching. Not only that, but it was apparent that the pupils did not always see the teacher's aims in the way that the teacher did, and adjusted their responses in lessons accordingly.
>
> Of course, it could be that the pupils were adjusting their responses to John Elliott in a similar way, and so in one case at least, a further discussion took place involving John Elliott, the pupils and the teacher. From our point of view this was a very important tape because it seemed to show us just how careful one had to be in accepting as evidence the responses of pupils in a group situation with or without the teacher. Notwithstanding this, there was certainly food for thought in the tapes, which were then discussed at central conferences.

It is evident from these remarks that the interviews with students were a source of considerable anxiety. Teachers frequently cited the collection of student data as that part of the process that aroused the greatest anxiety for them.

Here are some excerpts from one of the triangulation studies (Elliott and Partington, 1975) referred to by the teachers just quoted:

Observer: Do you know that you use the words "Do we all agree?" quite a lot?
Teacher: No I didn't [pause] OK – I know I use that a lot.
Observer: Three or four times.
Teacher: I am asking for assent.
Observer: Are you? Is that what you are asking?
Teacher: I think probably I am. I think possibly I use that when I don't get... if I make a statement and I haven't got a... I don't know sometimes if it is a rhetorical question or whether it is a question I want an answer to or whether it is just a statement, but I make a statement and I hope the response will come from it. If a response doesn't come from it, you either repeat it in a different way to a single individual and put them on the spot, or you perhaps get over it by saying OK or "Do you all agree with that?" I suppose they can possibly con me by saying yes and carrying on. It is something I hadn't thought of.
Observer: Do they all say yes?

Teacher:	Well they didn't all say no. I reckon if you take a non-negative approach to be an affirmative, which is perhaps a big thing to do. I don't think you ought to do that really. Yes that's naughty isn't it!
Observer:	Well the thing is I suppose when you say "Do we all agree?" they can say no.
Teacher:	I give them the opportunity to say no.
Observer:	They can say no, but how do they see it. If they see it as your seeking agreement...
Teacher:	I think a lot of the time one must be seeking agreement...what I am trying to put forward is what I feel to be a reasonable statement; a true statement. Although I didn't today, I do in fact sometimes put forward daft statements and you do usually find that they disagree if there is something stupid. It was a bit tame today – I mean you were coming in part way through a situation which wanted finishing and therefore I finished it. In terms of them going away and doing things – and I thought you would be more interested in discussion because of the material you had got – your recording technique...

Extract from observer's notes (written during lesson)

Look at old tables of results. "What's happened?" Teacher asks specific pupils questions. When he disagrees raises his voice quizzically as if he disagrees. Question and answer. Hints. When right answer is given it is reinforced by the teacher. "Right" [guessing game]. Do you all agree with that? Reply by one boy "Mm." When boy responds in a way which doesn't fit what teacher wants it is chopped. People not encouraged to elaborate on ideas. Wants to get them critical of John Innes compost manufacturer. John Innes made by pupils promotes growth better than commercial product. Asks why paper pots are better than plastic pots. Often makes an interpretation. Asks pupils if it is a "reasonable guess." Someone murmurs again "yes."

Interview with pupils

Pupil:	But he wouldn't ask you what you think your conclusions were, he'll put his own conclusion up on the board, and you have to write it. He says do you agree, not always but he don't want to rub it off so you just say yes to keep him quiet.
Observer:	You say yes to keep him quiet?
Pupil:	Keep him happy...
Observer:	There was a time when he said he was making a guess and he asked you if you agreed whether it was a reasonable guess. I don't know if you remember that?
Pupils:	Yes.
Observer:	And one person said yes and everybody else kept quiet. Now what I want to know is whether the person who said yes really did agree with him or just said yes because they thought he wanted them to say yes, and why everybody else kept quiet?
Pupil:	Well he would have liked us to say yes, really, cause I mean you could see it.
Pupil:	If you'd said no you'd waste time arguing wouldn't you.

Pupil:	Yeh, if you ever say no he'll stand there and just keep on and on.
Pupil:	He'll keep on till you come to his way of thinking.
Pupil:	So it's best to say yes to start with.
Observer:	So even if you did disagree when he said "Do you all agree?" you wouldn't.
Pupil:	If you said no he'd keep on to you until you said yes.
Pupil:	If you said no he's going to say why not.
Pupil:	And if you argued with him he'd come round to the same point where you left off.
Pupil:	Back to his way of thinking.

Excerpt from tape-recorded lesson

Teacher:	Yeh, do you all agree with that?
Pupil:	Mm.
Teacher:	What do you think Derek? I mean are you bothered?
Teacher:	… Would that be the only thing you want to know about a plant?
Pupil:	How to condition it Sir.
Teacher:	Yeh, do you all agree with that?

The anxiety our collection of students' accounts aroused was carried into local inter-school meetings. Those who had been involved in the triangulation studies discussed their experience with those who were not involved.

Here is an episode from one such discussion (Adelman *et al.*, 1975) held during the second term of the project:

Adviser:	Do children feel they are being inspected in any way?
Secondary Teacher (A):	No I don't think so – they will often open up with them.
Primary Teacher (B):	Pupils will open up with strangers who are just inquiring. Whereas they know the teachers are trying to find out what they know and therefore they try to give the 'correct' response.
Secondary Teacher (A):	…all that he [John Elliott] got from them was all criticism of the lessons.
Secondary Teacher (C):	This attempt to get frankness can obtain complete nonsense from the children and often means that later a more authoritarian approach has to be adopted with them.
Secondary Teacher (D):	I feel that this can cause trouble.
Secondary Teacher (E):	The children can in fact give false information. Children do not talk frankly.
Secondary Teacher (C):	Possibly children may like the idea that talking to the project team reflects an unfavourable image. To what extent do children realise the uniqueness of John Elliott's position? [as an outsider coming in to interview]….

Primary
Teacher (B):   It's easier in the Primary School.

Primary
Teacher (F):   Yes in the Secondary School you have the problem of adolescence, twisting of the evidence, etc. . . .

Secondary
Teacher (C):   By what criteria does a child get to know a teacher? Should we be judged by those we don't want to be judged by?

Primary
Teacher (G):   Children are used to visitors. I've had no trouble.

Secondary
Teacher (E):   Do children *really say* what they mean in the Primary School?

Primary
Teacher (B):   They try to reason out the correct response they ought to make.

Primary
Teacher (F):   Young children cannot rationalise the problems we are posing to them. They are not capable of making true judgments on effectiveness of lessons . . . etc.

Secondary
Teacher (E):   I have heard on tape some quite sensible judgments.

Primary
Teacher (F):   They become more coherent as they move higher up the school.

Primary
Teacher (B):   They still tend to give responses you expect.

Primary
Teacher (F):   Press the red button and you get the red response.

We attended the local inter-school meetings only on request, because we felt that our absence would allow teachers to feel freer to criticize our role. The verbatim account just quoted was sent to us by the Local Authority Adviser who chaired the meeting, having first obtained the permission of the teachers to do so.

Triangulation enables teachers to assess their ability to self-monitor in the teaching situation. The more congruent their own accounts are with those of their students and the participant observers, the more objective they are likely to be. Agreement does not necessarily indicate objectivity, though it merely means there is a prima facie case to be made for the objectivity of accounts that agree unless there is evidence to the contrary. We would, for example, be suspicious of any consensus that tended to suggest that no gaps exist between teachers' performance and their aspirations, a situation that would suggest that both the students' and the participant observers' accounts are distorted by their desire to reinforce the teachers' self-image.

As well, an absence of consensus should not necessarily be taken to indicate that the teacher's account is distorted by subjective factors. Majorities are not always right. Some evidence for assuming that a teacher's account is relatively objective would be its tacit acknowledgement of a gap between aspiration and practice. Such acknowledgement would suggest that the natural tendency to idealize practice had been resisted. In conclusion, then, I would simply assert that agreement and disagreement can be assumed to indicate objectivity and subjective distortion, respectively, only in the absence of any evidence to the contrary.

Some of the early triangulation studies I have described were, with the permission of the teachers involved and their head teachers, circulated to other teachers in the project. They also provided the basis for discussion at our interim conference at the end of the second term. At this conference they were used as data for testing the practical theories of the teachers studied.

Here is one teacher's account of the conference experience (Cooper and Ebbutt, 1974):

> These conferences were a new experience for the teachers. At the second one several transcripts of various lessons, together with three tape-slide compilations provided the raw data for discussion. It soon became apparent that the teachers at the conference had become much more sympathetic towards the teachers and children depicted on the tape-slides than they had been at the previous conference. One of our members felt that he was beginning to see his teaching in a different way. He was able to locate it within the general spectrum of the various inquiry/discovery approaches being adopted by project teachers, using terms that were beginning to emerge as a shared language for describing and talking about teaching e.g. formal/informal, structured/unstructured, guided/open ended. Whether this is going to prove valuable to him remains to be seen, but it is certainly true that he is thinking far more about the way in which he is teaching. Indeed the value of this research to us may lie in the analysis the teachers make of their methods and their whole approach to teaching.

A conference observer from New Zealand (Munro, 1974) noted:

> On several occasions I noticed considerable tension in some of the teachers. I suspect it was due to their recognition of the gulf that existed between the realities of their day-to-day teaching experience and the ideal inquiry/discovery environment which was unfolding at the conference. The tension was associated with defensive statements of the type: "No one can do inquiry/discovery all the time," "I teach...rigidly because I feel children need to be taught skills so they will avoid frustration," "some methods are better for only some children," "there's nothing new here...primary schools have been doing it all along."
>
> I estimated that roughly half of the teachers showed this kind of reaction at one time or another.

The circulation of triangulation data around schools, discussions between teachers at local inter-school meetings, and the experience of the interim conference began to take effect during the third term. Many teachers began to feel freer to look at, and share, their own classroom problems once others had demonstrated a willingness to do so. We discovered the crucial role local inter-school meetings and central conferences played in this respect. The school-based teams, with two notable exceptions, collapsed as a basis for sharing ideas and classroom data. The collapse was caused partly by lack of institutional support and partly by feelings of inter-departmental competition that prevented the inter-disciplinary team members from exposing their teaching to each other. Teachers felt more able to share their classroom data with teachers from other schools. Here the tape and slide recordings proved to be an invaluable tool. Some teachers were able to "take their classrooms" to the local meetings and discuss the events recorded with teachers from other project schools. The local meetings thus became the main setting for sharing ideas and experience for the majority of the 30 teachers who remained attached to the project.

During the third term 24 teachers were actively engaged in studying their own teaching in some form. Only six adopted the full-blown triangulation method, but the others began to use some of the methods suggested at the initial conference. Some tape-recorded lessons or parts of them regularly, others kept field-notes, and there was an increase in the general effort to obtain honest feed-back from students.

Initial attempts at obtaining student feed-back took an interesting form. Rather than collect students' interpretations and judgements about a particular situation, many teachers unwittingly interviewed, or held discussions, at the more abstract and less threatening level of pedagogic theory. For example, rather than ask students, "To what extent did I restrict your freedom to choose your own work?", there was a tendency to ask, "To what extent should teachers allow you to choose your own work?" Such discussions were valuable inasmuch as they clarified for teachers the value-systems of their students and thereby helped them assess some of the problems and possibilities of protecting and fostering self-directed learning. They also gave teachers an opportunity to clarify and discuss their own educational values with students. Discussions about pedagogic values appeared to be necessary before teachers felt ready to involve students in the more concrete activity of lesson analysis.

In general teachers tended to find their own level of research activity. They adopted methods that produced illuminating but not overwhelming data. They worked from the least to the most threatening gradually. Our observations of this process suggested that triangulation should appropriately come at the end of attempts to develop self-monitoring potential with teachers who are largely unreflective about their practice. We would in retrospect suggest that teachers need to work through the following sequence of activities:

1   Listening to or viewing recordings of their teaching situation.
2   Listening to or viewing recordings and then systematically noting salient patterns in their classroom behaviour.
3   2, plus dialogue with participant observer.
4   3, plus dialogue with students about pedagogic values.
5   Triangulation controlled by participant observer.
6   Triangulation controlled by teacher.

At the end of this process teachers should be able to act as participant observers in each other's classrooms. Indeed, during the second half of the project we found an increasing number of teachers able to do so productively. Their main problem, however, was gaining such opportunities in their schools. If these opportunities are not structured into the school time-table, the prospect of teachers being able to give each other this kind of support is rather gloomy. And in the United Kingdom there are few roles in the educational system that can be developed to provide such participant-observation support, at least at the level at which it needs to be sustained.

Developing hypotheses from classroom data

The data collected by triangulation and other methods enabled teachers, in dialogue with ourselves as participant observers, to clarify and test the theories implicit in their practice. As a result some teachers generated new theories. Since practical theories have normative implications, one would expect these new theories to be reflected in conscious changes in teaching approach. This is an important point with respect to the teacher's role in theory development. Since a theory generated from self-monitoring is consciously held, a teacher should be able, when called upon to do so, to make it explicit. However, the teacher need not necessarily explicate a practical theory in order to be said to have developed it.

I now use the triangulation data quoted previously to illustrate how teachers can use them to clarify, test, and generate their own theories of inquiry/discovery teaching.

The students argue that the teacher imposes constraints on their freedom to express their own ideas. They cite on their own initiative the teacher saying, "Do you all agree with that?" as a way of imposing constraints by indicating the idea wanted.

The participant observer notes both teacher behaviours that appear to indicate the outcomes desired and student responses to these behaviours. The observations are supported by the recording. The teacher accepts saying, "Do you all agree with that?" frequently, and describes the intention behind it as "asking for assent." Gradually the normative implications of the behaviour begin to dawn: "I don't think you ought to do that really. Yes, that's naughty, isn't it?"

The study of this triangulation data convinced the teacher that, in spite of professed aspirations to implement inquiry/discovery approaches, the teaching approach was in fact formal–structured–directed and that the behaviour cited deliberately fostered the students' dependence on his authority position. Having clarified and tested the theory implicit in the practice in this way, the teacher later dramatically switched to an unstructured–open-ended approach, to protect the self-directed learning of the students. The conscious switch to a new teaching approach reflected the development of a new theory, the applicability of which would require further self-monitoring.

The conscious development of new practical theories from self-monitoring we called "hypotheses," in order to highlight the fact that they are open to experiment. If a theory is held unconsciously, it is not open to experiment. But once a theory is consciously held, it is open.

From triangulation and other classroom data, we began to identify those practical theories that applied not only in individual instances but also in more general cases. These were identified from our dialogue with some of the teachers. By formulating them as general hypotheses and then circulating them to all teachers, we hoped that they would provide a focus for self-monitoring activity and that, in exploring their applicability, teachers would clarify and test their own practical theories. We realized there was a danger that teachers would simply accept or reject the hypotheses in the light of their perceived consistency or inconsistency with their own theories. However, this danger was somewhat reduced by the first batch of general hypotheses being introduced only towards the end of the second term, when many of the teachers had already begun to clarify and test their practical theories.

The general hypotheses introduced during the course of the project were as follows:

1. *Teachers are unlikely to move away from a formal situation if they adopt short-term structured approaches.* The adoption of a short-term structured approach tends to plunge the teacher into one of two possible dilemmas. First, students may adopt a line of reasoning different to the one the teacher wants. Given that the teacher has set a limited time in which to achieve the objectives, the teacher either has to make the objective more long term or exert more control over students' reasoning. If the latter is opted for, students' intellectual dependence on the

authority position is inevitably increased. Second, students may fail to do much reasoning of their own at all. Again, in order to realize the objectives in the time set, the teacher may lead students towards them by providing them with hints and clues. In this way a guessing game is initiated that caters to students' dependency needs, since it involves guessing what the teacher has in mind.

2. *To eliminate the guessing game and move from a formal to an informal situation, teachers may have to refrain from the following behaviours that tend to indicate a structured–directed approach to students:*

a. *Changing topic.* Teachers changing the topic under discussion may prevent students from expressing and developing their own ideas, since students tend to interpret such changes as attempts to get conformity to a particular line of reasoning.

b. *Positive reinforcement.* Utterances like "good," "interesting," and "right" in response to ideas expressed can prevent the expression and discussion of other ideas, since students tend to interpret such reinforcement as attempts to legitimate the development of some ideas rather than others.

c. *Selective critical questioning.* Teachers asking critical questions of some students rather than others may prevent the former from developing their ideas, since such questions tend to be interpreted as negative evaluations of the ideas expressed.

d. *Leading questions and statements.* Questions and statements containing information about the answer the teacher has in mind may prevent students from developing their own ideas, since they tend to interpret such acts as attempts to constrain the direction of their thinking.

e. *Inviting consensus.* Teachers responding to students' ideas with questions like "Do you all agree?" or "Anyone disagree with that?" tend to prevent the expression of divergence, since students interpret such questions as attempts to impose a consensus view.

f. *Question/answer sequences.* Teachers always asking a question following a student's response to a previous question may prevent students from introducing their own ideas, since students may interpret such patterns as attempts to control the input and sequencing of ideas.

g. *Introducing factual information.* Teachers introducing factual information in person, either in verbal or written form, may prevent students from evaluating it, since students tend to interpret such interventions as attempts to get them to accept its truth.

h. *Not inviting evaluation.* Teachers not inviting students to evaluate the information they are studying may prevent students from criticizing it, since students tend to interpret the situation as one in which criticism is not wanted.

It is perhaps worth pointing out the symbolic-interactionist perspective reflected in the formulation of these sub-hypotheses. Teacher influence is exerted via students' interpretations of teacher behaviour. Interviews and discussions with students elicited the rules they apply in interpreting what teachers mean by what they say. By studying such data, one can understand how teachers often unintentionally impose constraints on self-directed learning. The student data reminded teachers that good intentions are not enough; they must be clearly indicated to students. And if students strongly associate some behaviours with particular intentions, teachers may need to change their behaviour repertoire in order to make their intentions clearer.

3. *Teachers adopting long-term structured approaches in contexts where students are psychologically dependent on them are less likely to move away from a formal situation than are teachers who adopt unstructured approaches.* When students are psychologically very dependent on the teacher, the teacher may be able to decrease that dependency only by convincing the students that they cannot get the answers out of him/her. Any indications they have that a structured approach is being adopted, even in the long term, encourages them to devote much of their energies to getting the answers out of the teacher. Of course, a teacher may try to convince students that he/she doesn't have any answers they want, but an honest response would be to pursue more unstructured aims.

4. *In order to adopt convincing unstructured approaches and thereby move away from formal situations, it may be temporarily necessary to adopt open-ended rather than guided methods.* Guidance within a structured approach tends to take a different form than guidance within the unstructured approach. A clear indication of this difference can be found in the language of classroom questioning. Within the structured approach the teacher's questions tend to be subject-focussed, whereas within the unstructured approach they tend to be person-focussed. For example, compare the following two excerpts from the lessons of two teachers using the materials of the same curriculum project (The Schools Council Science 5–13 Project):

a. *Teacher:*   *what's happening?*
   Girl: Disappearing like Alkaseltzer.
   Teacher: What does that mean – it is disappearing like Alkaseltzer?
   Girl: Disappearing in the water.
   Teacher: What do you call that then, when something disappears in the water.... *Does it disappear altogether?*
   Girl: No.
   Teacher: *Where is it?*
   Girl: ...inside there and...
   Teacher: Have we lost it Christine? Have we lost the ammonium chloride – we have lost it – it has gone, we have got none left, *where is it?*
   Christine: It has dissolved in the water.
   Teacher: ...*what is this?*
   Christine: Substance.
   Teacher: *Substance?*
   Christine: Oh sorry.
   Teacher: *So what have you got here?*
   Christine: A solution.
   Teacher: How did you get a solution Christine?
   Christine: By putting the ammonium chloride in.
   Teacher: *And what has happened to it?*
   Christine: It dissolved.
   Teacher: So how do you get a solution? Dissolving something in –
   Christine: Water.

b. *Teacher:*   *Now what made you decide to build this one?*
   Boy: Because a triangle shape is better than a straight one.
   Teacher: *How do you know?*
   Boy: A straight one will crack, it will go like that. We are going to have one straight support.

Teacher: One straight up the middle. *What has been your biggest problem with this?*
Boy: Well they slip and the sellotape sometimes comes off.
Teacher: *So how can you overcome the problem?*
Boy: We haven't really, but we have made it.
Boy: We have got some string.
Teacher: Good.

Notice that in one excerpt the teacher's language refers to an objective event the students are being asked to explain, while in the other excerpt the teacher's language refers to the student's own mental processes and states. In the first, the teacher's questions normally indicate a concern for the subject matter while in the second they indicate a concern for the student's own perspective on the subject matter. The former normally indicates that the teacher is wanting certain answers. The latter indicates that the teacher wants the students to reflect on their own problems, decisions, beliefs, etc., and primarily expresses a concern to foster self-directed learning. Of course, subject-focussed questions, if they are responsive to problems in the task defined by students, do not preclude a concern to foster self-direction. The language simply indicates that the teacher also has other concerns in mind.

When students need to depend on the authority position of the teacher, and are not convinced that the teacher is not prepared to satisfy those needs, they tend to interpret person-centered language as the teacher's attempt to conceal the answers really wanted. Consider the following lesson excerpt:

Teacher: You have got quite a strong thing there. Do you need that?
Boy: No.
Teacher: I am not saying yes or no.
Boy: I don't think we need it anyway.
Teacher: Why not?
Boy: It isn't really helping much, look.

It is obvious that when the boy said "no" he interpreted the teacher's question as an indication, albeit masked, of the desired conclusion. In other words, his reply was based on guesswork rather than independent thought. The teacher then denied that his question was determined by any conclusions he may have had in mind, and implied it was intended to get the students to reflect on their own judgement. The boy didn't appear to be totally convinced that the teacher didn't want them to reverse their judgement, but the remark prompted him to assert that he had independent reasons for reversing it "anyway." In other words, he asserted the autonomy of his own judgement, which the teacher then made him demonstrate by giving reasons.

If the boy had valued independent reasoning less and wanted a more dependent relationship with his teacher, the situation would have been more difficult to retrieve. The informal pattern – students are forced to be independent but want dependence – is highly unstable. Our teacher was able to salvage the situation precisely because he was operating within a fairly well-established informal pattern in which the boy wanted to reason independently. The more unstable informal situation – with students still demanding the dependent relationship – can probably be stabilized only if the teacher is prepared to adopt a very unstructured approach and convince the students that it is being adopted by using completely open-ended methods, which merely indicate to students the freedoms they have in the classroom. This approach would involve refraining from using even person-centred guidance. As we have seen, students can be reluctant to believe that teachers mean what they say in asking person-centred questions, which they view instead as mere appearances masking the existence of preconceived objectives.

5. *In contexts where students are developing confidence in their own reasoning powers, teachers can change from unstructured–open-ended to unstructured–guided (person-centred) methods without imposing constraints on self-directed learning.* When students do not experience strong needs to depend on the authority position of their teachers, they are less liable to misinterpret person-centred guidance as concealed indications of the answers teachers want, and less liable to feel constrained by them if they do.

6. *In contexts where students are developing confidence in their own reasoning powers, teachers can adopt long-term structured approaches without imposing constraints on self-directed learning.* Once students come to value, and are more confident about, directing their own learning, they are less interested in eliciting answers from the teacher. And even if they are aware that the teacher wants certain answers, they try to reason them out for themselves – provided that the teacher does not prevent them from doing so by attempting to short-cut the reasoning process in favour of them giving quick answers.

These hypotheses locate teachers' practical theories in a developmental sequence. Overall they suggest that different theories are applicable at different stages of the innovation process, i.e., from a context in which students have strong dependency needs to one in which they have begun to value and develop some confidence in their own powers of self-direction.

The sub-hypotheses listed under 2 were formulated out of the initial triangulation studies in the second term and circulated throughout the project towards the end of that term. They aroused considerable interest amongst teachers. One secondary school teacher reported that he felt very strongly that they didn't apply to his teaching; having tested them, he then reported that he was rather surprised at the extent to which they did apply. A primary school teacher reported that his initial reaction was to argue that they applied to secondary but not primary teachers; he also was surprised to find that they were more applicable to his situation than he had expected. In fact, one effect of the teachers testing these hypotheses and then discussing their findings together at meetings was the virtual disappearance of the wide-spread belief in a radical difference between practice in primary and secondary classrooms.

The rest of the general hypotheses were formulated only towards the end of the final term of the project. They emerged partly as the product of further theory testing with teachers, and partly out of our monitoring of the autonomous studies that our teachers were increasingly able to initiate and sustain without heavy central team support. As hypotheses were introduced and tested by more and more individuals, we found that discussions at local inter-school meetings began to focus on the generalizable features of life in classrooms. In other words, teachers were increasingly able to monitor each other's studies and begin to formulate their own general hypotheses. During the final term of the project, several teachers embarked on case studies of work with a particular class. Twelve studies were eventually written up. They contain evidence of teachers clarifying, testing, and generating theory.

The shifts in central team and teacher roles in theory development during the life of the project can be crudely represented as in Figure 2.3. Of course, we found

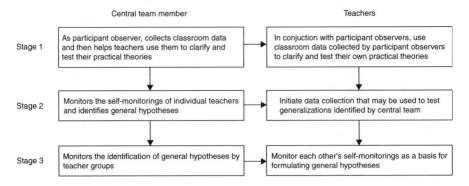

Figure 2.3 Shifts in roles of central team members and teachers in theory development.

ourselves in different role relationships with different individuals and groups at any one time. It is also possible to bring some teachers who are not normally self-monitoring in at stage 2, provided they have access to other teachers' classroom data.

Developing self-monitoring ability: some hypotheses

Earlier I explained how the project central team came to formulate a second-order action research role for itself. From reflections on our own practice, we have generated a number of practical hypotheses connected with the problems and possibilities of developing self-monitoring abilities in teachers. I now give a brief account of these hypotheses.

1. *The less teachers' personal identity is an inextricable part of their professional role in the classroom, the greater their ability to tolerate losses in self-esteem that tend to accompany self-monitoring.* In order to adopt an objective attitude to their practice, teachers need to be able to tolerate the existence of gaps between their aspirations and practice, with a consequent lowering of professional self-esteem. The more teachers self-monitor, the more mastery of their craft appears to elude them. As one teacher commented (Rowe, 1973):

> Nothing is ever in a state of stasis, nothing is ever finalised, always there is a reappraisal in the light of new experience. Like children we hanker after the finiteness of things, and like children, we are disturbed when there is frequent reassessment and modification.

Tolerance is difficult to achieve if the sole source of teachers' personal achievement and satisfaction lies in their classroom practice. To tolerate losses of self-esteem, it becomes necessary for them to get satisfaction from their performances in extra-professional situations. We had little success with those teachers whose personal identity was inextricably linked with their professional role in the classroom.

2. *The less financial and status rewards in schools are primarily related to administrative and pastoral roles, the more teachers are able to tolerate losses of self-esteem with respect to classroom practice.* This is particularly true in our expanding, reorganized, secondary schools. Systematic reflection on practice takes

time, and it was our secondary teachers who complained most about lack of time. Does this situation mean that they work harder than our primary and middle school teachers? Not necessarily. For primary school teachers, the demands of reflecting about the classroom constitute an extension of their existing commitment to the activity of teaching. But secondary school teachers are increasingly committed to administrative and pastoral functions that are only indirectly connected with the classroom. Thus, the demand to give more to the classroom situation generates conflict between alternative commitments.

Almost without exception those teachers with the least capacity for self-criticism have been those who have identified themselves strongly with roles outside the classroom situation. It is as if they can function without severe personal stress in a number of fragmented roles within the system only by maintaining a low degree of self-awareness about their classroom performance. The only way to resolve such stress is either to identify exclusively with the administrative or pastoral roles so that the quality of teaching no longer impinges on questions of self-esteem, or to withdraw from the former and sacrifice status and opportunity completely.

One of the current myths in education is that teaching experience necessarily qualifies a person to make educational policy decisions. Yet given the increasing role fragmentation in educational institutions, it is in fact extremely difficult for a person to move into a policy-making role without sacrificing depth for shallowness of understanding in the classroom. We reached a stage in the project where some of our teachers were faced with the problem of school and department heads who were so out of touch with the reality of the classroom they were incapable of responding supportively.

3. *The more teachers value themselves as potential researchers, the greater their ability to tolerate losses of self-esteem.* We found that once teachers began to perceive themselves as potential researchers, they developed a greater tolerance of gaps between aspirations and practice. An outside participant observer can do much to help teachers develop this alternative self by treating them as partners in research activities.

4. *The more teachers perceive classroom observers as researchers rather than evaluators, the greater their ability to tolerate losses of self-esteem.* For our teachers an "evaluator" ascribes praise and blame and allows few rights of reply. The "researcher" role we tried to adopt focussed on the practice rather than the practitioner. We tried to set out appraisals of practice in a context of dialogue with the teacher. Within this role teachers tended to perceive us as non-judgemental. Our refusal to ascribe blame helped at least some teachers to tolerate the gap between aspirations and practice.

5. *The more access teachers have to other teachers' classroom problems, the greater their ability to tolerate losses in self-esteem.* Once our teachers began to realize that others had similar problems and were able to study them objectively, they tended to tolerate losses in their own self-esteem more easily.

6. *The more teachers are able to tolerate losses in self-esteem, the more open they are to student feed-back.* Many of our teachers claimed that student feed-back was the most threatening kind of feed-back they could have. This is so possibly because students are in the best position to appraise teachers' practice. Openness to student feed-back, therefore, indicates willingness to change one's appraisal of oneself as a practitioner.

7. *The more teachers are able to tolerate losses in self-esteem, the more open they are to observer feed-back.* Even though not as threatening as student feed-back, observer feed-back is still threatening enough.

8. *The more teachers are able to tolerate losses in self-esteem, the more willing they are to give other teachers access to their classroom problems.* Our experience indicates that initially teachers are more open with professional peers from other schools, especially if they are teaching a different age-range, than with teachers in their own schools. Our inter-disciplinary teams tended to collapse because interde-partmental competition made openness between teachers difficult.

9. *The more open teachers are to student feed-back, the greater their ability to self-monitor in their classroom practice.* The reasons for this and the next two hypotheses have been explained in an earlier section.

10. *The more open teachers are to observer feed-back, the greater their ability to self-monitor in their classroom practice.*

11. *The more open teachers are to feed-back from other teachers, the greater their ability to self-monitor in their classroom practice.*

12. *The greater teachers' ability to self-monitor in their classroom practice, the more they experience conflict between their accountability as educators for how students learn (process) and their accountability to society for what they learn (in terms of knowledge outcomes).* Self-monitoring sensitizes teachers to account-ability issues. The issues presented themselves in the project as a dilemma between protecting self-directed learning and pursuing preconceived knowledge outcomes.

13. *The more able teachers are at self-monitoring in their classroom practice, the more likely they are to bring about fundamental changes in it.* This is the main premise on which the project was founded. Our experience tends to confirm it. Once teachers began to clarify and test their practical theories, the new theories generated tended to be reflected in changes in practice. The main problem is getting teachers to self-monitor in their practice.

We have attempted to formulate these hypotheses sequentially.[7] The relation-ships between the variables they specify are expressed by the basic theoretical model shown in Figure 2.4.

[. . .]

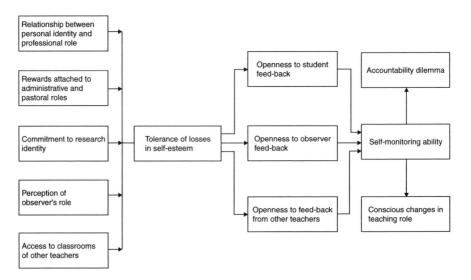

Figure 2.4 Model for development of teachers' self-monitoring abilities.

We hope that these second-order hypotheses about the problems and possibilities of initiating teachers into classroom action research make at least a small contribution to practical theorizing in the field of in-service teacher education.

Notes

This paper was prepared for a symposium on Modes of Thought among Teachers at the annual meeting of the American Educational Research Association, San Francisco, April 1976.

1 The Ford Teaching Project was sponsored by the Ford Foundation and based at the Centre for Applied Research in Education at the University of East Anglia, UK, from 1973 to 1975. In writing this account of the project's work I am enormously indebted to my ex-colleague Clem Adelman. Many of the ideas reported here were generated initially by him, especially those related to the eliciting of teachers' categories and methods of classroom observation.
2 It was called Document D. A few copies are available on request from me.
3 The idea of helping teachers to do so by investigating the meanings they ascribed to key terms came from Clem Adelman, who also devised the methods and techniques to be used.
4 It was called Document I, "Towards a General Methodology of Inquiry/Discovery Teaching." A limited number of copies are available from me.
5 See Adelman (1976) for a more detailed account of the triangulation techniques used in this project.
6 See Walker and Adelman (1975) for details of this recording technique.
7 I would like to thank Professor Louis M. Smith for his comments on an original draft of these hypotheses formulated by Clem Adelman, Don Cooper, Berris Bowen, and myself. In this reformulation I have tried to implement his suggestion of sequencing the hypotheses according to the extent to which a result in some appears as a determinant in others.

References

Adelman, C. On first hearing. Bulmershe College of Higher Education, Earley, Reading, 1976.

Adelman, C., Elliott, J., Sitte, K., and Ford Project teachers. *The stranger in the classroom.* Ford Teaching Project publication, Cambridge Institute of Education, Cambridge, 1975.

Cooper, D. and Ebbutt, D. Participation in action-research as an inservice experience. *Cambridge Journal of Education*, 1974, 4(2).

Elliott, J. and Partington, D. Three points of view in the classroom. Ford Teaching Project publication, Cambridge Institute of Education, Cambridge, 1975.

Hamlyn, D.W. Objectivity. In Dearden, Hirst, and Peters (Eds), *Education and the development of reason.* London: Routledge and Kegan Paul, 1972.

House, E. *The politics of educational innovation.* McCutchan, 1974.

MacDonald, B. and Walker, R. *Changing the curriculum.* London: Open Books, 1976.

Munro, R. *An observer's report.* Internal Report to Ford Project team, 1974.

Peters, R.S. Must an educator have an aim? In Macmillan and Nelson (Eds), *Concepts of teaching.* Chicago, IL: Rand McNally, 1968.

Rappaport, R.N. Three dilemmas in action-research. Paper presented to a Social Science Research Council conference, York, 1970.

Rowe, M. The cyclical structure of evaluating schemes. *The New Era*, 1973, 54, 216–218.

Stenhouse, L. Handling controversial issues in the classroom. *Education Canada*, 1969.

Stenhouse, L., Elliott, J., Plaskow, M., Ruddock, J. *The Humanities Project: An introduction.* London: Heinemann, 1970.

Walker, R. and Adelman, C. *A guide to classroom observation.* London: Methuen, 1975.

Appendix: Ford Teaching Project

1. *In-service materials*

Unit 1: Patterns of teaching
The language and logic of informal teaching, by J. Elliott and C. Adelman
Primary school – the tins
Primary school elective tasks
Primary school science
Paper structures – middle school
Social studies in a secondary school

Unit 2: Research methods
Support for research-based inquiry/discovery teaching, by Ford Project teachers
Ways of doing research in one's own classroom, by Ford Project teachers
Classroom action research, by J. Elliott and C. Adelman
The stranger in the classroom, by J. Elliott, C. Adelman, K. Sitte, and Ford Project teachers
Three points of view in the classroom – generating hypotheses from classroom observations, recordings, and interviews, by J. Elliott assisted by D. Partington
Team based action research, by Ford Project teachers
Self-monitoring questioning strategies, by J. Elliott assisted by T. Hurlin
Eliciting pupils' accounts in the classroom, by J. Elliott, C. Adelman, and Ford Project teachers

Unit 3: Hypotheses
The innovation process in the classroom, by J. Elliott and C. Adelman
Implementing the principles of inquiry/discovery teaching: Some hypotheses, by Ford Project teachers

Unit 4: Teacher case studies
A third-year form tries to enter a freer world – research into ways towards inquiry/discovery working, by B. Iredale
The castles group, by K. Forsythe
Inquiry/discovery learning in a science classroom, and The China project, by R. Pedler and A. Rumsby
Question strategies: A self analysis, by T. Hurlin
Identifying problems and strategies in the classroom, by Ford Project teachers

2. *Selected articles*

Bowen, R.B., Green, L.L.J., and Pols, R. The Ford Project – the teacher as researcher. *British Journal of In-Service Education*, 1975, 2(1).
Cook, M. Where the action-research is – a look at the innovatory work arising out of the Ford Teaching Project. *Times Educational Supplement*, 11 July 1975.
Cooper, D. and Ebbutt, D. Participation in action-research as an in-service experience. *Cambridge Journal*, 1974, 4(2), 65–71.
Elliott, J. Sex role constraints on freedom of discussion: A neglected reality of the classroom. *The New Era*, 1974, 55(6).
Elliott, J. Classroom accountability and the self-monitoring teacher. Cambridge Institute of Education, 1975.
Elliott, J. Preparing teachers for classroom accountability. Cambridge Institute of Education, 1975.
Elliott, J. Objectivity, ideology and teacher participation in educational research. *Research Intelligence B.E.R.A. Bulletin 1976*.
Elliott, J. and Adelman, C. Inquiry and discovery teaching – a new Ford Teaching Project. *The New Era*, 1973, pp. 115–117.
Elliott, J. and Adelman, C. Reflecting where the action is: The design of the Ford Teaching Project. *Education for Teaching*, 1973, pp. 8–20.
Elliott, J. and Adelman, C. Supporting teachers' research in the classroom. *The New Era*, 1973, 54(9).

Elliott, J. and Adelman, C. Aspirations into reality: Approaches to inquiry/discovery teaching. *Education 3–13*, 1975, 3(2).

Elliott, J. and Adelman, C. Teacher education for curriculum reform: An interim report on the work of the Ford Teaching Project. *British Journal of Teacher Education*, 1975, 1(1), 105–114.

Elliott, J. and Adelman, C. Teachers' accounts and the control of classroom research. *London Education Review*, 1975, 4(2/3).

Munro, R.G. Self-monitoring teachers. *Times Educational Supplement*, 21 June 1974.

Rowe, M. The cyclical structure of evaluatory schemes. *The New Era*, 1973, 54(9).

Thurlow, J. Eliciting pupils' interpretations in the primary school. *The New Era*, 1973, 54(9).

Walker, R. and Adelman, C. Developing pictures for other frames: Action research and case study. In G. Chanan and S. Delamont (Eds), *Frontiers of classroom research*. London: National Foundation for Educational Research, 1975.

3. Reviews

Almond, L. Ford Teaching Project. *Journal of Curriculum Studies*, 1975, 7(2).

Cook, M. Bridging the gap between theory and practice; a review of Ford T Project publications. *Times Educational Supplement*, 18 July 1975.

Maw, J. The Ford Teaching Project: A review of published documents in relation to in-service education. *British Journal of In-Service Education*, 1976, 2(2).

PART 2

HOLDING TEACHERS TO ACCOUNT

CHAPTER 3

PREPARING TEACHERS FOR CLASSROOM ACCOUNTABILITY[1]

Education for Teaching, pp. 49–71, Summer 1976

Towards a genuine and fair model of classroom accountability

Educational thinking in the 1960s and early 1970s was dominated by the issues raised by the emergence of the curriculum reform movement in this country. I will predict that in the late 1970s it will be dominated by issues raised by the emerging teacher accountability movement. The movement has been in full swing in the USA for some time. Recently Alec Clegg (1975) warned us in the *Times Educational Supplement* of the dangers of adopting the sort of accountability systems which dominate the American scene. America's strongest critic of such systems, Ernest House (undated), has argued that they share the following characteristics:

> First, there is a small set of prespecified goals. Second, some measure of output is established...often only one measure like achievement scores. Third, people with good results are rewarded or people with bad results are punished. The output measures are maximised with little concern for limits or side effects.

This model of classroom accountability assumes:

1   That teachers have a responsibility to bring about only a limited range of outcomes.
2   That achievement scores can be used to assess the causal effectiveness of what teachers do in classrooms.
3   That teachers can be praised and blamed and even rewarded and punished on the basis of causal evaluations of their performance.
4   That teachers have no rights of participation in evaluations of their moral agency in the classroom.

By reflecting upon these assumptions in turn we can grasp some of the limitations of the model as a whole.

1   The first assumption implies that there exists a limited range of audiences to whom teachers are accountable and whose valuations of what is worth learning ought to determine the aims of teaching. Who is this audience? House believes that in the USA it is the society's most powerful economic institutions backed by central government bureaucracy. The emergence of the demand for

accountability to the centres of economic power he suggests coincides with periods of inflation and the need to cut costs. The real aims are to cut costs rather than to improve teaching. We should not be too surprised therefore in these inflationary times when our Government shows signs of wanting to exercise greater control over what teachers do in classrooms. ... We are witnessing a general decline in the powers of the LEAs and their advisory services to teachers and the emergence of monitoring systems from the centre operated by Her Majesty's Inspectors.[2] It is also perhaps not over-speculative to suggest that the Schools Council for Curriculum Reform, with its emphasis on the professional autonomy of teachers, is on its way out – or at least having a severe identity crisis.

I would be the last to argue that teachers should not be accountable to members of society. But what benefits members of our society cannot necessarily be equated with what benefits its most powerful institutions. There is a tremendous danger in adopting 'the maximisation of utility for society' as a criterion of classroom accountability. As John Rawls (1971, p. 26) in his *A Theory of Justice* has pointed out, the utilitarian constructs the well-being of society out of the net balance of satisfactions gained by its members. It is only too easy to do this sum in order to justify maximising benefit for our society's most powerful institutions to the disadvantage of weaker institutions and groups. As House points out, concentration on maximising achievement scores in schools may benefit the dominant middle class sectors of society to the disadvantage of minority communities.

The utilitarian model of accountability criticised by House fails to take into account the requirements of social justice. Rawls points out we all know intuitively that:

> ... justice denies that the loss of freedom for some is made right by a greater good shared by others. It does not allow that the sacrifices imposed on a few are outweighed by the larger sum of advantages enjoyed by many. Therefore in a just society the liberties of equal citizenship are taken as settled; the rights secured by justice are not subject to political bargaining or to the calculus of social interests.
>
> (*op. cit.*, pp. 3–4)

For Rawls justice is not synonymous with equality. It requires that inequalities should benefit all, even though some will benefit more than others. Injustices are inequalities that do not benefit all.

If social justice replaces utility as a criterion of teacher accountability in the classroom it would place teachers under the following obligation:

> All social values – liberty and opportunity, income and wealth, and the bases of self-respect – are to be distributed equally unless an unequal distribution of any, or all, of these values is to everyone's advantage.
>
> (*op. cit.*, p. 62)

Teaching which fostered inequality of opportunity might be socially just if it brought greater opportunity for all. The criterion does not rule out responding to the needs of society's powerful institutions. It only rules out maximising their needs to the disadvantage of other institutions and groups.

This alternative to the utilitarian model of teacher accountability could be described as a *democratic model*. It implies that teachers should be accountable to a variety of 'audiences' in society. In deciding what is worth teaching, and how, they should take into account what is worthwhile from a range of different points of view. Central and local government, parents, minority groups, and the pupils themselves may all qualify on the democratic model as audiences to whom teachers are accountable within the limitations imposed by social justice. Democratic accountability is similar to House's 'responsive' accountability, where teachers are responsive to a range of social groups.

Within the democratic model teachers as educators have rights as a profession. The utilitarian model weakens educational institutions by making them totally parasitic for their values on other institutions. One of the great contributions of the analytic philosophy of education[3] is to remind us of a conception of education where value resides in the teaching-learning process itself rather than in its outcomes. Such values as 'rational autonomy' and 'a concern for truth' specify not so much learning outcomes as the manner in which they are to be acquired by pupils. They place limitations on the means teachers *qua* educators should adopt to achieve socially valued ends of learning. A utilitarian system of accountability completely ignores these distinctively educational values and in so doing threatens to destroy schools as places where *education goes on*. A democratic system would recognise teachers' *professional accountability* to each other. Justice requires both that they do not benefit outside groups in ways which prevent them from protecting and fostering educational values, and that they do not do the latter while neglecting the former.

2   The assumption that achievement scores provide a valid indication of teaching effectiveness is false. Such tests may evaluate what pupils have learned,[4] or even if they have learned what was intended, but not necessarily what has been learned as a result of what teachers do. Numerous factors operating in classroom situations influence pupil performance and are difficult for teachers to control e.g. those related to social background, peer group norms, and school ethos. Achievement scores alone cannot tell us which factors in the situation are the cause of learning or learning failure. Robert Stake (undated) argued that major differences in standardised test scores cannot be explained by differences in teaching method and pointed out the fact that achievement tests were designed as predictors of future academic success rather than measures of teaching effectiveness.

Test scores might discriminate effective from ineffective teaching if it were true that all classroom situations are easily manipulated by teachers. Even if this is normally true, which I don't believe, it may not be true in particular circumstances. Therefore, if a particular teacher's class scored high on tests this would at best only make it probable that his teaching was effective. Accountability systems which rely on tests mistakenly and conveniently assume that teachers can be omnipotent in their classrooms.

The only way to determine the causal significance of teaching in particular situations is *via* case studies of patterns of teacher-pupil interaction. In other words evaluations of teaching are appropriately based on the study of what is actually happening in the situation where it is going on. As Joseph Schwab argues, this approach on a large scale

> will require new mechanisms of empirical investigation, new methods of reportage, a new class of educational researchers, and much money. It is an effort without which we will continue largely...ignorant of what real consequences, if any, our efforts have had.

(1970, p. 31)

3   Ascriptions of praise and blame impute moral agency or responsibility for the consequences of actions. Even if current accountability systems evaluated the causal significance of teachers' actions on less dubious evidence than test scores, it still wouldn't follow that teachers should necessarily be held morally responsible, let alone punished, for consequences they have a moral responsibility to avoid. Considerations other than the causal significance of what a teacher does, have to be taken into account in evaluating moral responsibility in the classroom.[5]

People can be blamed for what they do on the following sorts of grounds:[6]

(a)   For acting with wrong intentions.
(b)   For failing to exercise the care and effort required to prevent consequences which are foreseeable.
(c)   For lack of skill i.e. bringing about the very consequences they are trying to avoid.

These grounds imply different degrees of blame (a) implies greater blame than (b) or (c), and (b) greater blame than (c). As Feinberg (1968) has pointed out, the expression of blame in punishment could not possibly improve the performance of someone who was unskilful, and there is increasing evidence that such 'remedial' treatment is self-defeating with respect to (a) and (b). To blame someone is to express disapproval of them, but does not imply any particular form of 'remedial' treatment.

The criteria cited pick out not so much what is brought about by a person's actions as his moral relationship to his actions and their consequences. In other words they are used to identify the manner in which the agent performs rather than merely what he performs. 'Descriptions' of performance may simply pick out what a man does (what he brings about) or they may pick out both this and the manner in which he does it. In the latter case 'the description' ascribes moral responsibility over and above causal responsibility.

[. . .]

The particular circumstances in which a teacher is working may be such that no amount of good intention, effort and normal skill will enable him to prevent his actions having the consequences they do. 'Accountability' systems which ascribe blame to teachers purely on the basis of causal evaluations of their actions, however well founded, are quite unfair. Such ascriptions should be based on considerations which are above and beyond those relevant to evaluations of causal significance.

4   The assumption that teachers have no rights to participate in evaluations of their own moral agency contradicts the values embodied in the concept of accountability. A person is accountable to others when he is obliged to respond to their ascriptions of blame by providing an answering account of his actions. The concept of accountability entails *the right to evaluate the evaluation* and therefore the right to self-evaluation. In a genuine accountability context ascriptions of moral agency (praise and blame) are what Hart has called *defeasible* ascriptions (1948). The term is taken from property law in which legal claims are called defeasible because they are vulnerable to defeat by the defendant. The task of the claimant is to establish a *prima facie* case

which is strong enough to oblige the defendant to answer it. Only if the defendant fails to justify or excuse his conduct sufficiently can the claimant's ascription of blame hold. The concept of accountability specifies a fair method of teacher evaluation in which the outsider's judgment is open to defeat by the agent's. It is fair because the agent is in a special position to evaluate his own moral agency. *Via* introspection he has direct access to his own intentions in, and beliefs about, his situation. He is also in a good position to assess the freedom of action open to him.

For these reasons outsiders' evaluations of teachers must pass the test of teachers' own judgments in any genuine system of classroom accountability. The model criticised by House is not in fact a model of accountability. The systems which embody it misdescribe themselves.

I have sketched what I see to be the main conceptual, methodological and ethical limitations of the sort of 'accountability' systems teachers are in danger of having imposed upon them. I have sought to avoid reacting to the idea of accountability in a negative way by trying to construct out of my criticisms an alternative model which I hope is conceptually, methodologically and ethically sounder.

In the next section I shall suggest some ways in which a teacher educator can prepare students and practising teachers for participation in a professionally fair and socially just system of classroom accountability.

Developing self-monitoring capabilities

If teacher education is to prepare students or experienced teachers for accountability then it must be concerned with developing their ability to reflect on practical classroom situations. By 'practical reflection' I mean reflection with a view to action. This involves identifying and diagnosing those practical problems which exist for the teacher in his situation and deciding on strategies for resolving them. The view of accountability which I have outlined, with its emphasis on the right of the teacher to evaluate his own moral agency, assumes that teachers are capable of identifying and diagnosing their practical problems with some degree of objectivity. It implies that the teacher is able to identify a discrepancy between what he in fact brings about in the classroom and his responsibilities to foster and prevent certain consequences. If he cannot do this he is unable to assess whether or not he is obliged to render an explanatory account of his performance, since such an obligation at least presupposes that the challenger ascribes blame on an accurate appraisal of the consequences of his actions. The identification of such a discrepancy would constitute a practical problem for the teacher to resolve. Accountability also implies that the teacher is capable of diagnosing his problems objectively. Otherwise what is the point of inviting him to defeat a challenge? Diagnosis will involve determining the extent to which his performance is best explained in terms of wrong intention, negligence, lack of skill or in terms of justifying or excusing conditions.

The fact that any genuine accountability system embodies the view that teachers are able to identify and diagnose practical problems objectively is very important because it indicates a respect for the teacher as an autonomous person who is capable of improving his own performance in the light of reflection. The fact that this view is not implicit in many current 'accountability' systems is indicative of the low esteem in which teachers are held.

To say that accountability assumes teachers are capable of identifying and diagnosing practical problems is to say that no genuine system of classroom accountability can be established unless these capabilities exist. But we need not assume that they do in fact exist. Nor should we assume that they are initially best developed within actual accountability contexts. My experience in the Ford Teaching Project[7] has taught me that teachers find it extremely difficult to be objective about their own performance and that outsiders' evaluations of their moral agency in the classroom can make things even more difficult by increasing their feelings of anxiety and defensiveness.

With these two points in mind I shall address the question of how these capabilities of practical reflection can be developed. The task is in my view one of the major tasks for teacher education in the near future. What I have to say is largely drawn from my own attempts with Clem Adelman to develop these capabilities with practising teachers involved in the Ford Teaching Project.[8]

The context was therefore one of Field Based Inservice Training. I hope that what I say has implications for Field Based Initial Training and the rethinking that is going on about the functions of school experience for student teachers. But I don't want to be labelled as an advocate of this approach as opposed to college centred teacher education. In the third section I shall look at the possibilities for developing practical reflection 'off the field'.

Stages in self-monitoring

Accountability gives practical reflection a certain focus. The emphasis is on the person and actions of the teacher. I am aware that this is a partial focus and that the problems in the classroom may lie elsewhere. However, this is a useful starting point for practical reflection because if teachers lack self-awareness they are in no position to identify *any* practical problems. I have known many who believed their problem to lie outside themselves in 'lack of resources', 'time-table provision' 'parental expectation' etc., because they were unaware of the constraints they actually imposed on pupil learning; constraints which self-awareness would have helped them to remove. In my experience teachers always have more autonomy in the classroom than they like to think they have. A teacher has the right to claim that the problem lies outside his own sphere of influence only if he has evidence that the fault does not lie with him.

In the Ford Teaching Project we called the agent's activity of practical reflection about himself and his actions 'self-monitoring'. In self-monitoring the teacher becomes aware of his own actions, their consequences, and the extent of his moral responsibility for these consequences. The process involves three distinct activities:

1   Self-ascribing personal agency for direct actions accurately i.e. actions which can be performed at will rather than indirectly as a consequence of some prior action. Compare 'asking a question' with 'eliciting an answer'.
2   Assessing the consequences of direct actions accurately.
3   Assessing moral responsibility for consequences accurately.

The activities constitute a logical sequence which simply means that one cannot do (2) without (1), or (3) without (2). However, in a teacher education context I think there are sound practical reasons for treating the order as a developmental sequence as well. This is because (1) alone involves less anxiety for the teacher than (2), and (2) than (3). If he merely identifies those actions he can normally perform directly rather than indirectly, he doesn't have to face questions about their causal significance and his accountability immediately. Therefore his self-ascriptions are likely to be more objective because less biased by the desire to select only those actions which have desirable consequences. Once an objective attitude towards his agency for direct actions has been developed, the teacher is less likely to allow his feelings of anxiety at (2) to influence his self-monitoring at (1). It is at this point that an attempt can be made to develop capabilities at (2).

Although assessing causal significance can raise questions about moral agency, the teacher does not have to face them. However, once he develops an objective attitude towards the consequences of his actions he should be able to reflect about moral agency without allowing his desire to escape blame to distort his assessments of consequences. It is only when teachers are capable of self-monitoring at each of these three levels to some degree that they are ready to participate rationally in accountability systems.

I believe that being plunged into a context where outsiders evaluated their moral agency without this kind of developmental preparation would be self-defeating since the anxiety generated would render the achievement of an objective attitude at any of these levels extremely difficult.

Self-monitoring agency for direct actions

Teachers should initially try to monitor their agency for those actions which are most likely to influence pupil performance. Such actions can be monitored without actually having to determine their consequences. There are *prima facie* reasons why some actions rather than others are likely to influence pupil performance. The following criteria[9] will pick out the most likely candidates:

(i) *Frequency of recurrence.* Persistent and recurring elements (patterns) in a teacher's performance should be selected because pupils' responses will be greatly influenced by those actions which are perceived to reflect their teacher's stable identity *qua* teacher. Frequently recurring actions which tend to persist over time are most indicative of a teacher's identity as it is embedded in the social context of the classroom. Their influence is cumulative so that the consequences of later recurrences will be greater than earlier ones. Isolated elements are not so influential. For example, if a teacher 'changes topic' only a few times during the course of class discussions his pupils will feel freer to bring him back to the point than if it is something which he does frequently and persistently.

A teacher's capacity for objectivity about his performance in a situation is strengthened by awareness of his tendencies to engage in certain kinds of patterned behaviour. This awareness makes it difficult for him to ignore evidence that past patterns still persist.

(ii) *Normative significance.* Actions which proximate to norms of action within the teaching profession and thereby reflect the institutional characteristics of schools are more likely to influence pupil performance than those which are relatively unique to particular individuals. Again the cumulative effects of such actions are likely to be greater than the effects of actions which are unique to individuals.

For example, a teacher who engages in a question-posing as against a didactic teaching style is unlikely to foster autonomous reasoning if the vast majority of his pupils' teachers, past and present, have collectively reinforced dependent thinking through didactic teaching.

In order to apply this criterion, teachers will need to know what the norms are, and the fact that observation and discussion of other teachers' classrooms is not easy to get access to may mean that teachers are surprisingly ignorant of professional norms. The provision of such opportunities should be a major task of teacher education since teachers' anxieties and fears about taking a hard look at their own performance are often the result of mistaken beliefs about how it relates to what is normal. In the Ford Teaching Project it made an enormous difference to teachers' capacities to look at their actions objectively when they discovered that they were not so idiosyncratic as they feared.

(iii) *Theoretical significance.* Actions which are significant in theories of teaching are more likely to influence pupil performance than those which are not. For example, Flanders claims that indirect actions correlate with learning achievement better than direct actions, and advocates of discovery approaches claim that 'implicit indications' of objectives correlate with autonomous reasoning more than 'explicit indications'. Statistical correlations of, and generalisations about, various categories of teacher behaviour can all be utilised to identify actions which are candidates for causal appraisal. Indeed, use of the criterion of theoretical significance places the teacher in a position to reflect about theories of teaching by testing their validity in his own classroom. Perhaps this is a better way of coming to understand theories than dealing with them outside the context of practical reflection on particular situations, as often happens in teacher education courses. I shall return to uses of theory for practical reflection in the third section.

(iv) *Structural significance.* Here a variety of actions falling under different categories are related together under a superordinate category because of certain structurally significant features they share in common. By 'structurally significant features' I refer to features of the teacher's primary aims in the situation. For example, the teacher may discover that a variety of actions falling under a number of different categories – such as questioning, rewarding, confirming – can all be related together under the category *subject-centred* because they express the aim of getting the pupils to learn the facts of the subject. Another teacher may discover that a variety of categories which apply to him can all be subsumed under *child-centred* because they express the process aim of getting pupils to direct their own learning.

Actions which are relevant to some structurally significant category are by virtue of this fact likely to influence pupil performance more than structurally insignificant acts. Pupils are unlikely to be heavily influenced by conduct they believe to be unconnected with the teacher's primary aims and objectives.

Perhaps the most important criterion of the four is that of frequent recurrence or patterning (although (i) and (iv) are mutually interdependent *via* intention). But the more additional criteria are satisfied the more confidence a teacher can place in a pattern's causal significance. The collective application of these criteria enables a teacher to monitor his personal agency for actions selectively and economically because he attends only to those actions which are most likely to influence pupil performance.

Monitoring consequences of actions

Stage 2 of the developmental sequence raises the question of how consequences are to be assessed. And indeed my experience with teachers in the Ford Project suggests they find it extremely difficult to gather sufficient and relevant evidence which places them in a position to make informed judgments. As I argued previously, test situations do not provide such evidence. What is required is evidence which enables teachers to identify what pupils do *as responses* to what *they do*. What sort of evidence is this? Well there is not one sort but two sorts, which can be labelled *objective* and *subjective* evidence respectively as long as the use of these terms here is not confused with their qualitative use to indicate the extent to which judgments are biased.[10] Objective evidence is not necessarily less qualitatively subjective than subjective evidence in this context. The former is simply evidence which can be verified by mere observation and is to that extent quantifiable, whereas the latter is evidence which is accessible only via participants' introspective accounts of their subjective states. The latter need not be more subjective in the qualitative sense than quantifiable evidence.

Teachers' observations of what pupils do in classrooms are I believe relevant, but not sufficient, for assessing consequences of actions. For example, a teacher observes that whenever he says 'Do we all agree?' during class discussions, his pupils remain silent. On the basis of this objective evidence he interprets the silence as the response 'We have no ideas on the subject'. This assumes that his pupils interpreted 'Do we all agree?' as 'I am trying to find out what your ideas are on this issue'. But suppose they in fact interpreted such behaviour as 'You had better agree with that'; in which case a better interpretation of the silence would be 'We are not free to express our own ideas'.

How pupils interpret teachers' behaviour places certain logical limitations on what can count as an intelligible response. It is only if the teacher's assumptions about how pupils 'take' his behaviour are well founded that he is likely to interpret the meaning of their behaviour accurately. In the Ford Project teachers invariably assumed the existence of agreed rules for interpreting behaviour. The result was that they frequently made wrong assessments of the causal significance of their actions.

Thus interpretations from objective evidence need to be checked from time to time against pupils' own accounts of their responses and the interpretations on which they are based. Honest accounts from pupils provide subjective evidence for self-evaluating the causal significance of teachers' actions.

Of course, one has to face the fact that pupils' accounts are not necessarily reliable. They may either consciously or unconsciously distort them in order to present the teacher with a false view of his agency. In other words they may well be subjective (in the qualitative sense). But this doesn't mean that non-quantifiable evidence is necessarily qualitatively subjective. The assumption that quantification is a necessary condition of objectivity has prevented classroom research in the past from providing teachers with adequate support in reflecting about their practice. To my knowledge the breakthrough in this country came in the late 1960s with Stenhouse's Humanities Project (1970). This project developed hypotheses about classroom problems partly based on data derived from interviews with pupils. The approach has been further developed by the Ford Teaching Project (1975). Robert Goldhammer working in the USA during the 1960s, had also grasped some of the possibilities of the approach for the supervision of teachers. He noted that

> Although wonderful opportunities exist, in this connection, for systematic phenomenological research, I am not aware of any that has been undertaken so far.
>
> (1969, p. 102)

It is my view that teachers' accounts of the causal significance of their actions based on observation need to be checked against pupils' accounts of causal significance.

But I also believe that the subjective 'evidence' provided by pupils needs to be checked against objective data. For example, suppose pupils say they interpret the teacher's behaviour as 'trying to prevent the expression of their own ideas', then an interviewer can ask them to cite the observable evidence on which this interpretation is based. If no such evidence exists then one has grounds for doubting the reliability of what pupils say. By cross-checking one sort of data against another teachers can evaluate the consequences of their actions with at least some degree of objectivity (in the qualitative sense).

In the Ford Teaching Project we developed a method of helping teachers to produce objective accounts (qualitative sense) of their performance. It is called *triangulation* and involves the collaboration of three parties – the teacher, his pupils, and an observer. Each is in a special position. The teacher is in the best position to know what he means by what he does and how he interprets pupils' responses. The pupils are in the best position to know the meanings of their behaviour and the interpretations of teachers' actions on which they may be based. The observer is in the best position, by virtue of his detachment from the requirements of action, to gather accurate evidence of observable behaviour. In our experience it is possible to use the observer's and pupils' accounts as a check on the teacher's accounts of the causal significance of his actions in at least the following ways:[11]

1   The accuracy of the account should be doubted if the observer disputes the observable evidence cited in support.
2   The accuracy of the account should be doubted if pupils who know the teacher well dispute it and the observer confirms the observable evidence they cite to support it.
3   The accuracy of the account should be doubted if it implies no gap between the teacher's aspirations or ideals and practice, and is confirmed by pupils.

The last criterion stems from the fact that teachers will tend to distort their own accounts in order to place their actions in a favourable light, and pupils will normally tend to avoid being critical of their teachers when accounts are elicited in their presence. So a teacher's account which places his actions in a favourable light and is confirmed by pupils should be treated with some suspicion although, of course, it is not necessarily false. One can place the greatest amount of confidence in those accounts where the teacher acknowledges a problem by implying a gap between his aspirations and his practice, and which are confirmed by the observer and pupils.

Monitoring moral agency

A teacher who is able to produce accurate accounts of his own actions and their consequences in the classroom can identify problems in his teaching because he will be aware of any discrepancies between his conception of his responsibilities as a teacher and the consequences of his actions. This awareness will perhaps inevitably raise questions for him about whether he can be blamed for such consequences. These are questions he can reflect on or avoid if left to do so. However, I believe if he was not prepared to face them eventually he would not have got as far as the second stage of the sequence. But this doesn't mean that pressurising him to face them by calling him to account will do much good. Such pressure may be useful once he has begun to assess his moral agency for himself. It is only when he has begun to call himself to account that he is ready for participation within some kind of accountability system. And here I think the teacher should still retain some initiative so that evaluations of his moral agency are made in response to his invitations. He becomes a 'collector of value judgments'[12] rather than merely their recipient.

In 'collecting judgments' the teacher gives people independent access to class-room data and uses their judgments of his moral agency to check his own. He then gives his audiences answering accounts. In terms of what I have called 'the democratic model' it is desirable that the range of audiences is gradually increased. It is perhaps best for a teacher to begin in the confines of his classroom with his own pupils. Inasmuch as he tries to elicit their accounts of the causal significance of his actions he will hardly be able to avoid eliciting ascriptions of praise and blame at the same time. When he is able to cope with and utilise pupils' challenges productively and rationally he can extend the range of his audiences to his fellow professionals and eventually beyond the school to inspectors, parents, the community, etc.

There are ontological reasons why other people's judgments of moral agency are necessary for self-evaluation. People construct their moral identities through interaction with the evaluations of others rather than introspection alone. If they were denied access to such judgments, or believed they were being dishonestly expressed, they would lose any sense of a stable moral identity. There are also not unrelated epistemological reasons. The honest reactions of others are necessary as a check on self-deception and subjective bias.[13] In this respect 'collecting value judgments' serves a similar function to triangulation in monitoring consequences of actions. The method is also an excellent way of reflecting about the responsibilities of the teacher in the classroom, since implicit in other peoples' judgments are views about the sorts of things teachers ought to bring about, or refrain from bringing about, in the classroom. From an analysis of the value judgments collected from a range of audiences teachers can come to understand a variety of different conceptions of their responsibilities, which ought to be taken into account in deciding what sort of teachers they ought to be.

[. . .]

The role of 'the outsider'

At this point I would like to say something about the role of classroom observers in developing self-monitoring capabilities. There is a distinction to be made between the role of observers operating 'inside' accountability contexts and those operating 'outside' them. The former role is concerned with ascribing praise and blame and thereby calling teachers to account. The latter role is concerned not so much with calling teachers to account as with developing those capabilities which help teachers to participate in accountability contexts. The adopter of such a role is in many ways a 'marginal man' operating outside the system *for* the system. In the Ford Project we labelled the role *'the outsider'*. It was the role adopted by the central team.

In preparing teachers for accountability I would argue that the teacher-educator's role is that of 'the outside' rather than 'the inside' observer. It is his job to prepare teachers to relate to the latter in ways which help him to make rational responses to evaluations of his moral agency in the classroom. But it is not his job to make those evaluations. Since the traditional role of the supervisor in the classroom is very much that of 'the insider', there are important problems of role change for teacher-educators which there is not space to explore here. How then does 'the outsider' observer prepare teachers for accountability?

His main contribution is to help them monitor the consequences of their actions. He is the observer in the triangulation. In the Ford Project 'the outsider' observed teachers and constructed hypotheses about the causal significance of their actions. He selected consequences in the light of teachers' conceptions of what they had a responsibility to promote or avoid. In other words he viewed the classroom situation from the teacher's conception of his role rather than his own. In constructing hypotheses he tried to avoid ascribing praise or blame either explicitly or implicitly. He aspired to accounts which left open questions about the moral quality of the teacher's intentions and the amount of care, effort and skill displayed in bringing about consequences. Consider the following hypotheses developed from observations of Ford Project teachers:[14]

(i) When teachers *change the topic* under discussion they prevent pupils from expressing and developing their ideas, since pupils interpret such actions as attempts by teachers to get conformity to their views.

(ii) Utterances like '*good*', '*interesting*', '*right*', prevent the expression of divergent ideas in the class, since pupils tend to interpret them as attempts by teachers to legitimate the expression of some ideas rather than others.

(iii) When teachers *do not invite* pupils to evaluate the information they are studying they will not criticise it because they interpret the situation as one in which the teacher does not want criticism.

None of these hypotheses expresses the observer's view of teachers' moral agency. They simply ascribe causal significance to certain actions on the basis of how pupils are believed to interpret them and his own observations. The question of whether pupils' interpretations are correct is left open.

By generating such hypotheses out of his classroom observations 'the outsider' can help a teacher assess the consequences of his actions objectively by using them alongside pupils' accounts as a check on his own.

Why might an observer restrict his role to that of 'the outsider'? Well, if he doesn't do this at stage 2 he may prevent teachers from objectively assessing the consequences of their actions by producing a degree of anxiety which reinforces their tendency to distort the facts of their situation to escape blame. It is only when teachers have developed a concern for the truth about the consequences of their actions that 'insiders' are likely to elicit 'answering accounts' based on accurate assessments of consequences. Since accurate assessments of consequences are conditions of accountability it is 'the outsider's' job to help teachers establish those conditions, but not his job actually to call them to account. At stage 2 the observer helps teachers to assess consequences, but leaves them free to ask or avoid asking questions about their moral responsibility for them.

When teachers begin to ask such questions (stage 3) they are ready for 'inside' observers. However, the emergence of this stage doesn't dispense with the need for 'the outsider's' support. Both teachers and 'inside' observers will require continuing assistance in checking tendencies to distort their observations to fit their biases. 'The outsider' can help to sustain a genuine accountability context where both the teacher and his audiences are evaluating moral agency on the basis of accurate assessments of consequences. Thus in the Ford Teaching Project, a teacher and his professional colleagues, observing his performance on tape-slide, were able to check the assessments of causal significance implied in their respective accounts against 'the outsider's' assessments.

In the third stage 'the outsider's' role in relation to teachers should be rather different from that in the second stage. When teachers lack methods and motivation for producing reliable accounts of actions and consequences, he needs to take many initiatives e.g. asking for observation opportunities, interviewing the teacher and his pupils, supervising checking procedures. But at stage 3, teachers should be in a position to request observation, spontaneously produce their own assessments, interview their own pupils and 'the outsider', and cross-check accounts.

Theory and preparation for accountability

In the previous section I outlined some methods and techniques for helping teachers to self-monitor their practice in the classroom. Little has been said about the contribution of theory to practical reflection. I am an advocate of field-based teacher education, but believe that theory contributes to practical reflection. Here it is necessary to make a distinction between what Schwab (1970, pp. 1–5) calls 'theoretic' and 'eclectic' inquiries.

Within 'theoretic inquiries' theories determine the problems to be studied, the selection of data, and the knowledge sought. According to Schwab particular theories or theoretical systems are limited as tools for reflecting about practical situations in two respects. The first is that of incompleteness of their subject-matter. Thus if sociology takes over educational studies on the teacher education curriculum, its theories will tend to reduce personality 'to an artifact of society'. We can already see a tendency in educational research to focus attention at the macro level of the educational system rather than at the micro level of the teacher in his classroom. The second weakness of theory is the partiality of view a particular theory embodies even of its own subject-matter. Schwab takes the Freudian treatment of personality as an example here. In viewing personality after the analogue of a developing, differentiating organism, it fails to deal satisfactorily with many practically important features of interpersonal relations.

However, Schwab believes that theories are useful for practical deliberation so long as their users are not dominated by the context of their normal use within the theoretical mode. First, they can free the deliberator from having to rely on first-hand information about the subject-matter. Thus Skinnerian theory can be used as knowledge of the way people learn, without having to investigate the matter at first hand for oneself. Second, the concepts used in a theory can be brought to bear practically. For example, in my argument about why current accountability systems were unfair, I made use of the distinction between action and agency which is made by many philosophers of action.

The eclectic mode consists of the use of theories for the purposes of practical deliberation. It therefore wrenches them out of their normal context of use within a theoretical mode of inquiry and subordinates them to the purposes of practical reflection. This requires the eclectic use of many theories and types of theory to avoid the limitations of both 'incompleteness of subject-matter' and 'partiality of view'. The subjects of 'eclectic' inquiries are therefore practical situations calling for a decision or policy, rather than knowledge, to resolve them. Practical problems are not determined by any single theory or theoretical system. They are initially experienced as obstacles to action without knowing what sort of obstacles they are. 'Eclectic' inquiries involve as much a search for the problem as for its practical solution. As the data of the situation is searched, certain theories seem to be better ways of making sense of it than others, and the problem appears to grow clearer. As this happens 'the problem' begins to direct the selection of data. But as more data are selected, the enquirer may experience the need to change or modify his conceptualisations of the situation and so on, until the inquiry gradually becomes the search for practical solutions. In 'eclectic' enquiries, relevant theories cannot always be selected in advance of the problem or the search for data because of the constant interaction between data and theory.

The main reason for the current reaction against theory in teacher education is the fact that theories have been taught to students as ways of initiating them into different modes of theoretical discourse and have not been used 'eclectically' to help them reflect about practical educational situations. The 'holy trinity' of the teacher education curriculum – philosophy, psychology, and sociology of education – are not in themselves concerned with the identification and solution of practical problems in the classroom situation. Education is merely the territory on which the theoretical interests of these disciplines are pursued. Of course, the theoreticians believe that pursuing their discipline in the teachers' 'patch' will bring greater benefits than working elsewhere. I often doubt this. As a sort of eclectic researcher engaged in trying to understand practical problems faced by teachers I read less 'educational' theory as the years go by, finding that my reading in sociology, philosophy and psychology beyond the field of education contributes as much, if not more, to my understanding. I would not deny the need to initiate people into theoretical pursuits as a precondition of professional preparation. But I take teacher education to be primarily about initiating students and teachers into a mode of professional discourse which contributes to practical reflection. And in my view this is essentially 'eclectic' discourse about practical situations, drawing on relevant theories from a variety of 'theoretical inquiries' regardless of whether these theories have been used in theoretical inquiries about education. The so-called disciplines of education should cease to dominate the educational studies curriculum and be replaced by kinds of educational situations which require 'eclectic' treatment.

Only if this happens can teacher-educators select and organise theories in ways which help teachers to self-monitor problems in their teaching and thereby prepare them for accountability. In addition to helping the teacher use the sort of practical methods I outlined in the second section, the teacher-educator should be concerned to give him access to the range of theories he needs to understand and resolve problems in his teaching. I would argue that this cannot always be predetermined because of the interaction between data and theory in 'eclectic' inquiry. What theory is required will depend on the data collected. And even theories which are known to be relevant will hardly be understood outside the context of their application to the data. So theories need to be introduced during the course of 'eclectic' inquiries while the teacher is reflecting about the data he is gathering in his situation. They may be introduced directly by the teacher-educator/s in conversation, or indirectly through the study and discussion of eclectic research such as case studies on similar situations and selected reading in philosophy, sociology, psychology etc.

[. . .]

In this chapter I have tried to suggest ways in which teachers can be prepared for classroom accountability, and have, I hope, made it clear that it will demand a radically different sort of teacher education curriculum from the one that has been established over the last fifteen years. The drift of change must be a change of focus away from knowledge-orientated 'theoretical' studies to practically orientated 'eclectic' studies. I am not too optimistic about the possibilities of such change so long as teacher education seeks, misguidedly in my view, to validate itself in the eyes of the 'theoreticians' rather than the teaching profession in our schools.

Acknowledgements

I would like to thank Clem Adelman, Stephen Kemmis, Barry MacDonald and Hugh Sockett for helping me in various ways to write this chapter.

Notes

1 This chapter was written for the 'Curriculum development in teacher education seminar, Committee for Research into Teacher Education Conference, September, 1975.
2 I have the DES 'Primary Assessment Unit' in mind here.
3 Notably through the seminal work of R.S. Peters.
4 Although I doubt if even the best tests can always do this reliably. See Stephen Kemmis's unpublished paper presented to the BERA seminar on 'Conceptualising attainment criteria' at the Annual Conference, 1–4 September, 1975.
5 See Feinberg (1968).
6 See Feinberg (1968).
7 See *The Stranger in the Classroom, Unit 2 Research Methods*, Ford Teaching Teaching Project (1975).
8 See *Classroom Action Research, Unit 2 Research Methods*, Ford Teaching Project (1975).
9 These criteria are adapted from Robert Goldhammer (1969), Chapter 4.
10 For an excellent account of how the conflation of these two uses of objectivity and subjectivity has functioned in educational research, see Michael Scrivens' 'Objectivity and subjectivity in educational research', in *Philosophical Redirection of Educational Research*, University of Chicago Press, 1972.
11 These tests have been slightly modified since I last described them in 'Teachers' accounts and the objectivity of classroom research', *London Educational Review*, 4 (2/3), Autumn, 1975.
12 See S. Kemmis and R. Stake, 'Operational versus judgmental assessment of teacher competence', *Educational Leadership*, 31 (4). The writers argue that 'collecting value judgments' from audiences should be a central feature of Competency Based Teacher Education.
13 The ontological and epistemological reasons are cited by David Wood in 'Honesty', in *Philosophy and Personal Relations*. A. Montefiore (ed.), Routledge and Kegan Paul. 1973, pp. 196–199.
14 For a full list of hypotheses see *Implementing the Principles of Inquiry/Discovery Teaching, Unit 3 Hypotheses*, Ford Teaching Project (1975).

References

Clegg, A. (1975) 'Battery fed and factory tested', *Times Educational Supplement* 11 July.
Feinberg, J. (1968) 'Action and responsibility', in *The Philosophy of Action*, A.R. White (ed.) Oxford University Press.
Ford Teaching Project (1975) Centre for Applied Research in Education, University of East Anglia. Materials now available from the Centre at the Cambridge Institute of Education.
Goldhammer, R. (1969) *Clinical Supervision: Special Methods for the Supervision of Teachers*, Holt, Rinehart and Winston.
Hart, H.L.A. (1948), 'The ascription of responsibility and rights', *Proceedings of the Aristotelian Society*, 49, pp. 171–194.
House, E. (undated), 'The price of productivity: who pays?', Center for Instructional Research and Curriculum Evaluation (CIRCE). University of Illinois, mimeograph. See also his 'The dominion of economic accountability', *Educational Forum*, November 1972.

Rawls, J. (1971) *A Theory of Justice*, Oxford University Press.
Schwab, J. (1970) *The Practical: A Language for Curriculum*, Washington, DC: National Education Association Publications.
Stake, R. (undated) 'Measuring what learners learn', CIRCE. University of Illinois, mimeograph.
Stenhouse, L.A., Elliott, J., Plaskow, M., Ruddock, J. (1970) *The Humanities Project: An introduction*, Heinemann Educational.

CHAPTER 4

SELF-EVALUATION AND TEACHER COMPETENCE

Irish Educational Studies, Proceedings of the Annual Conference of the Irish Educational Studies Association, 1994

Self-evaluation is often advocated when the teaching profession comes under pressure to be more publicly accountable for its practices.

[. . .]

Although the professional autonomy of individual teachers is an idea deeply embedded in the occupational culture, the idea of self-evaluation is not. It is culturally naive to assume that the vast majority of teachers will embrace self-evaluation as a means of safeguarding their autonomy. Indeed I would argue that self-evaluation schemes are usually perceived by teachers as a threat to their autonomy as this has been traditionally construed.

Helen Simons (1985) has pointed out the problems any school-based evaluation runs into if it contradicts the major values embodied in the occupational culture of teachers; namely, those of privacy, territoriality, and hierarchy. The proposed self-evaluation frameworks may appear to outsiders to be consistent with the protection of professional autonomy, and for this reason to lack credibility as instruments of public accountability, but from the perspective of the professional culture they threaten it. This is because the idea of teacher autonomy is shaped by the professional culture and, therefore, constructed in terms of the values cited by Simons. This culture construes the professional autonomy of the teacher in terms of the individual's right to practice in private free from external surveillance and scrutiny. Inasmuch as self-evaluation schemes involve individuals in the production of public representations of their practices, they render it open to a measure of external surveillance, albeit indirect and under the control of practitioners. Any form of formalised and systematic professional self-evaluation constitutes a shift in favour of someone's "right to know" what is going on away from the presumption of an unconditional right to privacy. The presumed right to total privacy is of course closely linked to a right to territory. The former rests on the presumption that the teacher in some sense owns the practice site; it is "his" or "her" classroom rather than the children's. And this suggests that it is the site where the teacher exercises authority and power. Knowledge implies power to influence, and any diminishing of privacy increases the power of someone else to influence what children learn in classrooms and thereby decreases the power of the teacher. Teacher self-evaluation threatens the value practitioners place on their capacity to control what happens in their territorial space; the classroom. Why might any teacher want to voluntarily engage in an activity that diminished their control in classrooms? Well some might for reasons I will explore later, but they won't find the rationale for it in a professional culture shaped by the values of privacy and territoriality. Teachers who commit themselves to self-evaluation activities commit themselves to the enterprise of transforming their professional culture.

Within schools and the educational system at large a considerable administrative hierarchy has functioned to maintain and protect the professional values of privacy and territoriality. Students are organised into classes which are then allocated to individual teachers at particular physical locations for specified periods of time. The organisational system represented by the school time-table and administered by the "hierarchy" maintains the conditions of privacy and territoriality that enable teachers to exercise a certain kind of power over children's learning. In this context "autonomy" is simply defined by the presence of such enabling conditions.

As Giddens has pointed out (1984) it is a mistake to view systems solely as constraints on human agency. They may also constitute enabling conditions for exercising a certain kind of agency (see also Elliott, 1993).

Formal self-evaluation procedures may threaten the traditional forms of organisation in schools and in doing so undermine the systems maintenance functions of the hierarchy. What happens if teachers lose their commitment to the values of privacy and territoriality as a result of their self-evaluation activity? It threatens the capacity of the administrative hierarchy to maintain and protect pedagogical conditions which enable teachers to control the processing of large amounts of information about students in a system of mass education. We should expect resistance to self-evaluation to come as much from school administrators as classroom teachers.

Self-evaluation and methodological competence

I now want to explore what I called the competence factor in explaining why self-evaluation advocacy tends to fall on stony ground.[1] The traditional professional culture of teachers provides no resources to enable teachers to become competent self-evaluators in the sense in which it is advocated. Of course, teachers are in a trivial sense right when they argue that they are self-evaluating all the time. Such activity is a normal part of what Giddens (1984) calls "practical consciousness." In participating in the routinised and habitual practices of everyday life human beings are aware of what they are doing inasmuch as they are intentionally trying to bring about certain effects and monitoring their actions in the light of their intentions. But such self-evaluation operates quite unselfconsciously in the flow of action. It is very different from what Giddens calls "discursive consciousness," being able to describe and explain one's practices in language to both oneself and others. This involves becoming reflexively self-aware, inasmuch as the "self's" role as agent in practical situations becomes an object of reflection for itself.

The traditional professional culture does not require teachers to be competent as self-evaluators at the level of discursive consciousness. Mere advocacy to be self-evaluating or reflective about one's teaching is futile when teachers don't know how to be [...]

The problem was that much of the advocacy which surrounded the self-evaluation movement was infected with assumptions taken over from the traditional professional culture. Thus the activity was frequently construed in individualistic terms. It was something teachers did in private, even if the outcomes were subsequently reported to, and discussed with, an audience. Moreover, it was assumed that data gathering is largely a private process of introspection rather than a matter of observing one's conduct, or eliciting the observations of others.

For example, "keeping a diary," "taking video and tape recordings of lessons," "using peer observations" and "the observations of external observers," "eliciting children's perceptions and understandings of their classroom experiences" are all self-evaluation methods. Evidence of other people's observations and children's experiences can provide fresh angles from which to view classroom situations and evaluate one's agency in them. They can enhance rather than diminish a teacher's capacity for self-evaluation. Similarly, in making sense of such multi-perspectival evidence, a process sometimes described as triangulation, the self-evaluating teacher operating at the level of discursive consciousness will not wish to reflect in isolation from others. S/he will seek opportunities for free and open dialogue about the evidence with peers, children, parents, outsider researchers and others as a means of self-evaluation. Self-evaluation is best construed as grounded in a social context of interacting minds collaborating with each other to improve the quality of their agency in classrooms and schools. To assume, as the check-list driven teacher self-evaluation movement in the UK did, that the activity of self-evaluation, if not the outcome, constituted a largely private process of introspective navel gazing, deflected attention away from the methodological competencies teachers need to develop to become self-evaluating teachers. Thus the question "Do I ask children leading questions?" is not best answered by private introspection but by discussing observational and pupil data with peers, pupils, and others. Accommodating self-evaluation activity to the assumptions that underpin the traditional teacher culture is a self-defeating strategy for its advocates.

In the UK we no longer use the term "self-evaluation" but a similar idea is now in widespread circulation in the field of initial teacher training; namely, of the teacher as a reflective practitioner. Inspired by the work of Donald Schön (1983, 1987) every Higher Education Institution (HEI) appears to be claiming to prepare student teachers to become reflective practitioners. What is so often missing is any detailed specification of how methodological competence as a reflective practitioner is to be developed. It is often simply presumed that reflection is a largely solitary and private process, albeit facilitated by a mentor who alone secures access to it, and aided by the keeping of a diary, journal or log. In my view such an account of reflective practice is totally inadequate as a basis for developing a level of methodological competence which enables the student teacher to withstand the pressures favouring rapid occupational socialisation into the traditional professional culture.

Such competence I have argued consists of capacities to participate in a form of social discourse which I have somewhat controversially described as "practical science." David Carr (1993), for example, finds such a term highly misleading because he believes the aim of a science is to produce causal knowledge, either for purely theoretical ends of explaining phenomena, or for the practical ends of technical control. It is therefore misleading, Carr argues, to use "science" to describe a form of moral discourse which generates neither theoretical "knowledge that" or technical "know how" but wise judgements about ethically appropriate ways of influencing children's learning. I used the term to refer to the latter because I wanted to convey the message that teacher self-evaluation, conceived as a form of moral/social discourse, involves the generation and testing of action hypotheses about which course of action in the situation is ethically consistent with one's educational ideals and values. In other words I wanted to highlight by using the term "science" the experimental as well as the social dimension of teacher self-evaluation. The significance of doing so should be fairly obvious.

Self-evaluation is not a distinct and separate activity running in parallel to that of teaching. It is a particular mode of teaching which operates at the level of discursive consciousness and, therefore, takes the form of a continuing moral experiment in a social context of dialogue with others. It would, therefore, be a mistake to construe the teaching competence of teachers as something quite separate from their methodological competence as self-evaluators. The competence of teachers operating purely at the level of unselfconscious practical consciousness must be distinguished from the kind of competence exercised by the self-evaluating teacher.

Carr pinpoints an important ambiguity in the sense in which the term "competent" is employed. It illuminates a lot of the current discussion in the UK which surrounds the Department for Education's (DFE) competency criteria for initial teacher training (see circ.9/92 and 14/93), and the possible use of the Department of Employment's "standards methodology" to generate National Vocational Qualifications (NVQs) for the teaching profession. Carr contrasts what he calls the "dispositional" and "capacity" senses of the term "competence." In the first sense we are referring to an individual's causal powers, which enable them to perform a task or function according to certain standards of technical efficiency/effectiveness. Thus we may deem a teacher competent in performing the discipline function if he or she can "keep children quiet in the classroom" or get them to "pay attention." Competence in this sense is always judged in terms of precise, pre-specifiable behavioural standards. In the second "capacity" sense of competence we refer to a person's general capacity to perform their functions in ways that are ethically consistent with some personal or professional ideal. Thus a teacher who asks "leading questions" in the classroom may be very competent in the dispositional sense of getting children through tests and exams, but nevertheless judge him or herself to be very incompetent in the capacity sense because s/he holds "fostering autonomy in learning" as an educational ideal. It should be noted that the latter judgement does not depend on whether the teacher's questions actually suppress autonomous learning. It is because the intention in asking the questions is ethically inconsistent with the ideal that the teacher judges him/herself to be incompetent.

When we use "competence" in the capacity sense we can still refer to how well a teacher performs his or her functional responsibilities, but the criteria or standards for judging "how well" will be predominantly ethical in character. They do not refer to quantifiable evidence or "measures" but to what Richard Peters (1968), and following him Lawrence Stenhouse (1975), called "principles of procedure" which can be analytically derived from an educational ideal and used to guide and evaluate the intentions of the teacher as a moral agent. Stenhouse's Humanities Project (1970) is a fine example of such an analysis, in its attempt to derive professional standards for handling socially controversial issues in classrooms from "Understanding" as an ideal in education.

In the UK the production of competence frameworks for initial teacher training by the DFE has, to date, not significantly gone beyond specifying competencies in terms of teachers' functional responsibilities in classrooms and schools. The standards for judging how well these are performed remain open, but there is a danger that attempts will be made to specify standards largely in terms of measurable behaviour using the DFE's standards methodology. There are certainly problems about specifying competencies in terms of ethical criteria. It can be argued that educational ideals and values are controversial both within the teaching profession and the broader society. For this reason they should not be included in national specifications of professional standards. Some have argued that the specification of standards in terms of criteria of technical efficiency alone can be justified as "minimal competencies" which provide through initial training a necessary foundation for good professional practice although they are not sufficient. Competence in the "capacity" sense can be developed at a later stage of professional development after the foundations of dispositional competence have been laid. It is this kind of argument that is being used to legitimate the removal of initial teacher training from HEIs, or at least to make it predominantly school-based. From this point of view it can be admitted that knowledge input is necessary for developing competence, but it takes the form of technical knowledge of causal principles, rules, and relationships. Its acquisition, therefore, does not need to be separately assessed from the evaluation of performance. If a teacher's performance conforms to the necessary standards of technical efficiency, then s/he has necessarily acquired the technical knowledge. Proponents of this view acknowledge that HEIs may still play a role in contributing "knowledge inputs."

As David Carr has pointed out, the problem with the "minimal competence" argument is that questions about what constitute desirable technical competencies cannot be separated from questions about the nature of education. Thus certain established techniques for keeping control in classrooms may be ethically inconsistent with some people's interpretation of what is involved in "developing children's understanding." Statements of educational aims embody controversial conceptions of value. There can be no ideologically neutral national framework of dispositional competences. Carr is right to point out that the two senses of competence are necessarily intertwined in any appraisal discourse which focuses on teaching. Just as a teacher's ethical competence is constituted by technical skills, such as an ability to elicit children's authentic ideas through open-ended questioning, so what constitutes technical competencies will always be governed by some view of what performances are educationally worthwhile in the ethical sense of "education."

One of the objections teacher educators in HEIs may have to school-controlled training is that it will reinforce the technical competencies embodied in the traditional occupational culture which constitute the power to control children's behaviour in ways that effectively get them to process large amounts of information. Such dispositional competencies may be viewed as educationally unsound because they do not value what we now understand about the nature of human knowledge, children's minds and how they learn with understanding and which should now shape teachers' educational ideals. However, one does not go about getting teachers to value these understandings of "education" by simply prescribing an alternative list of dispositional competencies that are consistent with them.

This is because learning is posited as an active process in which children construct knowledge and understanding from experiences provided by teachers, and do so in ways which are shaped by their personal characteristics, their individuality. This means that teachers have to view learning as a dynamic rather than passive process, and teaching as a responsive activity requiring the development of skills which are heavily dependent on context. With experience in many different classroom situations teachers may develop a repertoire of technical skills they know they can select from in the light of their understanding of a particular classroom situation. This implies that teaching which is orientated towards the realisation of a learning process defined by the kinds of understandings and values I have cited, requires competence in both its ethical and technical dimensions to be continually developed through a process of self-evaluation. This doesn't mean that techniques, which the collective wisdom of self-evaluating teachers suggests are ethically appropriate in certain kinds of classroom situations, should not be specified, but they need to be formulated as action hypotheses for teachers to test in certain kinds of situations. A competency framework of this kind would never be fixed, but open to revision and extension in the light of experience. It would both support and be continually developed in the kind of social and experimental process of self-evaluation I have described.

In my view it would be quite wrong to specify a mandatory framework of competencies which go beyond the formulation of role functions to trying to specify in detail the ethical and technical standards governing appraisals of how well they are performed. The clarification of such standards should emerge from within the kind of self-evaluation process I have depicted: in the dialogue between all the partners in the appraisal process – teacher, peers, pupils, and external observers – as they seek to understand similarities and differences in judgement between themselves.

When self-evaluation, conceived as a practical science in the terms I have depicted, is established as the context in which teachers develop their teaching competence, it implies that teaching competence not only involves technical skills and moral qualities but capacities which are intrinsic to the methodology of reflection. Elsewhere I have articulated these as the "generic qualities" teachers need to develop as practical scientists or action researchers. They constitute capacities which are activated and developed in reflective teaching. Drawing on the work of Klemp (1977) and other associates of McBer & Co. (Spencer, 1979), I have argued that these generic qualities fall into three broad categories: cognitive, interpersonal, and impacting abilities. Thus abilities to identify patterns in complex human situations or to understand different sides of a controversial issue are capacities which can be linked to the need of the self-evaluating practitioner to develop his or her understanding of the particular situations in which they are required to perform. But in order to exercise these capacities the self-evaluating practitioner will need to possess interpersonal abilities which can be linked to an empathetic understanding of the thoughts, feelings, and experiences of others, so necessary to the kinds of data gathering and analysis methods I sketched earlier. Finally, the experimental dimension of self-evaluation requires practitioners to develop impacting abilities associated with a belief that one can always initiate some course of action, whatever the situation, to create a better match between reality and ideal. Such abilities include exercising initiative and taking moderate risks in pursuit of one's ideals.

Conclusion

In my view the only form of self-evaluation which has emphasised the development of methodological competence is that which has become known as educational action research. In the UK it finds its expression in many part-time post-graduate degree courses for teachers in HEIs. Such courses focus on developing in teachers the methodological competence to research their own practice. But the aim of the research is not the production of value-free knowledge. It is the improvement of the moral quality of the agency the teacher exercises in his or her professional practices *qua* educator. HEIs in the UK have generated local networks which have sustained for teachers a professional counter-culture to the traditional craft culture of teaching. ...Although I believe that teacher self-evaluation can only be sustained through networking that permeates every level of the educational system, I am convinced from my own experience that it will collapse and die if the staff of HEIs are by-passed as senior partners in the provision of support for the professional development of teachers.

Note

1   Teacher self-evaluation was heavily promoted within the UK during the late 70s and early 80s by local education authority advisers and inspectors. Teachers were asked to work their way through self-evaluation check-lists published by local authorities.

References

Carr, D. (1993) "Questions of competence" *British Journal of Educational Studies*, Vol. XXXXI, No. 3, September.

Department for Education (1992) *Circular 9/92* Initial Teacher Training (Secondary Phase) Annex 1, September. London.

Department for Education (1993) *Circular 14/93* The Initial Training of Primary School Teachers: New Criteria for Courses, November. London.

Elliott, J. (1993) "What have we learned from action research in school-based evaluation?" *Educational Action Research: An International Journal*, Vol. 1, No. 1.

Giddens, A. (1984) *The Constitution of Society*. Cambridge: Polity Press.

Klemp, G.O. (1977) *Three Factors of Success in the World of Work: Implications for Curriculum in Higher Education*. Boston, MA: McBer & Co.

Peters, R.S. (1968) "Must an educator have an aim?" in MacMillan, C.B. and Nelson, T. (eds), *Concepts of Teaching*. Chicago, IL: Rand McNally.

Schön, D. (1983) *The Reflective Practitioner*. London: Temple Smith.

—— (1987) *Educating the Reflective Practitioner*. London: Jossey Bass.

Simons, H. (1985) "Against the rules: procedural problems in school self-evaluation," *Curriculum Perspectives*, Vol. 5, No. 2.

Spencer, L.M. (1979) *Identifying, Measuring and Training Soft Skill Competencies which Predict Performance in Professional, Managerial and Human Service Jobs*. Boston, MA: McBer & Co.

Stenhouse, L. (1975) *An Introduction to Curriculum Research and Development*, Ch. 7. London: Heinemann.

Stenhouse, L., Elliott, J., Plaskow, M., Rudduck, J. (1970) *The Humanities Project: An Introduction*. London: Heinemann Educational Books.

PART 3

PARADIGMS OF EDUCATIONAL RESEARCH

CHAPTER 5

CLASSROOM RESEARCH
Science or commonsense?

Understanding Classroom Life, pp. 12–25 (eds) R. McAleese and D. Hamilton, NFER, 1978

Concept and purpose

Researchers in the field of education often assume that the practitioner's own commonsense concepts of educational situations are too vague and imprecise for the purposes of theory development. Commonsense is *vague* sense. Research must establish conceptual schemes in which the empirical content specified by concepts is clear and distinct, and in which the relationships between concepts are compatible with the principles of formal logic. Only if concepts conform to this criterion can theories be developed which provide reliable predictive generalizations. In other words, researchers tend to assess commonsense concepts in the light of their commitment to a procedural criterion which has its home in a context of scientific inquiry aimed at developing reliable predictive generalizations. But as Popper has argued, the degree of conceptual precision necessary is relative to the purposes for which the concepts are employed.[1] The fact that commonsense concepts of classrooms are not precise enough for scientific purposes does not mean that they are not sufficiently precise for others. They may well be precise enough for the purposes of action in particular classroom situations. In fact I would argue that commonsense concepts are generated for such purposes. They orientate the practitioner to practically relevant features of particular situations.

Two types of concept

Herbert Blumer has made a useful distinction between *definitive* and *sensitizing* concepts.[2] The definitive concept 'refers precisely to what is common to a class of objects, by the aid of a clear definition in terms of attributes or fixed bench marks' and serves 'as a means of clearly identifying the individual instance of the class and the make-up of that instance that is covered by the concept'. The sensitizing concept on the other hand 'lacks such specification of attributes or bench marks and consequently it does not enable the user to move directly to the instance and its relevant content. Instead, it gives the user a general sense of reference and guidance in approaching empirical instances'. Blumer sums it up by suggesting that definitive concepts tell us what to see while sensitizing concepts merely give us a general direction along which to look. I find this distinction illuminating in terms of the different purposes for which out concepts are developed. Definitive concepts may well be necessary for the development of reliable predictive generalizations. But within the practical context of everyday life the practitioner has to act and react in relation to a particular situation and particular people and events within it. He needs to understand things in all their particularity.

Now, of course, he cannot do this without concepts which refer to features this situation may have in common with others. But these common features will take a distinctive form from instance to instance. They have a particular mode of expression in each case under study. As Blumer argues 'What we are referring to by any given concept shapes up in a different way in each empirical instance.' The practitioner's concepts guide him towards practically relevant features of the situation but in order to understand them he has to study their distinctive mode of expression in that situation. This understanding of the situation may in turn lead to a revision and modification of the concept. The practitioner may discover relevant features of the situation which do not quite fit the sorts of things he presumes the concept to cover and may change the concept accordingly.

With the employment of sensitizing concepts we have a constant interaction going on between the particular and the general. One can only understand a particular instance by studying features it has in common with other situations and yet 'paradoxically' we can only understand what situations have in common through studying particular instances.

The sense of a definitive concept can be communicated through a formal operational definition which describes the empirical content specified by the concept. Such concepts are 'empty' in the sense that they are mental constructs which may or may not refer to properties which actually exist in the real world. Whether the properties specified exist is something to be discovered. Thus one can understand a theory employing definitive concepts without in any way having to commit oneself to its truth or falsity. A theory can be communicated entirely through a formal statement, which one understands by knowing the meaning of the terms in which it is expressed. One cannot communicate the sense of a sensitizing concept through formal operational definitions. This is because such concepts are not simply mental constructs. They are 'embedded in the objective structure of the world'.[3] One can only develop them through concrete experience. Sensitizing concepts are *concrete-universals* which, in the words of Iris Murdoch, 'we do not simply, through being rational and knowing ordinary language, "know" the meaning of...'[4] She suggests that 'we may have to learn the meaning' of concrete universals through personal experience, and cites 'courage' as an example. 'Words may mislead us here since words are often stable while concepts alter; we have a different image of courage at forty from that which we had at twenty. A deepening process, at any rate an altering and complicating process, takes place' (Iris Murdoch, *op. cit.*).

Since one can only develop an understanding of the meaning of sensitizing concepts through concrete experience one can only communicate one's understanding to others through case study: what Blumer calls 'an exposition which yields a meaningful picture, abetted by apt illustrations'. But this presupposes that others have also experienced instances of the concept. Case study appeals to a world of common experience that enables others to generalize from the case to their own experience in a way which both increases their understanding of the concept and illuminates that experience. Robert Stake has described this kind of process as 'naturalistic' generalization in contrast to 'formalistic' generalization in science.[5]

The connection between sensitizing and commonsense concepts should now be obvious. They are descriptions of the same concepts because sensitizing concepts – concrete universals – get their sense from a world of common experience. They are the concepts of commonsense.

Commonsense theorizing

I would suggest that one can theorize either from the standpoint of science or from that of practice, and that the latter consists largely of developing our understanding of commonsense concepts through the study of concrete particulars. In other words practical theorizing explores commonsense concepts through case study. It is therefore through case study that the sensitizing concepts which guide practice can be improved. My previous remarks about the necessary vagueness of sensitizing concepts should not be interpreted as an excuse for the obvious deficiencies of commonsense. In attempting to give some account of them I have argued that sensitizing concepts can be infinitely learned and developed. And this suggests that the employment of such concepts in conceptualizing practically relevant features of an instance can be far from satisfactory. I agree with Blumer when he argues that 'the enormously wide-spread vice in the use of sensitizing concepts is to take them for granted – to rest content with whatever element of plausibility they possess'. When a concept is taken for granted it takes the form of a vague stereotype into which instances in the world are made to fit. As such its adequacy as a means of understanding the instance cannot be tested against the study of the instance in all its particularity. Case study then is necessarily the means by which commonsense conceptualizations of the world are tested and improved. There is a tendency among researchers and some philosophers to characterize commonsense conceptualizations as essentially taken-for-granted and to account for their vagueness in these terms. For example, Richard Pring, a philosopher of education, defines commonsense as 'that range of beliefs which people share and hold in an unquestioning sort of way, and which provide a basic view of the world, of their position in the world, and how they ought to act'.[6]

For Pring this unquestioning attitude conditions the nature of the beliefs themselves and the concepts they embody. Vagueness can be accounted for in terms of this attitude. As soon as rational criticism begins a person moves out of the domain of commonsense into that of the traditional disciplines of thinking. His concepts are no longer those of vague commonsense but gain precision and clarity from their location in the 'disciplines'. It is this characterization of commonsense belief as essentially 'taken-for-granted' which leads many 'theorists' to conclude that there is no room for rational inquiry within the domain of commonsense. 'Rationality' is defined by 'disciplines', which operate in a separate domain of thought. Therefore commonsense concepts cannot be improved by rational inquiry within the domain of commonsense. They can only be *improved upon* and superseded. Hence the tendency to 'redefine' commonsense concepts operationally. However, if there is such a thing as valid commonsense theorizing, if commonsense concepts can be improved rather than superseded, then the translation of sensitizing concepts cannot occur without the distinctive character and meaning of the data from which they derive their sense being lost. Severyn Bruyn argues that sensitizing concepts have a right to their own existence, and provides an illustration of the dangers of redefinition: 'Defining an emotion or sentiment, for example, as that which is measured by certain visceral responses, cannot convey the true meaning of that feeling.'[7]

In my view the assumption that commonsense conceptualizations are necessarily 'taken-for-granted' is based on a confusion between contingent and necessary features of commonsense belief. The fact that people tend to take their commonsense beliefs for granted does not mean they have to.

Commonsense theorizing through case study doesn't function to generate reliable predictive generalizations like scientific theorizing. Rather it helps people to orientate their actions towards others by increasing the likelihood of the actions and reactions they anticipate taking place. Alfred Schutz writes:

> The ideal of everyday knowledge is not certainty, nor even probability in a mathematical sense, but just likelihood. Anticipations of future states of affairs are conjectures about what is to be hoped or feared, or at best, about what can be reasonably expected. When afterwards the anticipated state of affairs takes some form in actuality, we do not say that our prediction has come true or proved false, or that our hypothesis has stood the test, but that our hopes or fears were or were not well founded.[8]

Stenhouse echoes Schutz when he talks about testing our commonsense conceptualizations by 'our experience of surprise'. He suggests that surprise 'is not experienced because of the negation of predictions based upon general laws but because of either the negation of predictions based upon diagnostic judgments or the experienced difficulty of making those judgments'.[9]

Having argued for the possibility of commonsense theorizing as distinct from scientific theorizing, I wish to assert that there are certain basic commonsense concepts of persons, actions and the natural world which must be taken-for-granted, simply because they constitute the presuppositions which make practical life possible. In inter-personal contexts, for example, the experience of other people and their behaviour is structured by concepts like motive, intention, disposition, and rôle. Without such concepts interaction with others would be impossible. Inasmuch as people need to anticipate and explain each other's behaviour in order to interact satisfactorily they cannot avoid seeing each other as persons whose conduct can be interpreted in terms of their subjective meanings. In other words inter-personal situations are necessarily experienced as inter-subjective situations.

It is because our practical purposes in inter-personal situations necessitate structuring our experience in terms of basic subjective categories that the less fundamental concepts we employ specify subjective phenomena. Attempts by behavioural 'scientists' to operationally define those concepts can only result in making them largely irrelevant for practical purposes. In the context of action mental concepts are essentially sensitizing.

Schutz distinguishes between two categories of subjectivity.[10] One may interpret an act by grasping the agent's intention in performing it. This he calls the act's in-order-to motive. The interpreted act can then be explained in terms of either dispositional characteristics of the agent or some external causal influence. Schutz calls dispositional explanations because-of motives. These may be traits, policies, creeds, attitudes or emotions etc. However, according to Schutz, subjective elements such as intentions and dispositions are not experienced directly but in their typicality. This is done by employing constructs of minds in which particular motives are assigned to 'any act that repeatedly achieves the same end through the same means'. Particular human acts are interpreted and explained in terms of patterns of motivation which Schutz calls 'types'.

For Schutz the assumption that some correspondence exists between the motive specified by 'the type' and that of the agent is based on the fact that in inter-personal situations people want to be understood and will therefore ensure that their actions conform to a particular typification. Philip Pettit, writing on Schutz's theory of typification, endorses this point with respect to the interpretation of intentions: 'Every action of mine is a potential interaction and every interaction supposes that I fit what I do to a standardized description so that the other person can understand it and know how to react.'[11]

However, with respect to 'because-of' motives, Pettit argues that explanation does not depend on the agent ensuring that his act will exhibit his motives. If he does, however, try to ensure this he will fit his actions not so much to a standardized description as to a standardized story, expressed either in style of behaviour or speech, e.g. 'I am angry', or 'I am taking a hard line'. Although people will always want their actions to be interpretable they may not always want them to be explicable. In spite of Pettit's point it remains the case that one can grasp a person's *because-of* motive because he can exhibit it either at the time in behaviour or later in speech as a result of discussion.

Schutz calls concepts of 'in-order-to' motives *course-of-action types* and concepts of 'because-of' motives *personal types*. He explains how the two kinds of concept function in a two-fold method for conceptualizing other people's actions: 'I can begin with the finished act, then determine the type of action that produced it, and finally settle upon the type of person who must have acted in this way. Or I can reverse the process and, knowing the personal ideal type, deduce the corresponding act.'[12]

It is clear that person types operate rather like theories. However, as sensitizing rather than definitive concepts they orientate one in the direction of, rather than 'tell you', the type of action one might expect to occur. One tests such 'theories' by studying the particular action which occurs. If it does not fit the person type employed then one may modify one's understanding of the sort of actions people of this type tend to perform. Case study in inter-personal contexts is a method of theorizing because it enables the practitioner to test and modify his anticipatory theories.

Pettit has pointed out that Schutz's theory of typification is a theory of rôles in the popular sociological sense. 'Personal' typifications predict roles while 'course-of-action' typifications identify them. The implication of this is that the concept of rôle, like so many 'psychological' and 'sociological' concepts, is a commonsense concept. And this raises the question as to whether the so-called 'behavioural sciences' should not be appropriately viewed as disciplined commonsense rather than scientific disciplines which define a perspective 'beyond' the domain of commonsense experience. Blumer's distinction between definitive and sensitizing concepts arose out of this sort of issue, and he argued that the concepts of social science are essentially sensitizing.

Implications for educational research in classrooms

I now want to spell out the implications of what I have said for educational research in classrooms (Table 5.1).

1. *A distinction can be drawn between educational research and research on education.* Educational research conceptualizes the classroom from within the action perspective of the participants, i.e. teachers and their pupils. It aims to improve commonsense conceptualizations rather than to supersede them, and constitutes what R.K. Elliott has called a natural – objective mode of understanding. Elliott writes:

> Common understanding...might appropriately be called 'natural' understanding. However, a group of persons in regular discourse together might make a more extensive use of criticism, answering objections to their opinions

beyond the usual point of refusal, reformulating their views and obtaining a clearer and deeper understanding of the matter with which they are concerned. Such persons would differ from the rest in being more disciplined in their thinking, but one would hesitate to regard them as practitioners of a special discipline. Everyone attaches importance to criticism to some degree; these men attach rather more importance to it than the others, and use it more effectively as a means to knowledge and understanding.[13]

Aiming at natural – objective understanding educational research does not constitute 'undifferentiated mush' as R.S. Peters once described educational theory.[14] It is disciplined even though it does not constitute a discipline which goes beyond commonsense experience.

Research on education conceptualizes the classroom from a scientific perspective 'beyond' that of action. It may fall within the domain of a particular science or it may be inter-disciplinary. Whatever form it takes, its concepts will supersede those of commonsense.

2. *Educational Research employs sensitizing concepts while research on education employs definitive concepts.* Inasmuch as the dominant tradition of classroom research stresses operational definitions of variables in advance of the research it constitutes research on education rather than educational research.

3. *The data of educational research in classrooms are qualitative data while those of research on education are quantitative data.* This follows from the different sorts of concepts employed by the two modes they operate in.

4. *Educational research aims to develop a substantive theory of classroom action while research on education aims to develop a formal theory.* Here I am relating the two modes of research to two kinds of theory suggested by Glasser and Strauss.[15] A formal theory explains the behaviour of non-natural classes as defined from the perspective of a scientific discipline, e.g. in the behavioural sciences there may be formal classes such as those of 'formal organization', 'deviant behaviour', 'status congruency', 'cognitive dissonance'. A substantive theory explains natural classes of action as they are specified by commonsense course-of-action concepts. A substantive educational theory of classrooms is a theory about such natural classes of educational action as those of 'teaching' or 'learning'.

Table 5.1 The distinctions between educational research and research on education

Parameter	Educational research	Research on education
Perspective	Natural – objective	Scientific
Concepts	Sensitizing	Definitive
	A posteriori	*A priori*
Data	Qualitative	Quantitative
Theory	Substantive	Formal
Method	Case Study	Experimental
Generalization	Naturalistic	Formalistic
Participation in data analysis	Teachers and pupils participate	No teacher/pupil participation
Techniques	Participant observation and informal interviews	Non-participant observation using *a priori* category systems

5. *Educational research adopts qualitative case study as its principle method of theorizing while research on education adopts the experimental method.*

6. *Educational research in classrooms generalizes naturalistically while research in education generalizes formalistically.* The two kinds of research are related here to Stake's naturalistic – formalistic distinction.[16] One *generalizes from* the case studies of educational research naturalistically; that is, to one's own experience. Generalization here is not the principle task of educational researchers but of their audience, classroom practitioners.

Naturalistic generalization validates case study as a method of illuminating general truths which cannot be fully understood in terms of formal statements. It is therefore teachers and pupils which validate educational research and not the procedures of science.

Research on education *generalizes about* a class of action on the basis of a sample study. Here one does not generalize from the research but through it. It is the researcher rather than his audience who generalizes, and he will do so by making formal statements. The truth of such statements are validated quite independently of his research audience's experience of classroom life.

7. *The concepts of educational research are* a posteriori *while those of research on education are* a priori. A priori definitions of the concepts to be employed are a characteristic feature of research on education. The use of *a priori* category systems in classroom interaction studies locates these studies as research on education rather than educational research.

The development, modification, and revision of concepts through case study is a characteristic feature of educational research. This follows from the fact that sensitizing concepts are embedded in the world.

In educational research the relationship between instance and class is the problem for case study. Research on education proceeds on the assumption that this relationship is non-problematic.[17]

8. *Educational research in classrooms necessarily involves teachers and pupils as active partners in the research process. Research on education treats teachers and pupils solely as the objects of research. They may be involved in applying or communicating research findings (sometimes called 'collaborative research') but not as people whose ideas can influence the conceptualization of data.* The actions studied in educational research have subjective meaning for those who perform and react to them. Participants are 'closer to the data' than 'the outsider' and in some respects in a better position to interpret and explain them. The performer of an act has direct access to his intentions and dispositions via introspection. The people who are influenced by his acts *have to* interpret and explain them in terms of their subjective meanings in order to respond successfully. Consequently they have an interest in 'getting it right'.

The demands of objectivity would require 'the outsider' to check out his own accounts of classroom action against those of teachers and pupils, thus involving participants in the process of conceptualizing the classroom. This kind of dialogue with teachers and pupils has been an integral feature of my own classroom research with Clem Adelman in the Ford Teaching Project.[18]

9. *In educational research in classrooms 'the outsider's' principle techniques are those of participant-observation and informal interview. In research on education in classrooms the principle technique is that of non-participant observation using a priori categories.* The informal (or unstructured) interview method arises out of the necessity for 'the outsider' to check out his own accounts against those of the participants. Participant observation is a method of observing close to the data,

of getting into the action sufficiently to begin to see things from the participants' perspective. Its skill lies in avoiding a disruption of the normal patterns of interaction.

In research on education the researcher will be concerned not to contaminate the situation and to detach himself as much as possible from the action. The use of *a priori* categories operationally defined expresses this concern.

Notes

1   A concise summary of Popper's views on conceptual precision can be found in Bryan Magee's excellent little book *Popper*, Fontana, 1973, especially pp. 49–51.

2   Blumer, H. (1970). 'What is wrong with social theory'. In: Filstead, W.J. (Ed.) *Qualitative Methodology*, Chapter 4. London: Rand McNally.

3   See Pivčevic, E. (1975). 'Concepts, phenomenology and philosophical understanding'. In: Pivčevic, E. (Ed.) *Phenomenology and Philosophical Understanding*, Chapter 16, pp. 185–186. London: Cambridge and University Press.

4   Murdock, I. (1970). 'The idea of perfection'. In *The Sovereignty of Good*, pp. 28–30. London: Routledge and Kegan Paul.

5   Stake, R. (1978). The Case Study Method in Social Inquiry'. *Educational Researcher*, 7, 2, 5–7.

6   Pring, R. (1976). *Knowledge and Schooling*, Chapter 5. London: Open Books. This chapter is entitled 'On respecting commonsense' and, as this suggests, Pring is sympathetic to commonsense in certain respects. For example, he argues that although the phenomena specified by the concepts of commonsense and a discipline are different the latter must always be related to the points of reference of commonsense. His views on commonsense discourse are further elaborated in 'Commonsense and education', a paper which can be found in the *Proceedings of the Philosophy of Education Society of Great Britain*, January 1977.

7   Bruyn, S.T. (1970). 'The new empiricists: the participant observer and phenomenologist'. In: *Qualitative Methodology*. (See Note 2.)

8   Schutz, A. (1970). 'The problem of rationality in the social world'. In: Emmett, D. and Macintyre, A. (Ed.) *Sociological Theory and Philosophical Analysis*, Chapter 6, p. 98. London: Macmillan.

9   Stenhouse, L. (1977). Case Study as a Basis for Research in a Theoretical Contemporary History of Education. Centre for Applied Research in Education, University of East Anglia (mimeo).

10   See Schutz, A. (1970). 'Interactional relationships'. In: Wagner, H.R. (Ed.) *On Phenomenology and Social Relations*, Chapter 8, pp. 163–199. Chicago: The University of Chicago Press.

11   Pettit, P. (1975). 'The Life-World and Role-Theory'. In: *Phenomenology and Philosophical Understanding*. (See Note 3.) Pettit's paper is a critical study of Schutz's theory of commonsense typification.

12   Schutz, A. (1970). 'Interpretative sociology'. In: Wagner, H.R. (Ed.) *On Phenomenology and Social Relations*, p. 284. Chicago: University of Chicago Press.

13   Elliott, R.K. (1975). 'Education and Human Being I'. In: Brown, S.R. (Ed.) *Philosophers Discuss Education*, pp. 45–72. London: Macmillan.

14   Quoted by Harry Judge in 'Was R.S. Peters nearly right?', *IES*, March 18, 1977.

15   See Glasser, B.G. and Strauss, A.L. (1967). *The Discovery of Grounded Theory: Strategies for Qualitative Research*, pp. 1–35. Chicago: Aldine Press.

16   See Note 5.

17   See Kemmis, S. (1977). Case Study Research: the Imagination of the Case in the Invention of the Study. Centre for Applied Research in Education, University of East Anglia (mimeo). This paper explores in depth the problematic nature of the instance – class relation in naturalistic case study research.

18   See Elliott, J. and Adelman, C. (1976). 'Innovation at the classroom level'. In: *Innovation, the School and the Teacher* (1) Units 27 and 28, Course E203 on Curriculum Design and Development, The Open University.

CHAPTER 6

EDUCATIONAL THEORY, PRACTICAL PHILOSOPHY AND ACTION RESEARCH

British Journal of Educational Studies, Vol. XXXV, No. 2, pp. 149–169, June 1987

The demolition of the disciplines in the development of educational theory

In 1966 Paul Hirst, in the context of a philosophical debate with the neo-positivist D.J.O'Connor, produced an influential account of educational theory which dominated teacher education in the UK for a decade.[1] After the mid-1970s this account began to lose its hold in the field of inservice teacher education, and later in the early 1980s its more tenacious hold over initial teacher education also began to fail. In 1983 Hirst published a critique of his earlier views and, in the course of it, 'reconstructed' the theory-practice relationship. He reflected:

> It is not so much that what I wrote in 1966 was mistaken as that what I omitted led to a distorting emphasis. Educational theory I still see as concerned with determining rationally defensible principles for educational practice. The adequate formulation and defence of these principles I now see as resting not simply on appeal to the disciplines but on a complex pragmatic process that uses its own appropriate practical discourse.[2]

In the 1966 debate with O'Connor, Hirst argued that educational theory is a form of practical theory, which can be sharply distinguished from domains that are concerned with purely theoretical knowledge and divorced from any direct practical concerns. The function of a practical educational theory is to justify principles for the rational determination of educational practices. The function of purely theoretical knowledge is to explain phenomena. Educational theory aims to provide a basis for rational action rather than simply rational understanding. Nevertheless, the practical principles it specifies must be justified in terms of rational understanding. And, for Hirst, rational understanding is structured by quite distinct 'forms of knowledge'. His main contention with O'Connor lay in the latter's view that beliefs only have the status of theory if they can be subjected to empirical tests using the methods of science. Hirst's 'forms of knowledge' thesis enabled him to posit different kinds of tests for truth. Standards of rationality can be brought to bear on moral values and religious beliefs, and not simply on empirical beliefs of a psychological or sociological kind.

In a subsequent debate with O'Connor,[3] Hirst agreed that all theory is explanatory, but argued that 'explanations' cover reasons as well as causes. Although the empirical sciences aim to produce rational understandings of causal phenomena, there is also a sense in which both moral and religious discourses produce rational understanding, for they provide reasons for commitment to certain action guiding values and beliefs.

For O'Connor, scientific theories can and should be applied to the determination of the technical means of education, and in any strict sense educational theorising involves no more than that. However, for Hirst it involved discourse about the ends of education as well as means. Educational theory consisted of all those 'rational explanations' that are relevant to the task of justifying the practical principles of education. On this view the development of a theory of education, derived from the relevant disciplines of knowledge, is a necessary basis for justifying educational principles and practices.

In his 1983 paper, Hirst argued that by the early 1970s it was clear that the foundation disciplines of education are problematic as a source of reasons justifying practical principles, for 'how can such diverse, partial and limited theoretical studies ever provide a satisfactory justification for any set of practical principles?' He concluded that:

> there is no reason whatever to suppose that these abstractions when put together begin to give any adequate understanding of the situation for practical purposes...the very character of the disciplines seems such that they must prove inadequate as a basis for practical principles.

As he pointed out, his previous account of educational theory was widely misinterpreted as an outline of a methodology when it was intended only to serve as an outline of the logic of educational discourse.

> Whether or not the pattern for the justification of an individual action is by appeal to principles and thence to the disciplines, it does not follow from this that in developing educational theory one must follow a method of deriving principles from the disciplines.

He pointed out that questions about how to generate principles are quite different from questions about how such principles once generated might be justified.

So what was problematic in Hirst's 1983 paper was, not how to produce principles from theory, but how to justify them in terms of theory. The foundation disciplines were no longer viewed as a sufficient source of justification. He argued that questions about the logic of justification for practical principles rest on an adequate account of the nature of rational action. The view that rational action is derived from a knowledge of principles was now explicitly rejected by Hirst. Following Ryle[4] and Oakeshott[5] he claimed that rational action is logically prior to rational principles. Indeed, the latter are the result of reflection upon the former. Practices are underpinned by principles and rules which can be tacitly followed as opposed to explicitly applied. Such tacit principles, Hirst argued, can be made explicit and subjected to critique. However, in so explicating principles one is abstracting them from their relationship with other elements within the total practice. Therefore, critiques of principles, when abstracted from the context of practice, are inevitably only partial critiques. The theories such critiques utilise can never be sufficient to justify modifications and changes to a practice.

Hirst concluded that in developing rational education practices:

> It now seems to me we must start from a consideration of current practice, the rules and principles it actually embodies and the knowledge, beliefs, and principles that the practitioners employ in both characterising that practice and deciding what should be done.

He called such knowledge, beliefs, and principles *operational educational theories*. In order to produce rational critiques of them, 'the concepts and categories that practitioners use implicitly and explicitly' have to be articulated because 'it is only from descriptions and principles formulated in these terms' that such critiques are possible.

For Hirst, critiques based on a knowledge of teachers' operational theories can be of two kinds:

- assessments of performance in which practice is evaluated in terms of the operational theories teachers bring to the situation;
- critiques of the operational theories themselves.

He pointed out that assessments of performance may raise questions about the validity of the operational theories employed. The distinction again is one of logic rather than method. Educational theory, in what Hirst called its 'wider sense', consists of critiques of teachers operational theories rather than assessments of performance as such, although the latter may well provide a stimulus for the former.

Questioning the validity of operational theories – the second kind of critique – has, according to Hirst, two dimensions. First, in justifying a belief or principle the practitioner must appeal to the 'results of individual activities and practices'. Hirst claimed that only principles generated from experience can 'do justice to the necessarily complex tacit elements within practice'. I interpret him to mean that any rationally defensible practical principle must be grounded in a largely tacit knowledge of complex and particular situations. In justifying an operational theory one needs to provide evidence that it applies to such situations because the actions it specifies produce worthwhile results.

Second, in justifying an operational theory in relation to experience, account must be taken of the validity of the wider framework of knowledge in which it is generated and tested. 'The very concepts in which our implicit and explicit understandings of practice occurs are tied in', Hirst argued 'with concepts of knowledge and understanding of many kinds'. Such concepts have not always been evolved in relation to immediate education practice but in the pursuit of scientific, historical, religious and other forms of understanding which employ their own distinctive conceptual schemes. Advances in the development of understanding within these conceptual schemes progressively modify the concepts and principles of everyday practice. Practitioners' operational theories can therefore be scrutinised in relation to the validity of the wider frameworks of belief and value they presuppose. And this is where the disciplines have a role, albeit an indirect one, in influencing the development of operational theories. The foundation disciplines of education provide a context in which the wider framework of understanding can be critiqued.

Hirst's position therefore has basically changed to incorporate the centrality of pragmatic tests of experience in justifying practical principles. In doing so he set aside his previous view that the foundation disciplines are central to the task of justification. But Hirst retained a role for them: as a source of criteria for a critique of the broader framework of ideas, presupposed by the way principles are articulated and tested in practical discourse.

Do the disciplines have any role at all?

In a critical response to Hirst, Pat and John White[6] [. . .] challenge Hirst's account of the justificatory role of the traditional disciplines. They pointed out the paradigm clashes within disciplines, and asked what role a paradigm has when it conflicts with commonsense ways of thinking. Why, for example, should we decide that the mechanical causal explanations of a dominant behaviourist paradigm in the discipline of psychology are preferable to the 'disreputable' teleological explanations of behaviour which people employ in everyday life? And why, the Whites asked, are traditional disciplines like philosophy, psychology, history, and sociology to be preferred as foundations for justification to newer disciplines like curriculum theory, political philosophy, economics, and comparative education? The forms of disciplined thought are subject to historical change. The retention of the traditional canon of four foundation disciplines needs to be justified.

The Whites argued that the appropriate starting point for teachers, concerned with improving their operational theories, is the asking of questions. The theoretical constructs of disciplines may not employ the best answers. For example, questions about why individuals fail to learn may not be best answered from the perspective of formal psychological theories of learning:

> She (the teacher) may be able to get what she is after from her own resources, relying on the vast store of everyday psychological knowledge we all possess and quite non-technical capacity for sensible hypothesising...

Similarly, questions which fall in the realm of ends rather than means may not be best served by the resources of academic philosophy. The question: 'Why is self-determination a good educational aim?' may not count as a proper question within a certain paradigm of academic philosophy but in everyday terms it would be. The Whites, therefore, wanted to open the door to the possibility that the disciplines may not always furnish knowledge and understanding that is relevant to critiques of the wider frameworks of belief and value which are presupposed by operational theories.

Now, this issue is not new to Hirst. It was originally posed to him by R.K. Elliott[7] in his paper 'Education and Human Being', in which a distinction was drawn between understanding structured by disciplines and 'natural understanding'. Certainly, Hirst's 1983 paper not only made the disciplines less central, but revealed a degree of ambiguity about whether they are at all necessary. At points he appeared to acknowledge the White's claim that some paradigms of disciplined inquiry may be quite incapable of supplying appropriate criteria for critiquing the constructs embedded in practical principles. For example, he argued that

> the role of such separate disciplines as, say, sociology of education and philosophy of education...must be the appropriate form of criticism of the sociological and philosophical elements that are significant for the formulation and practical testing of practical principles.

In other words, the theoretical constructs of the disciplines must be *appropriate criteria* if they are to provide a basis for a critique of the constructs presupposed by practical theories. What is fundamental to Hirst's account of the role of the disciplines is the kinds of questions one can ask about the wider context of values and beliefs in which operational theories are embedded. He claimed that such questions can be classified not so much in terms of disciplines as 'forms of knowledge'. The questions can be differentiated according to the kinds of conceptual schemes employed in posing them. Of course, Hirst assumed that the formal disciplines established to address such questions offer the best prospect of getting sound answers. But it seems likely that he would be prepared to acknowledge that the way some disciplines have evolved as paradigms of inquiry renders their 'knowledge and understanding' inappropriate as a basis for a critique of the 'belief structures' which underpin practical theories.

The Whites' paper classified the questions that can be asked about belief structures as philosophical, psychological, sociological, etc., and in doing so tacitly assumed them to be the foundation 'forms of knowledge' for educational theory. Their issue with Hirst is not really whether the development of educational theory requires some references to differentiated forms of understanding. It is whether the questions made possible by such 'forms' are best answered by the traditions of disciplined inquiry that have evolved to address them. Hirst has tended to say 'yes' with some reservations. The Whites have tended to be more open to the possibility that more informal everyday reflection about such questions may be quite appropriate as a basis for critique.

This issue has enormous relevance to any discussion about the role of educational research in the development of good practice. Such research has largely been conducted within the disciplines of psychology, sociology, history and philosophy, and has assumed that its findings provide a rational basis for deriving principles of practice. The implication of Hirst's account is that this rationalist assumption is no longer tenable. At best research findings within the disciplines of education can have an indirect influence on the development and justification of practical principles, providing they satisfy the criterion of appropriateness. Research within 'the disciplines of education' must enable questions, about the belief and value systems underlying educational practices to be answered. This means that research must be grounded in an awareness of the operational principles underlying actual educational practices and the contexts of belief and value in which they are embedded. Hirst claimed that

> there has, as yet, been little examination of such principles and their attendant beliefs and values by means of the relevant contributory disciplines.

If this is the case then he must surely also conclude that much of what has passed for educational research within the disciplines in the past would not satisfy the criterion of appropriateness. Instead of answering questions raised about the beliefs and values which underpin practice they have tended to define research questions in isolation from, and independently of, practitioners' perspectives.

For Hirst, the best answers to the questions which can be asked about the beliefs and values underpinning practice will be provided by the formal disciplines, but the Whites are open to the possibility that the more informal processes of everyday reflection and discourse are sufficient – what R.K. Elliott has called 'the natural understanding'. In this case educational research would not be conducted by specialists in a number of disciplines. It would constitute a process of self-reflection in which practitioners made their tacit values and beliefs explicit and then reflected about the questions they posed about them. Since this process would be a 'natural' one it is unlikely to occur independently of the explicit testing of operational principles. Engagement in the latter would stimulate reflection about the assumptions in which such principles are embedded, which in turn would suggest new possibilities for the development of practice. For natural everyday reflection, both practical and theoretical discourse proceed interactively with each other: two dimensions of a unified process.

The central issue raised by the White's response to Hirst is the relationship between the development of theoretical understanding and the development and testing of operational theories in practical discourse. In the last page and a half of his paper Hirst acknowledged the wider debate in social theory between Habermas and his critics on this very issue, and suggested that we need to look to this debate for illumination. The final part of the paper sketched out Habermas' account of rational discourse. The tacit principles, beliefs and values which underpin practices can, according to Habermas, be rationally criticised and validated in a context of free and open dialogue, in which no constraints operate on the conclusions drawn save the force of the better argument.[8]

Although Hirst mentions the controversy surrounding Habermas's contention that, in free and open discourse, the universal validity of theoretical beliefs and practical norms could be established – truth being that which everyone agrees about when power constraints are absent – he did not clarify what was at stake. He was content to put 'his money' on Habermas while 'covering his tracks' should the latter's critics win the day. This 'looking towards' Habermas rather than, say, Gadamer, whose debate with the former received no specific mention, can easily be explained in terms of Hirst's concern that practical principles, and the beliefs and values which underpin them, should be subjected to systematic tests of universal validity. His main criticism of attempts to grapple with the 'theory–practice' issue by other philosophers of education is that they call into doubt the possibility of developing universally valid principles.

This is precisely what is at stake in the Gadamer–Habermas debate.[9] For Gadamer,[10] theoretical understanding is constitutive of practical discourse, whereas for Habermas the way practical norms are justified in practical discourse needs to be subjected to an emancipatory theoretical critique. Gadamer rejected the argument for any distinction to be made between 'practical' and 'emancipatory' discourse. Since, unlike Hirst, my bias tends to be in favour of Gadamer's position, I will attempt to outline his theory of understanding and highlight what is at stake in the debate with Habermas. Also, I want to do this to provide a basis for discussing a whole trend in the development of a view of educational theorising which Hirst neglected in his paper. I am referring to the development of educational action-research and case-study methods inspired by the work of the Centre for Applied Research in Education (CARE). It is my view that these developments are grounded in a theory of understanding which is highly consistent with that expounded by Gadamer. However, the CARE tradition has come under increasing criticism from 'critical theorists' of education inspired by Habermas. As Habermas criticised Gadamer, so some educational theorists have criticised the work of CARE for emphasising the 'practical' rather than the 'emancipatory'.[11] At the present time the 'critical theorists' are in the ascendancy in developing action-research theory.[12]

Hirst's paper is so restricted in its literature base – he only refers by name to those who are identifiable as professional philosophers of education – that he is apparently unaware of the specific work of those who have been involved in the development of action-research and case-study theory. He is aware that some people concerned with curriculum studies and evaluation had begun to develop new approaches to the theory–practice relationship but apparently felt that their work lacked the necessary analytic rigour. Thus Hirst contented himself with such comments as:

> There has as yet been little examination of such principles and their attendant beliefs and values by means of the relevant contributory disciplines.
>
> The testing in experience of such principles is likewise in an embryonic stage…Nevertheless in a modest and as yet unsophisticated way, numerous curriculum evaluation and development projects have made a beginning. But at present it seems to me not possible to advocate any particular methodology for the development of educational theory.
>
> Though it is perhaps true to say that in curriculum work in particular, educational theory has begun to recognise something in the logic I have been defending, that recognition has been largely intuitive.

I would argue that in his 1983 paper Hirst doesn't even arrive at the level of discourse about the theory–practice issue which existed at the time within the field of curriculum studies. No reference, for example, is made to the elicitation and testing through action-research of teachers' practical theories in the context of the Ford Teaching Project[13]; to the seminal work on the logic of 'the practical' by Joseph Schwab[14]; to William Reid's 'Thinking about the Curriculum'[15]; to the work of Lawrence Stenhouse,[16] Barry MacDonald and others at CARE on case study methods as a basis for practical and theoretical discourse.[17]

In order to set such thinking about the theory–practice relationship in the wider context of social theory I will return to Gadamer's 'theory of understanding' and what is at issue between him and Habermas.

Gadamer on 'understanding and practice'

Gadamer's specific concern has been to develop a theory of understanding in relation to historical and legal texts (hermeneutics). But he sees his view of the relationship between understanding, interpretation, and application as valid for all inquiry concerned with the understanding of persons. Basically Gadamer claims that forms of understanding which have persons as their objects yield moral knowledge which guides choice and judgement in particular practical situations.

In developing his theory of understanding Gadamer drew not only on Heidegger, his former teacher, but on the Aristotelian tradition of practical philosophy. For Gadamer all understanding of human artefacts, institutions, and practices involves interpretation by an interpreter who confronts a particular concrete situation in which he or she has to make practical choices in the light of values and beliefs. These values and beliefs have been handed down from the traditions that historically shape our being-in-the-world and therefore our human practices. They are constitutive of our 'being', but since the latter is always in the 'process of becoming' they are open to continuous testing and development. The traditions of belief and value which shape our being-in-the-world, our practices, need not be static and lifeless. They maintain over time a continuous thread of being but at the same time, in the process of becoming, human beings modify, change, and enrich their traditions. Understanding is the means by which we reshape our being-in-the-world.

For Gadamer, the meaning of a situation is not an objective quality which can be grasped by setting aside the values and beliefs which are constitutive of our being and our practices in everyday life. These values and beliefs are projected into the situation as 'fore-conceptions' or 'prejudgements', which highlight some features rather than others and give it a particular meaning. Understanding involves this highlighting. The situation only speaks to us as we interpret it in terms of our own prejudgements. This doesn't mean that understanding is a purely subjective projection of meaning onto an essentially meaningless object. The object has meaning but only for some*one* who addresses it from the standpoint of his own historically located consciousness. What, for example, the texts of Aristotle say to 20th century man will be rather different from what they said to his contemporaries. Even a living cultural tradition will speak differently to contemporary observers. What Hinduism means to a Christian may differ somewhat from what it means to a Sikh. Understanding a cultural tradition from two different traditions, which stand in a different historical relationship to it, will yield different meanings.

'Meaning' is neither an objectively existing property nor a subjective projection. It emerges in the play between things-in-themselves and the historically constituted beliefs and values of the interpreter. Interpretation is therefore constitutive of understanding in the human disciplines. One does not first understand things and then interpret their significance for one's own values and beliefs and the practices they shape. Interpretation constitutes a moment within the process of understanding itself.

Gadamer stresses the importance of being open to the things we are trying to understand. Although our prejudgements are conditions of such openness they can, if not disciplined by the firm intention to let the objects speak for themselves, blind us to features which call for the development and reformulation of beliefs and values. Gadamer is concerned that 'the circle of understanding' should not be viewed as a vicious circle, and he emphasises Heidegger's point that

> our first, last and constant task is never to allow our fore-having, fore-sight, and fore-conceptions to be presented to us by fancies and popular conceptions, but rather to make the scientific theme secure by working out these fore-structures in terms of the things themselves.

In developing our understanding we have to risk our values and beliefs. As we open ourselves to the things we seek to understand they will force us to become aware of problematic pre-judgements and to critique them in the light of newly emergent meanings.

For Gadamer, there are no general or extrinsic standards of rationality which can be appealed to in deciding what constitutes a valid understanding. The same object can mean different things to people who view it from different cultural vantage points. Different vantage points have different horizons. What can be seen from one vantage point may be hidden from another. In developing one's understanding one always extends one's horizon, but in doing so one does not necessarily understand what others understand in extending their understanding under different historical and cultural circumstances.

This does not mean that there are no criteria for assessing whether it is understanding or misunderstanding that is being developed. A critique can always be exercised on the basis of the interpreter's attitude to the object. Suppose, for example, that the interpreter seemed unwilling to acknowledge that certain fore-conceptions were operating in his interpretation. Then one would doubt if he was working out his pre-conceptions in a form that was responsive to the object, and could begin to question the interpretation in the light of unattended-to features of the situation. Again, the interpreter might not ask certain questions of the object and thus avoid arriving at a particular interpretation which challenged his or her initial fore-conceptions. In this case a critic might begin to ask questions about the validity of the latter as an interpretative schema. The possibility of a critique of understanding, and of the beliefs and values which underpin it, does not depend on the existence of standards for demonstrating 'universal validity'. The standards the critic employs will be limited by his or her own particular vantage point.

For Gadamer misunderstandings are constituted by a failure to achieve an authentic conversation or dialogue with the object to be understood; to let the object speak and to let one's beliefs and values be challenged by 'what is said'. So as long as the appropriate attitude of openness and responsiveness to the object is present and dominant, the interpretation will necessarily move in the direction of understanding rather than misunderstanding. And since, in reality, this attitude will never be perfectly realised there will always be grounds on which to mount a critique of understanding.

In his theory of understanding Gadamer not only fuses interpretation and understanding but also application and understanding. He argues for 'an inextricable connection of the theoretical and the practical in all understanding'. One does not develop understanding of things and events in the human field and then apply this knowledge to one's practical judgements and decisions. The quest for understanding is conditioned and constituted by reflection about how to act wisely in a particular and concrete human situation.

In developing this aspect of his theory of understanding Gadamer draws on the Aristotelian tradition of practical philosophy and fuses it with Heidegger's theory of hermeneutic interpretation. In the Aristotelian tradition of practical philosophy phronesis is a form of reflection concerned with translating universal ethical values into concrete forms of action in a particular situation. Aristotle contrasts it with instrumental reasoning which is concerned with selecting means that will cause certain pre-defined objectives to be brought about. Phronesis is not a form of instrumental reasoning about methods and techniques for achieving pre-defined goals. It is not concerned with techne (instrumental action) but with praxis (moral action). Ethical values are realized *in*, rather than as a result of, praxis. Moreover, their meaning can only be grasped as a concrete form of action. In judging how a value is to be translated into practice in a particular situation one is making an interpretation of what that value means as well as what the situation means. The form of action chosen constitutes an articulation of both the meaning of the situation and the meaning of the value to be realised in it. Phronesis co-determines the means and ends together by reflecting on the former in the light of the latter and vice versa. The outcome of such reflection – a concrete form of practice – constitutes an achievement of understanding in which both interpretation and application have been integral features of the process.

General understandings of values tend to be encapsulated in sets of practical principles distilled from retrospective reflections on experience. Such principles guide phronesis but are not a substitute for it. Operating as fore-conceptions they help one to anticipate possibly relevant features of the new situation. But as one opens oneself to the new situation the principles get reworked and reformulated. And so do the general concepts of value and beliefs which underpin them. Phronesis is not only the context in which practical principles are tested, changed, and reformulated but the context in which their underlying values and beliefs are subjected to critique.

Gadamer claimed that all understanding in the human field is constituted by phronesis. Richard Bernstein[18] illustrates this claim in relation to Gadamer's own appropriation of meaning from Aristotle's texts:

> Gadamer brings his own awareness of our hermeneutical situation to his interpretation of Aristotle's text, emphasising...that we are confronted with a world in which there has been 'a domination of technology based on science', a 'false idolatry of the expert', 'a scientific mystification of the modern society of specialisation', and a dangerous 'inner longing...to find in science a substitute for a teacher's lost orientation'.

Gadamer was concerned to discover some resolution to this situation as interpreted in the light of his own beliefs and values. This interpretation governed his questioning of Aristotle's text. And the meanings he appropriated from the text spoke to the concrete situation he wished to change. They illuminated his practical situation in a way which suggests new forms of action for it; new interpretations of value.

Certainly, it can be argued that the human disciplines of philosophy, history, psychology, and sociology provide a basis for exercising critiques of the values and beliefs which underlie principles and practices. In allowing Aristotle to speak to his situation Gadamer risked the beliefs and values embedded in his interpretation of the problem. The meanings he appropriated from Aristotle's texts may have challenged his initial interpretation and resulted in reformulations of his beliefs and values.

What Gadamer's theory of understanding would deny is that the beliefs and values which underpin our practical principles can be appropriately critiqued from a vantage point which is not directly concerned with forming a practical judgement, for phronesis is always constitutive of the search for understanding in the human field. And it follows from this that just as phronesis is the context in which practical principles are tested and developed in relation to particular situations, so it is the context in which their underlying values and beliefs are made explicit and critiqued. The testing of practical principles and the critique of their underlying values and beliefs are just two aspects of a unified process of reflection.

Educational action-research, case study, and the disciplines

On a Gadamerian account of the development of educational theory, teachers would be involved in the reflective process of phronesis in which they deliberated about concrete practical problems in relation to the principles, values, and beliefs they brought to the situation. Such deliberations would benefit from eclectic appropriations of meanings distilled from a variety of sources, which might include the disciplines. But the appropriateness of ideas and knowledge drawn from the disciplines will depend on the extent to which teachers view them as speaking to their concrete practical concerns. The ultimate test of the usefulness of the disciplines as sources of ideas is whether teachers can use them to construct a workable theory of the case. I say 'workable' because in practical reflection the outcome is both a theory and a form of action.

The Action-Research movement arose in the context of collaboration between teachers and researchers in the development of the curriculum. It primarily addressed the problem of how best to realise fundamental educational values in action. It was, from the beginning, more concerned with the quality of educational processes than with the specification of outcome measured. This conception of educational action as a form of moral practice has been carried over into the teacher education field where action-research is increasingly viewed as central to the professional development of teachers. The swing away from a discipline-based towards an action-research based form of teacher education has meant less stress being placed on the traditional foundation disciplines. The emphasis is on a unified mode of practical reflection which focusses on the concrete cases of educational practice teachers are engaged with. Teachers are now expected to carry out their own research supported by facilitating teacher educators. Such research largely consists of the collection and analysis of case study data. Formal seminars and supervisions are concerned with helping teachers to generate their own theories of cases rather than simply to apply general theories culled from the literature.

In this context many teacher educators are struggling to reorganise the ideas and constructs to be found in the literatures of the disciplines so that teachers can use them eclectically as tools for the analysis of concrete practical problems and situations. And they are learning that much of the traditional content of teacher education conveys little meaning to teachers reflecting about particular cases in the light of their practical concerns. There is little 'fusion of horizons'. What is relevant and significant about educational situations from the vantage point of the specialist researchers does not speak to the situated concerns of practising teachers.

Specialist researchers within the disciplines can come to feel that the action-research movement despises research within the formal disciplines, and that its ascendancy is threatening. But there is a constructive response that specialist philosophers, psychologists, and sociologists can make. And that is to develop ideas and constructs within their disciplines in relation to the concrete situations and concerns of teachers and in dialogue with them. In order for this to happen there must be some degree of 'fusion of horizons'. The specialist researchers must be as committed as the teacher researchers to certain educational values and to the problems of realizing them in complex and particular circumstances. They too will be concerned to wrestle with cases alongside the teacher researchers. But whereas the latter will seek to utilise the ideas and constructs of the disciplines eclectically in their search for a holistic theory of the situation, the specialist will seek to iden-tify and develop those ideas and constructs in a discipline which can illuminate, albeit partially, the concrete situation of the practitioner. Case studies, therefore, provide the context for developing both a practical theory of the case, and the theoretical constructs of a discipline. And I include here the future development of the philosophy of education. Specialists ought to develop their discipline by going out into schools and doing collaborative case study research with teachers.

So I would wish to argue that the development of educational theory is appro-priately a collaborative enterprise which focuses on the study of cases. The practi-tioner's research will take the form of action-research aimed at generating and testing specific action-strategies. The specialist's research will aim to develop ideas and constructs of the situation which can be reflectively appropriated in action-research.

How far Hirst would accept this view of the relationship between the critique function of the disciplines and the development and testing of practical theories, I am unsure. But I suspect that he would not be entirely happy with the view that the constructs of the disciplines of education can only be validated in the self-understandings of practitioners as they deliberate about concrete situations.

Hirst would tend to argue that, although the theoretical constructs of the disciplines are a basis for a critique of practice, they can be developed and validated quite independently of any direct concern with concrete practical situations. This would, I think, be the central point at issue between us.

The Habermas–Gadamer debate

In recent years, Carr and Kemmis have introduced a 'critical theory' perspective into the literature on action-research.[19] Like their mentor, Habermas, they accept many of the presuppositions of the neo-Aristotelian practical paradigm of educational theory. The critical paradigm of educational theory, Carr argues,

> differs from the 'practical' view... in its explicit recognition of how the practitioner's own understanding of his educational values may become distorted by various non-educational forces and pressures and of how the practical realization of those values may be impeded by institutional structures and political constraints. The tasks of a critical approach to educational theory, therefore, are: to expose those false beliefs which sustain practitioners' misunderstandings of their practice, to identify those organizational arrangements which frustrate the pursuit of genuine educational aims and purposes, and to indicate to practitioners what needs to be done for these misunderstandings to be removed and the adverse effects of these organisational arrangements eliminated.[20]

The 'critical' approach is concerned with the development of explanations for the ways political and social forces in the society ideologically distort teachers self-understandings and practices. These explanations can then be appropriated by teachers as a basis for critical self-reflection on their own practical knowledge and understanding. But they initially depend for their source on the 'insights' of experts in the critical social disciplines.

The relationship of critical theory to practice is held to be quite different from the relationship posited by either a 'positivist' or 'moral' science. In a 'positivist science', theory is developed and validated independently of practice and then applied by the practitioner to it. In a 'moral science', theory is developed from practice and validated against it. According to Carr,[21] a moral science provides 'no critical basis for rendering this practice problematic'. Gadamer would certainly disagree with him. Carr argues that in a 'critical science' theory and practice are 'mutually constitutive and dialectically related'. The validity of a critical theorem depends upon its appropriation in the critical consciousness of the practitioner under conditions of free and open practical discourse. The fact that practitioners may reject critical theorems in the light of their own self-understandings does not invalidate a critical theorem. What would invalidate it would be its rejection under the very conditions it is intended to create; namely, free and open practical discourse. This is why critical theory and educational practice are posited as mutually constitutive and dialectically related.

As I have argued the justification for this critical paradigm of educational theory ultimately rests on the validity of Habermas's critique of Gadamer. Against Gadamer, Habermas argues that one cannot reduce all social understanding to an interpretative science. He accuses Gadamer of absolutizing language and tradition. Social inquiry is not simply the explication of meaning, and it does not have to accept the conceptual frameworks of traditions as the limits of understanding.

Tradition and culture are not self-sufficient but developed in relation to social, political and economic conditions of life. Traditional meaning-structures can mark and distort as well as foster an awareness of these conditions. For Habermas, quasi-causal explanations – showing how traditions of thought and practice mask and distort social, political, and economic conditions – are necessary for the growth of human awareness. Such explanations require a system of reference which goes beyond tradition and the historically situated consciousness of practical reason.

In responding to Habermas, Gadamer found his concept of critique too dogmatic. He argued that critical theory itself cannot escape from participation in a cultural tradition which is itself historically conditioned. Habermas establishes an unreal opposition between reflection and tradition. Interpretative understanding itself incorporates a critical perspective on the tradition one has drawn on in constructing meaning. Gadamer admitted that the critique of prejudgements is always limited and from a particular vantage point. One cannot question the whole of ones tacit anticipations at once, and what one questions is contained within the changing horizon of one's consciousness. But he argued that this is also true for critical theorems. They do not escape the conditions of finitude and the particularity of reflection which govern all attempts at human understanding.

Gadamer objected to the way in which Habermas separated the realm of language and culture from the realm of power relations. What Habermas designated as determinants of social processes are themselves accessible to interpretative understanding and practical reasoning. He writes:

> Understanding and coming to an understanding do not refer primarily or originally to a methodologically trained behaviour towards texts; rather they are the form in which the social life of men is carried out, a social life which...is a community in dialogue...Nothing is excepted from this community, no experience of the world whatever.[22]

In sum then, Gadamer denied that interpretative understanding in the context of 'the practical' fails to incorporate the possibility of a critical perspective. I have always been puzzled by those critics who have attacked CARE's work with teachers on the grounds that it didn't encourage them to critique the power relations in which their reflection and practice are situated. I have never experienced it that way. My experience has always been that teachers tend to develop critiques of the macro-context of their practices during the process of reflectively developing and testing their practical theories.

The moral science paradigm of educational research incorporates its own critical perspective. It does not need to be supplemented by a critical paradigm based on absolutist and objectivist assumptions about the nature of human understanding. The advocacy of such a paradigm could itself do with a little ideological unmasking, for does not it once more allow the academic experts to play God with teachers?

Notes and References

1 P.H. Hirst: 'Educational Theory' in J.W. Tibble (ed.): *The Study of Education* (Routledge and Kegan Paul, London, 1966).
2 P.H. Hirst: 'Educational Theory' in P.H. Hirst (ed.): *Educational Theory and Its Foundation Disciplines* (Routledge and Kegan Paul, London, 1983).

3 G. Langford and D.J.O'Connor (eds): *New Essays in the Philosophy of Education* (Routledge and Kegan Paul, London, 1973), Papers 3 and 4.

4 G. Ryle: *The Concept of Mind* (Hutchinson, London, 1949).

5 M. Oakshott: 'Rational Conduct' in *Rationalism and Politics and Other Essays*, (Routledge and Kegan Paul, London, 1962).

6 J. and P. White: 'A Critical Response to Hirst'. Presented at a seminar on Educational Theory and Practice at the London Institute of Education in 1984. Mimeo unpublished

7 R.K. Elliott: 'Education and Human Being' in S.C. Brown (ed.): *Philosophers Discuss Education* (Macmillan, London, 1975).

8 J. Habermas: *Knowledge and Human Interests*, translated by J.J. Shapiro (Beacon Press, Boston 1971).

9 A summary of this debate can be found in C. McCarthy: *The Critical Theory of Jurgen Habermas* (Hutchinson, 1978) pp. 187–193.

10 H.G. Gadamer: *Truth and Method* (Sheen and Ward, 1975).

11 G. Whitty: 'Curriculum Studies: A Critique of Some Recent British Orthodoxies' in M. Lawn and L. Barton (eds): *Rethinking Curriculum Studies* (Croom Helm, London, 1981).

12 R. Gibson: 'Critical Times for Action Research', *Cambridge Journal of Education*, (Cambridge Institute of Education, Cambridge, 1985) Vol. 15, No. 1.

13 J. Elliott: 'Developing Hypotheses about Classrooms from Teachers' Practical Constructs', *Interchange*, (1976/77) Vol. 7, No. 2; J. Elliott: 'Implications of Classroom Research for Professional Development' in E. Hoyle and J. Megarry (eds): *World Yearbook of Education 1980: Professional Development of Teachers* (Kogan Page, London, 1980); J. Elliott: 'Educational Action Research' in J. Nisbet (ed.): *World Yearbook of Education 1985: Research, Policy and Practice* (Kogan Page, London, 1985).

14 J.J. Schwab: *The Practical: A Language for Curriculum* (National Educational Association, Centre for the Study of Instruction, Washington, DC, 1970).

15 W. Reid: *Thinking about the Curriculum* (Routledge and Kegan Paul, London, 1978).

16 L. Stenhouse: 'The Conduct, Analysis and Reporting of Case Study in Educational Research and Evaluation' in R. McCormick (ed.): *Calling Education to Account* (Heinemann/Open University, London, 1982).

17 H. Simons (ed.): *Towards a Science of the Singular* (Occasional Publications No. 10, Centre for Applied Research in Education, University of East Anglia, Norwich, 1980).

18 R. Bernstein: *Beyond Objectivism and Relativism* (Basil Blackwell, Oxford, 1983).

19 W. Carr and S. Kemmis: *Becoming Critical: Knowing Through Action-Research* (Deakin University Press, Victoria, 1983).

20 W. Carr: 'Can Eductional Research be Scientific?' *Journal of Philosophy of Education* (1983) 17, 1.

21 W. Carr: 'Theories of Theory and Practice' (1984) mimeo.

22 Cited by McCarthy, *op. cit.*

CHAPTER 7

IMPLICATIONS OF CLASSROOM RESEARCH FOR PROFESSIONAL DEVELOPMENT

Professional Development of Teachers, World Yearbook of Education
(ed.) Eric Hoyle, 1980

Introduction

During the last decade the study of classroom events has become a major growth area for educational research. In this chapter, I shall not be reviewing specific research findings in order to discuss their relevance for teacher education. Rather I shall interpret my task as that of answering the general question, 'How can the study of classroom events contribute to the professional development of teachers?' I shall contrast two distinct approaches to classroom research in terms of their underlying assumptions about the relationship between teaching and learning, and in the light of these assess their potential for influencing professional development. It will be my contention that not every way of influencing the practice of teachers in classrooms contributes to their professional development. Such development is an educational process, and in order to influence this process, classroom research must possess educative potential.

Process-product studies

The 'triple-play'

To date, the dominant approach to classroom research has been that of the process-product study; these studies have been reviewed by Berliner and Rosenshine (1977) and Dunkin and Biddle (1974). Studies of this type attempt to describe observable regularities in teaching performance, and then to discover whether any causal relationships exist between such performances and learning outcomes as measured by achievement tests. In discovering these relationships, process-product researchers would claim to have identified certain elements of effective teaching, which can be formulated as technical rules to be applied in teacher education. Fenstermacher (1978) suggests that the motive to furnish 'imperatives for teacher training' is so strong that process-product researchers tend to engage in a kind of 'triple-play'. He argues that research findings are usually based on statistical correlations which answer the general question 'What relationships obtain, if any, between teacher performances P1, P2, P3, ... Pn and success at learning tasks K1, K2, K3, ... Kn by students assigned to complete these tasks?' Having isolated a positive correlation, say 'P1 and P2 are significantly correlated with success at task K1 by students assigned this task', researchers tend to conclude that teachers should do P1 and P2 in answer to the question 'What should teachers do in order to be effective in getting students to succeed at K1 and tasks like it?'

Now Fenstermacher claims that this leap from correlational findings to prescriptions for teacher training begs two important questions; first, the causal question 'Do teacher performances P1 and P2 *result* in success at task K1 by students assigned this task?' A correlational relationship does not necessarily imply a causal one. From the fact that a correlation exists between P1–P2 and K1, one cannot logically infer that a causal relationship exists between them. It could be that the causal relationship exists between both these correlated variables and a third. In order to establish where the cause lies, a researcher would have to embark on a series of experimental studies. Fenstermacher argues that the standard procedure in process-product research is to assume that the correlational question answers the causal question, 'Why do P1 and P2 result in student success at K1?' Thus process-product research rarely provides us with a theoretical explanation as to why the correlations or causal relationships it discovers obtain in the context of the study. Having ignored this question, the third and final move is to translate the assumed cause–effect relationships between teaching and learning into rules for teacher training.

I have dealt extensively with Fenstermacher's account of how process-product classroom researchers reason from theory to practice, because it enables me to spell out the implications of some key assumptions which underly their approach.

The assumption of teachers' causality

The first key assumption is that teaching *causes* learning. On the basis of this assumption the process-product researcher tends to focus on the performances of the teacher rather than those of students in the classroom, and to interpret correlations between these performances and learning outcomes as evidence that the former caused the latter.

This assumption also has implications for educational accountability. It suggests that teachers alone can be held accountable for student learning, rather than, say, the students themselves or educational managers and administrators. In the absence of the assumption of teacher causality the discovery of correlations between classroom events and learning outcomes might be a stimulus for entertaining the possibility that, rather than being causally linked with each other, these variables are caused by factors originating beyond the classroom in its institutional and administrative context. The assumption of teacher causality is bureaucratically and politically convenient since it suggests that deficiencies in educational provision can only be rectified by doing something about the way teachers perform in classrooms rather than by doing something about the way schools as institutions are organized, or the provision of educational resources administered.

The causal knowledge generated by process-product researchers can easily be formulated as sets of technical means-ends rules intended to govern teacher performance. One might argue that the researcher's knowledge is based on the view that teaching is a technology or form of instrumental action (see Habermas, 1972). Such action involves the agent (teacher) administering certain treatments (teaching methods) to passive objects (students) in order to produce preconceived outputs (objectives). In the field of social relations, instrumental action influences people's behaviour by securing compliance, and this involves the employment of power expressed in the use of positive and negative sanctions (rewards and punishments). Thus teaching conceived as instrumental action is power-coercive and its object, learning, is power-dependent.

When teaching is conceived as instrumental action, learning is conceived as passive behaviour directed by the teacher rather than self-directed by students. Presupposed in the process-product approach is a bias against the ideas of 'self-directed', 'discovery', 'inquiry' learning. If effective teaching is a set of causally efficacious performances then by definition it cannot result in learning conceived in these ways. It should hardly be surprising, then, that process-product correlations fail to demonstrate 'the effectiveness' of informal teaching methods when employed by teachers who construe learning in the terms cited above. Yet the failure to establish causal relationships here is interpreted by the researchers as an outcome of their research, rather than being an inevitable implication of their research design. There is no way in which progressive methods of teaching can 'look good' from the perspective of process-product research.

Finally, the assumption of teacher causality implies a division of labour between researchers who produce causal knowledge and teachers who apply it in practice. The causal statements produced by process-product researchers refer to publicly observable acts rather than the subjective states of teachers. They can be tested independently of any reference to the beliefs, intentions, and meanings teachers express in their actions. Thus the production of knowledge about teaching does not have to be validated against teachers' understanding of their own actions, and does not require their participation: their role is to apply the knowledge researchers produce. The process of professional development involves the application of research knowledge but not its production.

Generalizability

Let me now turn to the second key assumption underlying process-product research. Power (1976) sums it up neatly when he argues that for this kind of research, 'situations and events are not regarded as unique. This means actions can be repeated and probability statements linking situations and actions made ... Generalizations across classrooms about classroom phenomena, their antecedents and consequences are believed to be both possible and useful.' This is the assumption of *formal generalizability*, that there are general laws governing the relationship between classroom events to be discovered. This assumption explains the process-product researcher's apparent failure to explain why the causal relationships he infers from his correlations obtain. Such an explanation would be given only if the researcher thought that it might not be possible to generalize across all classroom contexts.

It is my view that process-product generalizations are applicable only to some learning contexts. Doyle (1979) argues that process-product research has tended to assume a homogeneity in the quality of learning tasks given to students, leading to the use of a single criterion for assessing outcomes. The result is a general focus on the quantifiable aspects of teaching and learning. Thus *how much* is learned becomes more significant than the type of learning involved, and in an attempt to discover correlations, quantifiable aspects of teaching, such as pacing of content and the amount covered, have priority over qualitative aspects.

Three types of learning task

Doyle distinguishes three types of learning task. First, there are 'understanding' tasks, requiring students to apply cognitive operations, such as classification, inference, deduction and analysis, to instances not previously encountered, or to comprehend information by reproducing it in transformed or paraphrased form.

Second, there are 'memory' tasks, requiring recognition or recall of facts, principles, or solutions the student has previously been acquainted with. Third, there are 'routine problem-solving' tasks, such as dividing fractions or squaring numbers, which require students to learn a standard and reliable formula or principle. Doyle goes on to argue that different types of learning tasks can be compared in the light of the degrees of ambiguity and risk inherent in them. Ambiguity inheres in a learning task, not because of the teacher's lack of clarity, but because it does not tell the student the exact performance that will be required and how to produce it. Risk refers to the likelihood of students being able to cope with the demands of a task. According to Doyle 'understanding' tasks score high on both ambiguity and risk. 'Memory' and 'routine problem-solving' tasks on the other hand are low on ambiguity and when the amount of content to be covered is small or the routines to be mastered simple, low on risk.

In the light of these qualitative differences between learning tasks, Doyle suggests that one can expect greater variance in learning outcomes, and therefore lower mean achievement, on 'understanding' tasks than on 'memory' or 'routine problem-solving' ones. This implies that it is easier for teachers to control mean achievement when the learning tasks are of the latter rather than the former kind. It follows that one is more likely to discover general rules for maximizing learning outcomes when the learning tasks are of the 'memory' or 'routine problem-solving' kind than of the 'understanding' kind. If this is correct, then we have a possible explanation for the causal generalizations established by process-product research. It is that they only apply to classroom contexts where students are performing on 'memory' or 'routine problem-solving' tasks. The fact that the criteria employed by process-product research tend to measure outcomes of these kinds of tasks reinforces this point.

The qualities of ambiguity and risk, intrinsic to 'understanding' tasks, indicate why process-product methodology is quite inappropriate for the study of classrooms where students are performing them. Such qualities imply that learning is contingent on the personal characteristics of individual students and thereby introduce an element of unpredictability into teaching. In 'understanding' contexts one can no longer assume that the relationship between teaching performance and learning outcomes is a causal one, let alone generalizable across students and classrooms. A new paradigm of classroom research is required, but before sketching it, I want briefly to return to the implications of process-product research for teacher education.

Teacher training and teacher education

Most educational theorists would view education as a process of 'teaching for understanding'. Process-product research therefore masks and distorts education. This is why I have elsewhere described such research as 'research on education' rather than 'educational research' (Elliott, 1978b). The outcomes of education cannot be detected by its methods, and *educational* methods are bound to show up rather poorly in its research findings. If these findings are then translated into prescriptions for competency-based teacher education and implemented on a large scale, the teachers of the future will certainly not be equipped to be educators of children. Moreover, the process of teacher training will also not be an *educational* one. All process-product research can do is to furnish rules governing teaching performance in typical situations. These rules are learned by applying them uncritically in such situations. In other words the process of teacher training will involve teachers performing 'routine problem-solving' rather than 'understanding' tasks. In my view the professional development of teachers is an educational process which involves developing understanding of the particular classroom situations in which they work. The application of general rules pre-empts such understanding.

Educational action research

Curriculum development as a context for research

It is no coincidence that action research in classrooms tended to emerge in association with the curriculum development movement in the 1960s and early 1970s. Many of the projects which constituted this movement were concerned with shifting the learning context in classrooms from 'memory' and 'routine problem-solving' to 'understanding' tasks. Such innovations tended to articulate this shift in terms of ideas like 'self-directed', 'discovery', and 'inquiry' learning. As I suggested earlier these ideas embody a more active and personal conception of the learning process than the one presupposed by process-product research. Each of the above terms picks out a particular aspect of this process. 'Self-directed' implies that learning outcomes are the result of the student's own autonomous activity and not of teaching. 'Inquiry' provides a general description of the kind of activity involved, constituted by the cognitive operations cited by Doyle in his account of 'understanding' tasks. 'Discovery' refers to the quality of the intellectual experience which results from this kind of activity, indicating both its personal and impersonal aspects. In its impersonal aspect an objective reality which exists independently of the student's own thinking is disclosed. In its personal aspect this reality can only be personally appropriated by the student as he brings his own cognitive structures to bear on the problems defined by the task. These orienting ideas, employed in the curriculum development movement, simply pick out different dimensions of performance on 'understanding' tasks in terms of its agency, the operations involved, and the quality of the intellectual experience which results.

The problems teachers experienced in initiating and sustaining student performance on 'understanding' tasks generated a whole movement of classroom research conducted largely by people attached to the development teams of national projects in collaboration with participating teachers (see Barnes, 1976; Elliott and Adelman, 1976; Elliott and MacDonald, 1972; Jenkins, 1977; Parlett and Hamilton, 1973; Smith and Schumacher, 1972; Walker and Adelman, 1972; Wild, 1973). Interestingly, this research conceptualized the problems of teaching in a radically different way from process-product research. In place of technical problems of selecting causally effective means for bringing about certain pre-specified learning outcomes, the problems were seen as ones of achieving a certain quality of communication with students about the problems and issues posed by learning tasks. Teaching was viewed as a mode of communicative rather than instrumental action (see Habermas, 1972).

In viewing teaching in this way classroom researchers were simply adopting the same perspective as the curriculum developers. Indeed, many of them, like myself, played the dual roles of developer and researcher. The reason I have called this alternative mode of research action research is simply because it adopts the action perspective of curriculum developers (Elliott, 1978a). I will now attempt to give a more detailed account of this perspective.

The action perspective of curriculum development

Many curriculum development projects neglected to spell out the pedagogical implications of 'teaching for understanding' in the content areas they were concerned with. Perhaps naively it was assumed that they would be tacitly understood by teachers. Stenhouse's *Humanities Curriculum Project* (1971) and Bruner's *Man: a course of study* (1970) were notable exceptions. Both formulated pedagogic principles which specified conditions of teaching and learning to be realized in classrooms rather than learning objectives. Stenhouse called them 'principles of procedure', while Bruner used the phrase 'pedagogical aims'. Such principles or aims specified intrinsically, rather than instrumentally, valuable qualities of teaching and learning tasks. Although some curriculum development projects attempted to fit their ideas to a behavioural objectives model of curriculum design, Stenhouse (1975) claimed that such a model was inconsistent with teaching for understanding and education. He argued that the Humanities Project's aim of 'developing an understanding of controversial issues' could not be broken down into specific learning objectives without distorting its nature. This is entirely consistent with Doyle's account of 'understanding' tasks as high in ambiguity, in the sense that there are no absolute rules for producing correct answers, and therefore no ways of predicting in advance exactly what constitutes successful performance.

Stenhouse posed the 'process model' of curriculum design as an alternative to 'behavioural objectives'. He claimed that the general aim of 'understanding' could be logically analysed into principles governing the process of teaching and learning in classrooms. For example, he argued that the teacher who used his position of authority in the classroom to promote his own views would necessarily impose constraints on the development of an understanding of controversial issues. The actions involved would be logically inconsistent with such development. From this consideration Stenhouse formulated the principle of procedural neutrality, i.e. the obligation to refrain from taking sides on a controversial issue *qua* teacher. Similarly, he argued that students would necessarily lack opportunities to develop their understanding of issues if the teacher denied them access to some views rather than others. Thus failure to protect divergence in classroom discussion was logically inconsistent with the project's aim. Only the teacher whose actions realized the principle 'protect the expression of divergent views' would be acting consistently. Stenhouse's 'procedural principles' functioned as criteria for selecting teaching acts which were logically consistent with the development of understanding on learning tasks. Acts which realized these criteria constituted a worthwhile form of teaching regardless of their outcomes. His inspiration for the 'process model' of curriculum design came from R.S. Peters' seminal paper entitled 'Must an educator have an aim?' (1968). In this paper Peters argued that *educational* aims specify what is to count as a worthwhile educational process rather than its extrinsic outcomes.

The process model embodies a radically different set of assumptions about the relationship between teaching and learning from the behavioural objectives model and the process-product research which matches it. The aim of teaching is viewed as 'enabling', 'facilitating' or 'providing opportunities for' the development of understanding. Such aim descriptions specify conditions to be realized by the teacher rather than his students. A teacher can *enable* pupils to perform certain learning tasks successfully without them then actually doing so. The student's task performance is ultimately his or her responsibility. The teaching aim of 'enabling the development of understanding' must be distinguished from the learner's aim of 'developing an understanding'. The teaching aim is concerned with establishing conditions in the classroom which enable students to develop their own understanding of the subject matter. The process model, inasmuch as it specifies enabling conditions, embodies an active conception of learning and does not assume that it is caused by teaching.

I will now examine more closely the nature of the enabling conditions specified by the principles of educational procedure which govern 'teaching for understanding'. I have argued that understanding is developed by the student from 'within', through the exercise of his own rational capacities, and therefore cannot be caused from 'without'. However, a student could hardly be described as exercising his rational capacities if he were closed to the reasons and arguments put forward by others. Intellectual development necessarily involves being open to discussion. The fact that it is not causally effected does not imply that it cannot be influenced in other ways. This kind of learning, although inconsistent with the employment of power strategies aimed at securing quasi-causal compliance from the student, can be rationally influenced by teaching which involves the student in discussion or discourse about the learning task. In discourse, the teacher seeks to influence a student's task performance by citing evidence, reasons, and arguments.

According to Habermas (1974) pure discourse constitutes 'the ideal speech situation' presupposed in all interpersonal communication. It is characterized by an absence of all constraints on people's thinking, save that of 'the force of the better argument'. For Habermas, the influence exerted through this ideal form of human communication is quite distinct from the power influence exerted in instrumental action upon another. The consensus which results between the participants in discourse is a justified or warranted one. But this raises the problem of how one distinguishes a warranted from an unwarranted consensus, a rational acceptance of another's argument from a non-rational one. Applied to 'teaching for understanding' the issue becomes one of how to distinguish the rational from the non-rational influences a teacher might exert. Habermas attempts to resolve this problem in terms of the formal properties of discourse. He argues that participants must have an equal opportunity to adopt dialogue roles, and in particular equal freedom 'to put forward, call into question, and give reasons for and against statements, explanations, interpretations and justifications'. Thus the conditions of discourse correspond with the liberal-democratic values of 'equality', 'freedom' and 'justice' and constitute the conditions which enable people to develop their understanding through communication with others. In educational contexts, where students encounter 'understanding' tasks, the provision of such discourse conditions is the *educational* responsibility of teachers.

Inasmuch as it is discourse which enables, rather than causes, the development of understanding, then teachers enable this development when they realize discourse values in their communications with students. The relationship between means and ends here is not a technical or instrumental relation. Discourse values are not extrinsic outcomes of communicative acts but intrinsic norms which ideal acts of this kind ought to satisfy. They are not so much realized *by* as *in* acts of teaching.

Stenhouse's 'principles of procedure' and Bruner's 'pedagogical aims' can both be interpreted as attempts to explain the implications of discourse values for teaching in their respective subject areas.

I described the classroom research generated by the curriculum development movement as action research because it conceptualized problems of teaching from the same action perspective as those involved in developing and implementing new curricula. This perspective defines *the educational perspective* on teaching and learning and can be summarized in terms of:

1   a focus on the quality of the teacher's discourse with students about learning tasks;
2   construing learning as a student-directed rather than teacher-directed activity;
3   construing teaching as a mode of exerting rational rather than causal influence on student learning.

It might be argued that classroom action research does not necessarily adopt an educational perspective. In some classroom research contexts the action perspectives of teachers may be very different. I would agree that classroom action perspectives may differ. However, it is not merely a contingent fact that research from an educational perspective appears to be the only mode of action research currently existing in classrooms. There are some kinds of human action which can only be described from a phenomenological perspective, i.e. by adopting the point of view of the agent. Other kinds of action can be described without any reference to the agent's point of view. Let us compare instrumental with communicative action in this respect. An instrumental action is one which is viewed by its agent as a means to an extrinsic end. But it can be described quite independently of the instrumental meaning ascribed to it by the agent, perhaps on the basis of observational criteria alone. A communicative action on the other hand is an action defined by rules which are logically presupposed by its occurrence. For example, an assertion is an action *in* which the agent places himself under an obligation to speak the truth. Thus one cannot describe the act independently of the agent's perspective in performing it.

It is only when the teaching acts to be described are defined by the teacher's action perspective that research needs to adopt it. Inasmuch as teaching for understanding involves communicative actions defined by the teacher's obligation to realize discourse values, research can only identify them by adopting the same perspective. But inasmuch as teaching for 'routine problem-solving' or 'memory' learning is a form of instrumental action, the activities involved can be identified and described quite independently of the teacher's point of view. It is only in the discourse context of teaching for understanding that classroom research must adopt the teacher's perspective if it is to produce valid accounts of such teaching. Process-product studies, by construing teaching as a form of instrumental action, assume that it can be described quite independently of the teacher's action perspective. Such studies therefore cannot be described as educational action research.

I now want to sketch out the main features of educational action research and explore its implications for the role of teachers in research, and their professional development.

Clarifying action perspectives

The first task of educational action research is the explication and clarification of the educational perspectives from which teachers identify and diagnose problems in their teaching. For classroom researchers working with teachers attempting to implement the Humanities Project, the action perspective of the project had already been clarified, through discussions between the project team and teachers prior to implementation. But for many classroom researchers the action perspective of the teachers they work with is not explicitly formulated. It is in this situation that the first stage of the research must involve an explication of action perspectives.

A good example here is the Ford Teaching Project (Elliott and Adelman, 1976), which was sponsored by the Ford Foundation. In this project we involved 40 British teachers in an investigation of the problems of implementing inquiry/ discovery approaches to teaching, in a variety of curriculum areas. All the teachers claimed to be actively involved in curriculum developments which employed these approaches, and to be interested in monitoring the problems of implementing them.

Initial discussions with participating teachers were concerned to elicit their understandings of the aims of inquiry or discovery teaching. They revealed that the majority saw the main aim as 'enabling independent reasoning'. We then studied tape-recordings of our teachers discussing transcripts and video-recordings of classroom situations with a view to extracting the main terms they employed in talking about them. The meaning of these terms was then clarified through further discussions and interviews with teachers. We finally produced three sets of categories which together defined the main features of the action perspective shared by our teachers. They were those of informal/formal, unstructured/structured, open-ended/guided-directed. The first set picked out the degree of intellectual independence the teacher allowed to students working on learning tasks. The second set picked out the extent to which teachers worked with preconceived task outcomes in mind, and the third the manner in which their intervention influenced students' thinking on tasks. It is obvious that all three sets of categories pick out dimensions which are pedagogically significant for teachers who aspire to enable independent reasoning.

Parallel to this elicitation exercise we analysed the idea of 'independent reasoning' into four constituent student freedoms:

1   to initiate and identify their own problems for inquiry;
2   to express and develop their own ideas;
3   to test ideas against relevant and sufficient evidence;
4   to discuss ideas with others.

From this analysis some pedagogical principles governing the selection of teaching acts were derived. We argued that teaching acts could only constitute an enabling influence on the development of students' powers for independent reasoning, if in performing them the teacher *refrained from*:

 I preventing them from initiating and identifying problems;
 II preventing them from expressing and developing their own ideas;
III restricting their access to relevant and sufficient evidence;
IV restricting their access to discussion.

We found that the above principles closely corresponded to the tacit criteria our teachers employed in distinguishing 'formal' from 'informal' teaching situations, and describing teaching strategies within them. For example, 'open-ended' questions were seen to constitute an informal situation, and 'leading' questions a formal one. 'Open-ended' questions imply that students are free from teacher – imposed constraints on their freedom to express their own ideas, while 'leading' questions imply the presence of teacher – imposed constraints.

The price which process-product research pays for neglecting teachers' perspectives is that it so often appears to them to be irrelevant to their practical concerns. This 'irrelevance' stems from the fact that the process-product perspective on the phenomena of teaching and learning differs radically from that of teachers themselves. When both parties talk about these phenomena, they find themselves talking about different things. This makes it impossible for process-product studies to appeal to a teacher's 'understanding' as a mode of influencing his practices, and explains the tendency for teacher education based on such studies to take the form of behaviour modification programmes in which the teacher's behaviour is manipulated in a quasi-causal manner.

Explicating and clarifying the action perspectives of teachers ensures that the phenomena of teaching and learning are understood from their point of view. Thus researcher and teacher are now able to speak the same language and engage in discourse with each other about classroom events. This enables classroom research to exert rational, as opposed to causal, influence on teachers' practices. Through discourse, the researcher can appeal to a teacher's 'understanding'. Such a solution to the familiar communication problem between teachers and researchers has two very important implications. First, in engaging teachers in dialogue and appealing to their 'understanding', action research submits itself to their judgement. There is an important sense in which classroom action research can only be validated in dialogue with teachers. It therefore involves them as active participants in the generation of research knowledge. Second, in making dialogue possible, action research enables teachers to use it as a tool for developing awareness and understanding of what they do in classrooms. Such self-knowledge is, in my view, at the heart of the professional development process. By involving teachers in dialogue, classroom action research itself constitutes an educational process.

Teacher education looks very different when examined from the point of view of action research rather than that of process-product research. From the former point of view it is a matter of rationally influencing the teacher's understanding of his classroom situation by engaging him in dialogue about it. From the latter point of view it is a matter of getting him to perform in accordance with certain technical rules.

Identifying problems in teaching

These rather abstractly formulated points about the collaborative and educative nature of classroom action research will be illustrated in a more concrete form later. After explicating and clarifying action perspectives, the second task is that of identifying and describing the problems teachers have in enabling the development of their students' understanding. This is a matter of identifying acts which constrain students' thinking in certain respects, e.g. the constraints cited in principles I–IV above. From the point of view of its power to rationally influence changes in teachers' classroom practices, it is obviously more important for action research to identify cases of failure to realize principles than cases of success, i.e. constraining acts rather than enabling acts. As Karl Popper claims, we make progress by reflecting about our errors rather than basking in our strengths. However, the identification of enabling acts may have the pragmatic merit of giving a teacher sufficient confidence in his strengths to face up to his weaknesses.

Criteria for identifying constraining acts will differ in one important respect from criteria for identifying enabling ones. Compare each statement in the following pairs:

1   (a) By performing X the teacher prevented students from developing their own ideas.

     (b) In performing Y the teacher gave students an opportunity to develop their own ideas.

2   (a) By performing Z the teacher prevented students from discussing divergent views.

     (b) In performing E the teacher protected the discussion of divergent views.

Statements 1(a) and 2(a) imply infringements, while 1(b) and 2(b) imply realizations of principles II and IV respectively. Whereas enabling influences – acts 1(b) and 2(b) – entail an absence of causal influence on students' thinking, constraining influences – acts 1(a) and 2(a) – entail its presence. In imposing a certain kind of constraint on students' thinking, a teacher must perform a separate act which has the constraining effect. Action research is concerned with identifying those teaching acts, which by virtue of their effects, constitute negative cases of the principles to be realized. For example, in the Ford Project, we discovered that when teachers initiated 'changes in topic' they often prevented students from developing their own ideas, and when they said 'Do you all agree with that?' following the expression of a student view, they often prevented students from continuing to discuss alternative views. Both these acts, cited above, can be identified on the basis of observable evidence alone, and the evidence extracted from recordings as well as direct observation.

I will now describe the methods action research employs for describing the effects of teaching behaviours on students' thinking. It should be clear that the effects to be described are on students' thought processes rather than directly on their behaviour. However, these subjective effects may be observably indicated by students' overt responses. Overt responses, like the acts which cause them, can be both directly observed and extracted from recordings. Participant observation, assisted by audio and audio-visual recordings, plays an important role in action research. Neither teachers nor their pupils, engaged as they are in interaction, are in a good position to isolate the observable elements of their interaction. The 'outside' observer has an epistemological advantage in this respect.

However, in order to describe the constraining effects of a teacher's acts, observation alone is not enough. Both the observable behaviour of the teacher and the observable responses of his students require interpretation. I will deal with the interpretation of students' responses first. An observed response may be susceptible to a variety of interpretations. In the Ford Project I often observed students responding to 'Do you all agree with that?' with silence. The teacher would then fix each student in turn with his eyes until someone said 'yeh' or 'mm, yes', before proceeding. Were the students silent because they felt unsure about whether they agreed or not, or because they were indifferent to the view expressed, or because they were reluctant for some reason to express any felt disagreement? The observer will tend to form his own judgement based on inference from observable evidence. But these judgements can be cross-checked against other evidence, namely students' accounts of their own subjective states. The best way of checking out an interpretation is to 'ask the students'. They are in the best position to know their own subjective states of mind. The observer can only infer them from behaviour, but the students have direct access to them through introspection. When I asked students how the 'Do you all agree?' behaviour influenced their responses they often said it made them reluctant to express any disagreement. If they are honest, then their reply is evidence that the behaviour is a constraining influence. But it does not explain how it influences their thinking in this way. In addition we need to elicit students' interpretations of what their teachers mean when they say 'Do you all agree?'. In my experience students frequently interpret their teachers to mean 'You had better agree', or words to that effect.

In communicative interaction the relationship between cause and effect is mediated by the hearer's interpretation of the meaning the speaker is trying to convey in his behaviour. Therefore, descriptions of the ways teachers constrain students' thinking should cite the latter's interpretations of the former's meaning in addition to effects. Interviews with students about the ways they interpret and subjectively respond to the behaviour of their teachers is a key action research method for cross-checking observers' interpretations.

In describing the constraints exerted by teaching behaviour on students' thinking we also need to know whether they were intended or unintended. To return to my 'Do you all agree?' example once again, the fact that students often interpret the meaning of this question as 'You had better agree' is not sufficient to warrant the conclusion that the teacher did mean that. An observer will interpret the meaning of teaching acts on the basis of inference from observed behaviour. But his interpretations need checking out. 'Do you all agree?' *may* mean 'You had better agree' but it may *also* mean 'I would like you to tell me whether you agree or disagree'. Since the observer is concerned here with the subjective meanings conveyed by a teacher through his observable behaviour, the person in the best position to know what they are is the teacher himself. The observer is methodologically obliged to cross-check his interpretations of teaching behaviour by interviewing the teacher concerned.

In order to understand the exact nature of the problems teachers have in enabling the development of understanding, the distinction between intended and unintended constraints is crucial. If in saying 'Do you all agree?' a teacher does not mean 'You had better agree' but his students take him to, then the constraining effect of this behaviour can be simply removed by the teacher clarifying what he really does mean. In other words, the problem is one of communication, of misunderstanding on the part of students. But if the teacher means what his students take him to mean then we have a different kind of problem, which requires the teacher to change his behaviour radically in order to solve it.

I am now in a position to define the main features of an action research account of teacher-imposed constraints on the development of students' understanding. They are:

1　A descriptive account of observed teaching behaviour and student response.
2　An interpretative account of the effects of teaching behaviour on student thinking.
3　An interpretative account of student interpretations of teaching behaviour.
4　An interpretative account of the meaning conveyed by teaching behaviour.

The observer's descriptive account (1) is cross-checked against recordings, but his interpretative accounts (2–4) can only be cross-checked against accounts provided by the teacher and his students. The production of an action research account involves the collection of accounts from three points of view: those of an observer, the teacher, and his students. In this way teachers and students are involved in the research process.

A question of procedure arises when either teacher or students disagree with the observer's, or each others' interpretation of their behaviour. The procedure we tended to adopt on the Ford Project was to allow all three parties access to the three accounts, and after a period for reflection bring them together to discuss inconsistencies. Inevitably, limitations of time may prevent issues from being resolved in dialogue. In this situation the dialogue must simply be reported, and the main areas of disagreement cited. The process of collecting accounts from three different points of view, and then contrasting them in a discussion involving all three parties, is called *triangulation* (Adelman, 1978).

Even when disagreements remain unresolved there are ways of assessing the degrees of confidence one might have in the accuracy of accounts. For example, if the observer and students agree in their accounts of constraints, but the teacher's account disagrees with theirs, one would be justified in suspecting the teacher's account to be an idealization of his practice. Again, if students support their teacher in denying that constraints cited by the observer obtain, then one would be justified in suspecting the observer's account.

This outline of the structure of action research accounts, and the methods employed in cross-checking and validating them, illustrates in concrete form the points I made previously about the collaborative and educative nature of action research. In involving the teacher in a triangulation procedure for cross-checking and validating his observer's interpretations, he is provided with opportunities for developing self-awareness and understanding.

Case study

The kind of accounts described are produced through case rather than sample study. Action research does not assume that its findings are generalizable. Which teaching acts constitute a particular form of constraint may vary from classroom to classroom. However, through the comparative study of cases it is possible to identify similar cases, and therefore teaching problems shared by different teachers.

The identification of common problems was one of the aims of the Ford Project, and was the reason it involved 40 teachers drawn from different curriculum areas and age levels of students. We wanted to discover the extent to which similar problems arose in apparently very different teaching contexts. At the end of the project we were able to describe some of the problems our teachers shared. They were stated in the form of 'general hypotheses' to indicate a contrast between the status we claimed for our findings and that claimed for the generalizations of process-product research. We wanted to encourage other teachers to test the extent to which the cases of constraining influence cited by the hypotheses could be generalized to their situation. The hypotheses expressed anticipations of classroom possibilities, derived from the common experience of a particular group of teachers. They provided an orientation for teachers wanting to examine their own classrooms.

In action research, generalization is an unstructured process of proceeding from case to case. In process-product research, it is a formal process based on theoretical sampling methods. Unlike the generalizations of process-product research, those of action research can only be validated in the self-knowledge of teachers working in particular classrooms. Action research does not prescribe rules governing the ways teachers enable the development of understanding in students. But it can give general guidance in the form of hypotheses, to teachers who wish to develop their understanding of the particular situations in which they teach.

The two tasks described so far locate classroom action research firmly in the 'interpretative', 'phenomenological' or 'hermeneutic' tradition of social inquiry. This tradition can be contrasted with the 'empiricist' tradition in which process-product research belongs. However, if classroom action research merely restricts itself to explicating teachers' perspectives and studying teacher-student interaction in the classroom, its educative power to influence the self-awareness and practice of teachers may be weakened.

Action research and critical theory

Such a restriction assumes that once a teacher becomes aware of the acts which constrain students' thinking, he is in a position to refrain from them. But in the Ford Project some of our teachers became increasingly aware of the gaps between their aspirations and practice, while at the same time claiming they lacked the freedom to do much about it. They cited various constraints originating in the institutional, social, and political contexts in which they taught. If such teachers are to increase their freedom of action at all, they need not only to understand what it is they are doing in their classrooms, but how their actions are influenced and shaped by institutional, social, and political structures.

The understanding involved in professional development transcends the boundaries of the classroom. Classroom action research therefore also has the task of developing what Habermas and other members of the Frankfurt school of social science might call a *critical theory* of the teaching situation. Such a theory would explain the ways in which teaching is constrained by factors operating outside the classroom in its institutional, social and political context. It would inevitably be conditioned by political beliefs and values. But this kind of bias, like the educational bias of classroom action research, need not imply a lack of objectivity.

If the practical interest served by process-product research is one of technical control over student behaviour, and that served by the interpretative tasks of action research is one of increasing the educational quality of teacher-student discourse, then the interest served by a critical theory of teaching is one of increasing the professional autonomy of teachers (see Habermas, 1974, on knowledge-constitutive interests). To my knowledge, few classroom action research programmes have, up to the present time, incorporated a highly developed critical perspective. They have tended to stop short at classroom-bound interpretative or phenomenological description, perhaps for prudential reasons. Power (1976) in his review of classroom research in science education, cites three research paradigms which roughly correspond to the empirical, interpretative, and critical traditions of social inquiry. He cites no examples of the latter, and names the Ford Project as an example of classroom research in the interpretative tradition. Certainly, we did not systematically provide critical explanations for the feelings of powerlessness which accompanied the development of self-awareness amongst some of our teachers, although such explanations were often subjects for discussion at meetings and conferences. However, a critical science of teaching should not merely be concerned with explaining why teachers act inconsistently with their educational values.

In the Ford Project, we tended to be rather preoccupied with teachers who resisted opportunities to develop their understanding and awareness through reflecting on the alternative 'understanding' held by students and observers. We eventually developed in a fairly systematic way a set of hypotheses about the conditions which enabled and constrained the development of self-awareness in teachers (see Elliott and Adelman, 1976). Here is one of the 43 hypotheses we generated:

> The less financial and status rewards in schools are primarily related to administrative and pastoral roles, the more teachers are able to tolerate losses of self-esteem brought about through increased self-awareness.

This cites an institutional constraint on the development of self-awareness and understanding. In order to participate fully in classroom action research at the level of describing problems in his teaching, a teacher must be open to having his understanding of problems rationally influenced through dialogue with observers and students. But we discovered a tendency, varying in its strength, for teachers to resist being so influenced, and sought explanations for such resistance in the institutional, social, and political settings of their classrooms.

How is this critical task of elucidating the structures constraining teachers' classroom practices, and their thinking about them, accomplished? First, like the task of describing constraining influences of teaching in the classroom, it will involve case study. The structures which constrain teachers' thoughts and actions may vary from one institutional, social or political context to another. General critical theorems must depend for their development on comparing similarities and differences between cases. The generalizability beyond the context of the research must be hypothetical and dependent on further grounding in case study. Second, the critical theorems of action research must be validated in dialogue with teachers; they are in the unique position to test critical hypotheses by negating them in action. But their participation in the validation of critical theorems also enables teachers to develop an understanding of the wider influences which impinge on their freedom of thought about, and action within, the classroom. Again, teacher participation in action research is potentially an educative one.

The professional development of teachers can be seen as possessing three aspects. The development of self-awareness in the classroom is one. But this assumes that the teacher is free to develop his self-awareness. In this respect an understanding of the institutional, social and political structures which constrain such development is a first step in his professional development. Finally, the development of self-awareness may not be sufficient for bringing about the improvements in his practice which he has come to desire. He may discover that he does not enjoy the freedom of action he once assumed he did. In order to implement the desired changes he must first understand the structures which constrain his freedom of action in the classroom. If action research is to contribute to all three aspects of professional development, it must go beyond the study of teacher-student interaction in classrooms to focus on the structures which distort its educational function.

References

Adelman, C. (1978) On first hearing *in* Adelman, C. (ed.) (1978) *Uttering, Muttering*, CARE: University of East Anglia, Norwich.

Barnes, D. (1976) *From Communication to Curriculum*, Penguin Books: Harmondsworth.

Berliner, D.C. and Rosenshine, B. (1977) The acquisition of knowledge in the classroom *in* Anderson, R., Spiro, R. and Montague, W. (eds) (1977) *Schooling and the Acquisition of Knowledge*, Lawrence Erlbaum Associates: Hillsdale, NJ.

Bruner, J.S. (1970) Man: a course of study *in* Bruner (1970) *Evaluation Strategies*, Educational Development Center: Cambridge, Mass.

Doyle, W. (1979) *The Tasks of Teaching and Learning*, Invited address at the Annual Meeting of the American Educational Research Association, San Francisco, April 1979.

Dunkin, M.J. and Biddle, B.J. (1974) *The Study of Teaching*, Holt, Rinehart and Winston: New York.

Elliott, J. (1978a) What is action research in schools? *Journal of Curriculum Studies* 10 4: 355–357.

Elliott, J. (1978b) Classroom research: science or common sense *in* McAleese, R. and Hamilton, D. (eds) (1978) *Understanding Classroom Life*, National Foundation for Educational Research: Slough.

Elliott, J. and Adelman, C. (1976) *Innovation at the Classroom Level*, Course E203 Unit 28, Open University Press: Milton Keynes.

Elliott, J. and MacDonald, B. (1972) *People in Classrooms* CARE, Occasional Publications No 1: University of East Anglia, Norwich.

Fenstermacher, G.D. (1978) A philosophical consideration of recent research on teacher effectiveness, *Review of Research in Education* 6.

Habermas, J. (1972) Technology and science as 'ideology' *in* Habermas (1972) *Towards a Rational Society*, Heinemann: London.

Habermas, J. (1974) *Introduction to Theory and Practice* Heinemann: London.

Jenkins, D. (1977) Saved by the bell *and* Saved by the army *in* Hamilton, D. *et al.* (1977) *Beyond the Numbers Game*, Macmillan Education: London.

Parlett, M. and Hamilton, D. (1973) Evaluation as illumination *in* Tawney, D. (ed.) (1973) *Evaluation in Curriculum Development: Twelve Case Studies*, Schools Council Research Studies, Macmillan Education: London.

Peters, R.S. (1968) Must an educator have an aim? *in* Macmillan and Nelson (eds) (1968) *Concepts of Teaching*, Rand MacNally: Chicago.

Power, C. (1976) *A Critical Review of Science Classroom Interaction Studies*, mimeo, School of Education, University of Queensland: Australia.

Smith, L. and Schumacher, S. (1972) *Extended Pilot Trials of the Aesthetic Education Program: A Qualitative Description, Analysis and Evaluation*, CEMREL Inc: USA.

Stenhouse, L. (1971) The Humanities Curriculum Project: the rationale, *Theory into Practice* 10: 154–162.

Stenhouse, L. (1975) *An Introduction to Curriculum Research and Development*, Heinemann: London.

Walker, R. and Adelman, C. (1972) *Towards of Sociography of Classrooms*, Final report, Social Science Research Council (Grant HR996–1): London.

Wild, R.D. (1973) *Teacher participation in research*, Unpublished conference paper, SSRC and Gulbenkian Project on Problems and Effects of Teaching about Race Relations, CARE: University of East Anglia, Norwich.

PART 4

CONCEPTIONS OF TEACHING AS AN EVIDENCE-BASED PROFESSION

CHAPTER 8

MAKING EVIDENCE-BASED PRACTICE EDUCATIONAL

British Educational Research Journal, Vol. 27, No. 5, pp. 555–574, 2001

Redirecting educational research in the service of outcomes-based education

There is a great deal of current debate about the future direction of educational research. According to some current commentators, like David Hargreaves, it has lost its way. Educational research needs to be redirected towards the systematic development of a body of knowledge that is capable of informing the practical judgments of teachers. The idea of 'evidence-based practice' is central to this redirection. It orients research towards the goal of maximising the utility of its findings for teachers. In this context, Hargreaves (1997) argues that:

> research should provide decisive and conclusive evidence that if teachers do X rather than Y in their professional practice, there will be a significant and enduring improvement in outcome.
>
> (p. 413)

More recently, Hargreaves (1999) has displayed an increasing sensitivity to accusations of 'positivism' (see Hammersley, 1997). He qualifies the idea of 'evidence-based practice' by suggesting that 'evidence-informed practice' is a less ambivalent expression. It more clearly indicates that relevant research *informs* rather than *displaces* the judgment of teachers. He also appears to qualify the injunction that research evidence should be *decisive and conclusive* for practice.

Such evidence does not presume the existence of universal causal laws as a basis for generating means–ends rules that are beyond doubt and the need for any further speculation.

Hargreaves sees the future of educational research to require more experimental studies and randomised controlled trials, in search of *what works* in practice to produce improvements in outcome. These studies investigate 'some "reasonably stable relationships" ' (1999, p. 247) but are open to revision in the light of exceptions and changing circumstances. Their generalisable findings deal in statistical probabilities only.

Moreover, in discussing the relationship between research and policy-making, Hargreaves acknowledges that practical decisions are context-bound. He argues that they need to be based on a wider range of considerations than 'relevant research'. Knowledge derived from research 'serves as a supplement to, not a substitute for, the policy-maker's existing knowledge' (1999, p. 246).

By attempting to uncouple educational experiments into *what works* from positivistic assumptions, Hargreaves (1999) aims to strengthen the case for an 'engineering model' of educational research, as opposed to an 'enlightenment model'. The former, he contends, aims to exert a direct influence on educational action in the areas of policy and practice, by generating evidence of *what works*. The latter, in contrast, aims only to shape the way people think about situations and the problems they raise. The influence of such research on their concrete decisions and actions is at best indirect. Hargreaves acknowledges that 'enlightenment research' can in the longer term indirectly impact on policy and practice by permeating the prevailing climate of opinion. However, this 'uncontentious fact', he argues, is no excuse for a *hermit stance*, 'in which the researcher withdraws from the messy world of short-term, practical problems into intellectual obscurities masquerading as profundities whilst dreaming of ultimate recognition' (1999, p. 243). Indeed, Hargreaves claims that the transmission of theories and ideas alone to 'enlighten' professional practitioners is a dangerous enterprise. By way of example, he points to the intellectual monopoly social scientists in education have, 'until recently', exercised over the initial training of teachers. In the process, they have purveyed the ideas of researchers like Piaget, Skinner and Bernstein (1999, p. 244) in distorted forms. Arguably, he contends, this has done 'untold damage' to teachers' professional practices.

Hargreaves portrays the 'enlightenment model' as an oppositional stance to an 'engineering model' framed by naive positivistic assumptions. By uncoupling the 'engineering model' from such assumptions, he aspires to disarm the opposition in the academy, and to reinstate it at the core of social science research generally and educational research in particular. In this way, the future of social and educational research can be redirected to generating *actionable knowledge* for both policy-makers and practitioners.

Has Hargreaves succeeded, in his latest writing, at finally uncoupling his endorsement of an 'engineering model' of social and educational research from the charge that it presumes a crude and naive positivism? Has he thereby exposed, as mere rationalisation, the grounds for opposing such a model with one that dissociates knowledge from any direct link with social action, and in doing so restricts its aim to influencing the 'climate of opinion'? I would argue that Hargreaves has only partially succeeded. From the standpoint of social philosophy, his arguments are not exactly novel ones. They echo in some respects those developed by Alasdair MacIntyre (1981) in chapter 8 of his seminal text entitled *After Virtue*.

Discussing *The Character of Generalizations in Social Science and their lack of predictive power*, MacIntyre identifies the discovery of statistical regularities as an important source of predictability in human behaviour. He argues that generalisations of this kind, couched in terms of probabilities rather than strict causal laws, do not entail explicability in terms of such laws. This point is echoed by Hargreaves (1997) in his rejoinder to Martin Hammersley's (1997) contention that many educational researchers would perceive his account of 'evidence-based practice' as positivistic. MacIntyre also argues that knowledge of statistical regularities plays an important role in informing human choices between alternatives, in terms of their chances of success and failure. They constitute what Hargreaves calls *actionable knowledge*. However, unlike Hargreaves, MacIntyre does not view the existence of exceptions to constitute a platform for improving the predictability of research findings and therefore their utility as *actionable knowledge*.

According to Hargreaves (1999), educational research evidence about *what works* in classrooms should be cumulative and based on a process of continuously investigating exceptions (pp. 247–248). He appears to assume that such exceptions constitute counter-examples in the sense that they expose deficiencies in the original generalisations which need to be improved upon by further research. However, MacIntyre argues that the probabilistic generalisations of social science are different in kind from those which obtain in natural science fields like statistical mechanics. Unlike the former, probabilistic generalisations in such natural science fields do not merely consist of a list of instances to which there are exceptions. Rather, they 'entail well-defined counter-factual conditionals and they are refuted by counter-examples in precisely the same way and to the same degree as other law-like generalizations are' (1981, p. 91).

Given this difference, Hargreaves's assumption that exceptions to social science generalisations can function as counter-examples, and thereby constitute a basis for cumulative research which improves the actionability of its findings, is an erroneous one. MacIntyre emphasises Machiavelli's point, that in human life people may act 'on the best available stock of generalizations' and yet, when faced with unpredicted exceptions, see no way to improve them or reason to abandon them (p. 93). Relatively speaking, such generalisations are predictively weak. Hargreaves's belief that they can be improved upon, rather than simply added to or changed, in a way which leads to a progressive diminution of unpredictability in human affairs, suggests that he has not entirely shed the assumptions of positivism.

However much Hargreaves has modified his position on evidence-based practice in response to accusations of 'positivism', there is a consistent theme running through his writing since the Teacher Training Agency (TTA) lecture he delivered in 1996. It is that the major task of educational research is to improve the *performativity* of teachers with respect to the outcomes of their teaching. At first sight, this view of the aim of educational research appears to be a matter of common sense and not open to question. Teaching is an intentional activity directed towards bringing about learning outcomes for pupils. What is more open to dispute (see Stenhouse, 1970a, 1975) is a thread of ideas which originally stemmed from Bloom's *Taxonomy of Educational Objectives* (1956) and Bloom's research into *Mastery Learning* (1971). In the 1980s, these ideas were further developed under the name of *outcomes-based education* (OBE). Within the thread of ideas that make up OBE are the injunctions that learning outcomes should be the same for all students, operationally defined as *exit behaviours*, and progress towards them measured against *benchmarks*. The terminology employed tends to shift over time and context, but its meaning remains constant. Hence, within the UK National Curriculum framework, specifications of *outcomes for all students* are referred to as 'standards', *exit behaviours* as 'targets', and *benchmarks* as 'attainment levels'.

One of the attractions of OBE is that it appears to provide a framework of practical rules for designing teaching interventions and measuring teaching effectiveness. In applying these rules to instructional design, the outcomes of teaching are conceived as measurable *outputs*. As such, they are specified in a form which renders them predictable and amenable to technical control by the teacher. Within the OBE framework, 'evidence-based teaching' can be characterised as a means of improving teaching as a form of technical control over the production of learning outcomes, thereby rendering them increasingly predictable. In spite of various adjustments Hargreaves has made to his accounts of 'evidence-based practice', and the role of educational research in relation to it, they continue to embrace and endorse the control ideology of OBE. In this respect, they remain open to the charge of positivism.

In what follows, the phrase 'outcomes-based education' will be used to refer to the particular strand of ideas sketched above. In so doing, I will in no way wish to deny the truism that teaching involves the intention to bring about worthwhile learning outcomes for students. What I would deny is that teaching to become effective has to take on the particular ideological baggage of OBE. The truism referred to does not necessarily entail that the teacher should have the same outcomes in mind for all students, or that he or she should specify outcomes in the form of exist behaviours or outputs, or assess the effectiveness of his or her teaching by measuring students' progress in learning against benchmarks. Hargreaves's account of the role of educational research can be interpreted as an attempt to reposition it as the handmaiden of OBE and the educational policies which are increasingly shaped by the ideology which underpins it.

I will return to the question of what constitutes *actionable knowledge* in the context of social practices like education shortly. First, I want to explore Hargreaves's view of the role of *educational research* in the prevailing policy context. I shall do so in the light of MacIntyre's account of the use of social science generalisations in the management of society.

The policy context of educational research

Hargreaves endorses political interventions to shape pedagogical practices in school classrooms so long as they are informed by research evidence rather than ideology. He writes (1999):

> In England and Wales policy makers were formerly limited, or limited themselves, mainly to decisions about the structure of the education service; the internal activities of what teachers did in classrooms, even the curriculum itself, was largely left to the discretion of teachers enjoying a high level of professional autonomy. Today a new link is being forged between what hitherto have been mainly distinct areas [of policy and practice] and marks the end to the convention by which ministers remain distant from classroom practice.
>
> Policy makers' interventions in classroom activities will, I suspect, increase, especially if the national literacy and numerary strategies succeed in raising levels of students' measured achievement. Ministers now recognize that standards of teaching and learning are unlikely to be raised by policy action that never penetrates classrooms. This is less dangerous than it initially appears, as long as ministers retain some distance by a pragmatic attention to 'what works' and by an acknowledgement that the discovery of 'what works' is more a matter of evidence, not just ideology or of political preference.
>
> (p. 246)

From MacIntyre's point of view, Hargreaves's optimism about the uses of educational research in the policy context, as depicted above, would appear to be ill founded. He argues (pp. 106–108) that the claims of politicians and bureaucrats to expertise in the 'social engineering' of society is a masquerade for a histrionic imitation of scientifically managed social control. Such claims, he argues, arise from 'the dominance of the manipulative mode in our culture', but which 'cannot be accompanied by very much actual success in manipulation' for 'our social order is in a very literal sense out of, and indeed anyone's, control'. MacIntyre concludes that it is 'histrionic success which gives power and authority in our culture' and not scientific evidence about how to manipulate/engineer the social order to achieve certain purposes. In doing so, he anticipates a likely response from social managers and bureaucrats that, interestingly, echoes Hargreaves's account of the role of educational research:

> We make no large claims [to expertise]...We are as keenly aware of the limitations of social science generalizations as you are. We perform a modest function with a modest and unpretentious competence. But we do have specialized knowledge, we are entitled in our own limited fields to be called experts.
>
> (p. 107)

MacIntyre argues that these modest claims do little to legitimate the possession and uses of power 'in anything like the way or on anything like the scale on which that power is wielded' in bureaucratic systems. He sees them as an excuse for continuing 'to participate in the charades which are consequently enacted'. His account of how political and managerial power is generated in our culture seems credible, in which case Hargreaves's account of the significant, if modest, contribution of educational research to the production of *actionable knowledge* in the current policy context is based on a fiction about the capacity of such research to inform and shape policy interventions. It is a fiction which, nevertheless, provides an excuse for an unprecedented extension of the operation of political and bureaucratic power to regulate the pedagogical activities teachers engage their students in within classrooms. Hargreaves, it appears, from this point of view, has cast educational researchers for a role in the histrionic production of the power and authority of the state and its officials over the processes of education. MacIntyre 'reminds' educational researchers that they also will need to be good actors when he writes:

> The histrionic talents of the player with small walking-on parts are as necessary to the bureaucratic drama as the contributions of the great managerial character actors.
>
> (p. 108)

I would contend that in giving the 'engineering model' of educational research a central role for the future, Hargreaves takes for granted a set of prevailing assumptions about the nature of social practices, like 'education', and their relationship to desirable social outcomes. These assumptions are embedded in a climate of opinion which currently surrounds the formation of social policy in the post-industrial nations and the systems of quality assurance associated with the process. In the field of education, such assumptions are embedded in the notion of *outcomes-based education* outlined earlier. They can be summarised as follows:

1   That social practices are activities which need to be justified as *effective* and *efficient* means of producing desirable outputs.
2   That means and ends are contingently related. What constitutes an appropriate means for bringing about the ends-in-view needs to be determined on the basis of empirical evidence.
3   That the determination of means requires a clear and precise pre-specification of ends as tangible and measurable outputs or targets, which constitute the *quality standards* against which the performance of social practitioners is to be judged.

The prevailing policy context in education, as in other areas of social policy, tends to reflect these assumptions, inasmuch as it prioritises *target-setting* and forms of evaluation and quality assurance which measure the *performativity* (efficiency) of practices against *indicators* of success in achieving the targets. In other words, it is a context in which practices are treated as manipulative devices (technologies) for engineering desired levels of output.

Hargreaves's vision of the future of educational research neatly fits this policy context and he apparently sees no problem with it. He clearly assumes that restrictions on the autonomy of teachers by the interventions of policy-makers to shape classroom practice are justified, so long as they are informed and disciplined by empirical evidence of *what works* to produce a given level of output. What he fails to consider is MacIntyre's point that such evidence can never provide 'the managers of society' with the amount of predictive power that is commensurate with the concept of *managerial effectiveness*. Such a concept, for MacIntyre, is a moral fiction (pp. 106–107). If we accept his line of argument, then, in a policy context characterised by 'managerialism', empirical evidence about statistical regularities is only *histrionically useful* as a masquerade for arbitrary preferences. In which case, Hargreaves's vision of government ministers distancing themselves from their ideological preferences and pragmatically attending to evidence of *what works* is somewhat fanciful and no basis on which to sanction restrictions on teacher autonomy. Indeed, the fact, evidenced by the limited forms of empirical generalisations produced by the social sciences, that human life is accompanied by a high degree of unpredictability as a permanent condition, is a good reason for giving teachers a measure of autonomy from political and bureaucratic control. Trusting in their capacities to exercise wisdom and judgment in the unpredictable circumstances they regularly encounter in the course of their activities is the wise policy.

We need a third vision of educational research to either the 'enlightenment' or 'engineering' models; one which places the judgment of teachers at the centre of the research process. It is the articulation of this third vision that the rest of this article is devoted to.

Hargreaves's vision of the future of educational research ignores a tradition of philosophical thinking about social practices, like education, which goes back to Aristotle and is exemplified in contemporary thought by MacIntrye's *After Virtue*. According to MacIntyre, this philosophical tradition defines a social practice as:

> any coherent and complex form of socially established cooperative human activity through which goods internal to that form of activity are realized in the course of trying to achieve those standards of excellence which are appropriate to, and partially definitive of, that form of activity, with the result that human powers to achieve excellence, and human conceptions of the ends and goods involved, are systematically extended.
>
> (1981, p. 187)

From this *ethical perspective*, goods internal to a practice are distinguished from external goods because one cannot specify them independently of the activities and processes the practice itself consists of. They are norms and values which define what are to count as the worthwhile activities and processes which make up the practice, and not some extrinsic goods which may result from participating in it. Moreover, unlike the latter, goods internal to a practice can only be identified and recognised 'by the experience of participating in the practice in question' (see MacIntyre, 1981, p. 189).

The concept of education and the role of educational research

In the field of education, such a perspective constituted in the 1960s and early 1970s a major resource for two highly influential and interlinked bodies of work. I am referring to Richard Peters's work in establishing the Philosophy of Education as a major discipline in education (see *Ethics and Education* [1966]) and 'Aims of education – a conceptual inquiry' [1973] and Lawrence Stenhouse's use of Peters's work in developing research-based teaching as a coherent and integrated form of educational practice (see Stenhouse, 1970b, 1975, 1979). In fact, the linkage between Peter's educational theory and Stenhouse's work in placing the idea of 'research-based teaching' at the core of the curriculum development process in schools, as exemplified by his Humanities Project (1970b), is not sufficiently acknowledged by either philosophers of education or educational researchers. Yet, it provides a significant exception to Hargreaves's contention (1999, p. 244) that the transmission of theories of education have not been accompanied in the past by a sound body of empirical evidence related to teachers' routine practices (see, e.g., Stenhouse, 1970b, 1977; Ford Teaching Project 1974; Elliott and MacDonald, 1975; Elliott, J., 1976–7; Stenhouse *et al.*, 1979; Ebbutt and Elliott, 1985; Elliott, 1991).

Peters was a member of the Humanities Project's Steering Committee, and Stenhouse viewed this project as an example of curriculum development grounded in a well-articulated philosophy of education. Consistently with this, Stenhouse sent a member of his team (me) to study the philosophy of education under Peters, on a part-time basis, at the London Institute of Education.

In this section, I will revisit Peters's work on the aims of education and their relationship to educational processes, and argue that its implications for educational research and evidence-based practice are very different from Hargreaves's position. In the final section, I will sketch out Stenhouse's vision of the relationship between educational research and teaching and indicate its congruence with the educational theory of Peters.

For Peters, *educational aims* do not refer to ends which 'education might lead up to or bring about' (1973). From his point of view, economic ends like 'providing students with jobs' and 'increasing the productivity of the community' are goods extrinsic to education. *Education*, Peters argues (1966), is not 'a neutral process that is instrumental to something that is worthwhile which is extrinsic to it' (p. 27). Such extrinsic ends are more appropriately referred to as *purposes* rather than *aims of education*. The latter refer to norms and values which define what it means for a person to become *educated*, and what is to count procedurally as a worthwhile *educational* process for realising such a state. They define 'goods' that are intrinsic to *education* as a process. A process which is solely directed towards *extrinsic* ends such as economic ones, Peters (1966) argues, is best described in terms of *training* rather than *education*. However, people can be taught a body of knowledge, such as science, or a practical skill, like carpentry, for both 'their own intrinsic value and because of the contribution which they make to extrinsic ends' (Peters, 1966, p. 29). *Education* and *training* are not necessarily discrete processes.

According to Peters, the norms and values which define the intrinsic goods of education fall into two closely connected clusters (1973, pp. 18–24). First, there are those which provide general criteria of education when it is viewed as an achievement. Peters claims that success at becoming an educated person involves:

- coming to care about an activity for 'what there is in it as distinct from what it may lead onto', e.g. 'the pursuit of truth' or 'making something of a fitting form' (p. 18);
- possessing 'depth of understanding' by grasping the principles which underpin an activity;
- not being narrowly specialised but able to see the connection between an activity one cares about and understands and a 'coherent pattern of life'. Peters calls this ability, to make connections between specific human activities (e.g. science, history, or engineering) and a wider pattern of meaning in life, *cognitive perspective*.
- having one's way of looking at things in life generally, one's *cognitive perspective*, transformed by what one has learned in pursuing specific worthwhile activities.

The implication of this analysis, of what it means to be *educated*, is that becoming such a person involves a process that is qualitatively different from one which involves merely learning bodies of knowledge and skills that are valued solely in terms of their relationship to extrinsic economic and social purposes. *Education*, for Peters, involves the transformation of a person's way of seeing the world in relation to him or herself. It is a holistic process. He argues that a person is never *educated* 'in relation to any specific end, function, or mode of thought' (1966, p. 34). The acquisition of specific competencies in these respects is more appropriately described in terms of *training*. Nor do people become *educated* additively, by virtue of the sheer amount of knowledge and skills they acquire. Knowledgeable or omnicompetent individuals are not necessarily *educated*. From this we might conclude that our Government's current project of 'driving up standards' in schools has little to do with improving the quality of *education* within them, since the acquisition of specific competencies are not in themselves *educational achievements*. The latter refer to the *manner* in which people learn and involve qualitative transformations in their general outlook on life, the conditions of which can be specified by the kinds of general criteria Peters has drawn our attention to. His purpose, in attempting to clarify aims which are intrinsic to the process of becoming educated, is 'to clarify the minds of educators about their priorities' (1973, p. 21). The need for such clarification is perhaps greater now at a time when the educational policy context is being driven by economic imperatives in an age of globalisation, and teachers at all levels of the education system are being held to account in terms of standardised learning outputs which are believed to posses *commodity value* for the labour market.

The second cluster of aims cited by Peters refers to procedural values and principles rather than the achievement aspect of education. Some of these aims, he argues, are linked to the claims of the individual in the process of education, and draw attention 'to a class of *procedures* of education rather than prescribe any particular content or direction to it' (1973, p. 22). Aims like 'self-realization' and 'the growth of the individual' imply procedural values such as 'learning by discovery', 'inquiry learning', 'autonomous learning', 'learning by experience'. Other procedural aims refer to the rules or standards that are built into *educationally* worthwhile activities, such as respect for reasons and evidence (1973, p. 25). Aims and Procedural values are emphasised, Peters argues, 'when the educational system is either geared towards the demands of the state...or when individuals are being moulded relentlessly in accordance with some dull and doctrinaire pattern' (1973, p. 23). Under these conditions, there is a point in stressing the need, e.g., to respect the individuality of learners by allowing them a measure of self-direction and control within any *educationally* worthwhile process. There may also be a point in emphasising the intrinsic value of procedural standards built into an activity, such as 'respect for evidence', in contexts where the activity is in danger of being valued only for its instrumentality as a vehicle for producing goods which are extrinsic to *education*.

If, for Peters, general aims function to remind educators of their priorities with respect to what they should be trying to achieve in *educating* students as opposed to merely training them, then procedural values and principles function to remind them that their methods should be consistent with both the standards that define and discipline *educationally* worthwhile activities, and the moral claims of individuals as learners. Procedural values and principles based on the latter remind educators of the ethical limits *education* as a task places on the pedagogical methods they employ to structure students' learning.

According to Peters, procedural values and principles cannot be characterised independently of his characterisation of education as an achievement. Although they specify criteria which characterise those processes 'by means of which people gradually become educated' (1973, p. 15), they do not, Peters argues, specify 'efficient means for producing a desirable end' (1973, p. 15).

The connection between *educational* processes and becoming an *educated* person is a conceptual rather than a contingent one. Why, he asks, are values and principles embedded in *educational* procedures treated as *aims* of education? The answer, he argues:

> is connected with the impossibility of conceiving of educational processes in accordance with a means–ends model and of making any absolute separation between content and procedure, matter and manner, in the case of education.
> (1973, p. 24)

Peters here is not denying that considerations of instrumental effectiveness, in achieving specific educational outcomes, are pedagogically relevant. What he is denying is their relevance to judging the *educational quality* of pedagogical methods. This is because, for him, both the achievement and procedural criteria of education characterise different aspects of the same process of *initiating* people 'into a public world picked out by the language and concepts of a people and structured by rules governing their purposes and interactions with each other' (1973, p. 26). The achievement criteria characterise *educational outcomes* in a form that renders them inseparable from the process of *becoming educated*. They characterise *qualities of being* which are manifested *in* a process of *becoming educated* and cannot be described independently of it. Such a process, Peters argues, is inconsistent with both the view of teachers as operators who shape minds 'according to some specification or "top them up" with knowledge' and the view that their function is simply to 'encourage the child to "grow" ' as if s(he) were an 'organism unfolding some private form of life' (1973, p. 26). The function of procedural criteria, according to Peters, is to act as a guide to teachers in helping learners, viewed as active and developing centres of consciousness, 'to explore and *share* a public world whose contours have been marked out by generations which have preceded both of them' (1973, p. 26). The central pedagogical problem for teachers as educators, Peters claims, is the procedural one of how to get students to enter into this public world and enjoy their public heritage. Procedural values and principles articulated as *aims of education* remind them that this can only be achieved by methods that acknowledge both the internal standards which govern the activities that people are being initiated into, and the moral standards appropriate to their status as 'developing centres of consciousness'.

Since there are multiple criteria for judging both what it means to become *educated* and what are to count as *educational* methods or procedures, it is obvious, Peters argues, that some will be emphasised more than others at particular times, 'according to the defects and needs of the contemporary situation' (1973, p. 20). The demand for aims in education serves to focus attention on a neglected priority. The existence of multiple criteria, for Peters, means that educators can be pulled in different directions by conflicting educational priorities, and that such dilemmas cannot be resolved by the formulation of a single overall aim of education which everyone could agree about. Which aim(s) should be emphasised in any particular circumstance must be left to the discretion and practical wisdom of the teacher(s) concerned (1973, pp. 27–29).

Let us now briefly explore the implications of Peters's theory of education for a future direction of educational research that is very different to the one enunciated by Hargreaves.

Hargreaves' account of the sort of research evidence which can be used to inform pedagogical development confines itself to evidence of 'instrumental effectiveness'. However, from Peters's account of the procedural aims and values implicit in the concept of education alone, one might argue that educational research, if it is to inform *educational* practice, should prioritise the gathering of empirical evidence which can inform teachers' judgements about the ethical consistency of the teaching and learning process with the procedural aims and values that define what is to count as a worthwhile process of *education* (see Elliott, 1989). The primary role of *educational* research, when understood as research directed towards the improvement of *educational* practice, is not to discover contingent connections between a set of classroom activities and pre-standardised learning outputs, but to investigate the conditions for realising a coherent *educational* process in particular practical contexts.

Both the indeterminate nature of educational values, and the context-dependent nature of judgements about which concrete methods and procedures are consistent with them, suggest that *educational* research takes the form of case studies rather than randomised controlled trials. The latter, via a process of statistical aggregation, abstract practices and their outcomes from the contexts in which they are situated. Case studies entail close collaboration between external researchers and teachers on 'the inside' of an educational practice. As Alasdair MacIntyre points out, the identification and recognition of goods which are internal to a practice depend on the experience 'of participating in the practice in question' (1981, p. 189). In the context of research directed towards the improvement of *educational* practice, teachers need to be involved in prioritising their *educational* aims in a given situation, in defining what is to count as relevant evidence of the extent to which they are being realised and interpreting its practical significance for them. In other words *educational* research, as opposed to simply research *on* education, will involve teachers in its construction and execution and not simply in *applying its findings*. Teachers engage in *educational* research and not simply with it.

The implications outlined above, of Peters's educational theory for educational research, are highly consistent with Stenhouse's *process model* of curriculum development and the central role of *research-based teaching* within it.

Stenhouse on research-based teaching

Stenhouse drew on Peters's work in *Ethics and Education* (1966) to develop his *process model* of curriculum and pedagogy in opposition to the emerging 'objectives model', which forged the basis of what has now become widely known as 'outcomes-based education'. In demonstrating the process model in practice through *the Humanities Curriculum Project*, Stenhouse saw himself to be addressing the issue:

> can curriculum and pedagogy be organised satisfactorily by a logic other than the means–ends model?
>
> (pp. 84–85)

He derived this alternative logic substantially from the arguments Peters sketched out in *Ethics and Education*.

> Peters (1966) argues cogently for the intrinsic justification of content. He starts from the position that education 'implies the transmission of what is worth-while to those who become committed to it' and that it 'must involve knowledge and understanding and some kind of cognitive perspective, which are not inert'. (45) Believing that education involves taking part in worthwhile activities, Peters argues that such activities have their own in-built standards of excellence, and thus 'can be appraised because of the standards immanent in them rather than because of what they lead on to'. They can be argued to be worthwhile in themselves rather than as means towards objectives.
>
> (Stenhouse, 1975, p. 84)

Stenhouse was emphatic that the intrinsic 'standards of excellence', which Peters links to the development of 'knowledge and understanding', could not be specified as 'objectives'. The term 'process objectives', used by some curriculum theorists, to refer to standards intrinsic to the learning process, was also misleading (1975, p. 39). In selecting content to exemplify 'the most important procedures, the key concepts and criteria and the areas and situations in which the criteria hold' (p. 85), one does not designate objectives to be learned by the students.

> For the key procedures, concepts and criteria in any subject – *cause, form, experiment, tragedy* – are, and are important precisely because they are, problematic within the subject. They are the focus of speculation, not the object of mastery. ... Educationally they are also important because they invite understanding at a variety of levels. ... It is the building of curriculum on such structures as procedures, concepts and criteria, which cannot adequately be translated into the performance levels of objectives, that makes possible Bruner's 'courteous translation' of knowledge and allows of learning which challenges all abilities and interests in a diverse group. ... The translation of the deep structures of knowledge into behavioral objectives is one of the principal causes of the distortion of knowledge in schools.
>
> (Stenhouse, 1975, pp. 85–86)

For Stenhouse, the dynamic nature of the procedural standards and principles that structure intrinsically worthwhile activities implies that they constitute *resources for thinking* about experience, and leave space for students' *individuality, creativity and imagination*. They structure thinking in ways which open rather than close the mind to new ways of interpreting the world. Stenhouse claims that 'the principles which obtain for knowledge within a field are problematic within that field' and therefore pedagogically should always be treated as 'provisional and open to debate'. This echoes Peters's view that procedural principles refer to both standards internal to an activity and the claims of individuals as learners participating in it.

I have argued elsewhere (Elliott, 1988, p. 51 and 1998, Ch. 2) that the translation of the structures of knowledge into objectives through the English National Curriculum was a considerable error, and has denied students in schools that 'courteous translation of knowledge' that is a condition of giving them equality of access to our cultural heritage. I predicted that it would result in widespread disaffection from schooling, and this now appears to be manifest, even to policymakers. The Secretary of State's proposals for revising the National Curriculum acknowledged that it 'was failing to engage a significant minority of 14–16 year olds, who were as a consequence becoming disaffected from learning' (see Elliott, 2000).

Stenhouse did not discount the appropriateness of an objectives model of curriculum design in particular contexts. He argues (1975, p. 80) that education in a broad sense is comprised of at least four different processes: *training, instruction, initiation,* and *induction.* Training is concerned with the acquisition of specific skills, such as speaking a foreign language or handling laboratory apparatus. The use of an objectives model in this context is quite appropriate, Stenhouse argues. Instruction is concerned with the retention of information, e.g. learning the table of chemical elements, dates in history, the names of countries, German irregular verbs, and cooking recipes. In this context too, the objectives model is appropriate. Contrary to Peters, Stenhouse views Initiation as 'familiarization with social values and norms' leading to a capacity 'to interpret the social environment'. As a process, it appropriately takes place as a by-product of living in a community and operates in schools as the 'hidden curriculum'. Induction, according to Stenhouse, appropriately describes the introduction of people to the thought systems of the culture and is concerned with developing their 'understanding'. This is 'evidenced by the capacity to grasp and to make for oneself relationships and judgments'. For Stenhouse, induction is at the core of any *educational process.* Within such a process, both training and instruction have important but subsidiary functions, for 'skills and information are often learned in the context of knowledge, which is, in one of its aspects, an organization of skills and information'. It follows that in designing an educationally worthwhile curriculum, there is a place for specifying objectives in terms of the information and skills to be learned. The danger, for Stenhouse, lies in extending its scope to include the most important aspect of education; namely, the process of inducting students into the thought systems of our culture. Its scope, he argues, should be confined to designing subordinate units within the curriculum that play a service role to the induction process.

One pedagogical implication of Stenhouse's account of the relationship between 'process' and 'objectives' models of curriculum design is that technical means–ends reasoning about the most *effective* and *efficient* training and instructional methods has a place, albeit a subsidiary one, in teachers' decisions about how to improve teaching and learning in an *educational* situation...

Stenhouse's idea of 'research-based teaching' is linked to a 'process model' of curriculum design. This, in turn, rests on the belief that the structures of knowledge into which students are to be inducted are intrinsically problematic and contestable, and therefore objects of speculation. This implies that teachers ought to cast themselves in the role of learners alongside their students. Stenhouse argues (1975, p. 91) that:

> Either the teacher must be an expert or he must be a learner along with his students. In most cases the teacher cannot in the nature of the case be the expert. It follows that he must cast himself in the role of a learner. Pedagogically this may in fact be a preferable role to that of the expert. It implies teaching by discovery or inquiry methods.

For Stenhouse, the teacher who casts him or herself in the role of a learner alongside his or her students must have 'some hold on, and a continual refinement of, a philosophical understanding of the subject he is teaching and learning, of its deep structures and rationale' (1975, p. 91). It is this depth of understanding in relation to the subject matter that makes the teacher into a learner with something to offer to students; namely, a research stance towards the content they teach. From such a stance, they model how to treat knowledge as an object of inquiry. Stenhouse argues that a teacher who casts him or herself in the role of expert, representing knowledge as *authoritative* and therefore beyond doubt and speculation, is misrepresenting and distorting that knowledge. His major objection to the use of the 'objectives model' to map learning in the fields of knowledge is that it reinforces authoritative teaching, and in the process compounds error. This argument was most developed in his *Inaugural Lecture* at the University of East Anglia entitled '*Research as a basis for teaching*' (1979), and subsequently published in a posthumous collection of his essays (1983). In it, he argued that:

> No teacher of normal endowments can teach authoritatively without lending his authority to errors of fact or of judgment. But my case goes deeper than that. Were the teacher able to avoid this, he would, in teaching knowledge as authoritative, be teaching an unacceptable proposition about the nature of knowledge: that its warrant is to be found in the appeal to the expertise of persons rather than in the appeal to rational justification in the light of evidence. I believe that most teaching in schools and a good deal in universities promotes that error. The schooled reveal themselves as uneducated when they look towards knowledge for the reassurance of authoritative certainty rather than for the adventure of speculative understanding.
>
> (1979, p. 6, mimeo)

For Stenhouse, *research-based teaching* is an implication of a theory of education that places induction into knowledge structures at its centre, and then characterises them as *objects for speculative thought*. This theory of education implies a logical framework for a teaching and learning process. At the centre of this framework is a pedagogical aim that he characterises in the following terms:

> to develop an understanding of the problem of the nature of knowledge through an exploration of the provenance and warrant of the particular knowledge we encounter in our field of study.
>
> (1979, p. 7)

As an aim for all learners, Stenhouse was aware that some would doubt its realism. However, anything less would consign many children to a permanent condition of educational disadvantage, for 'we are talking about the insight which raises mere competence and possession of information to intellectual power of a kind which can emancipate'. Such an aim, for Stenhouse, implied certain procedural values and principles governing methods of teaching and learning, e.g. 'inquiry' or 'discovery' learning, and 'teaching through discussion'. 'Research-based teaching' can also be regarded as a procedural principle implied by the aim, inasmuch as it characterises the personal stance to knowledge the teacher must adopt in support of the other principles of procedure.

As I indicated earlier, Stenhouse did not view his methodology of induction to be incompatible with instruction. He argues that in order to cover the curriculum, we need instruction and 'text-books too'. The key to the relationship between, say, 'discovery' or 'discussion' methods and instruction, he argues, lies in the pedagogical aim.

> The crucial difference is between an educated and an uneducated use of instruction. The educated use of instruction is skeptical, provisional, speculative in temper. The uneducated use mistakes information for knowledge. Information is not knowledge until the factor of error, limitation or crudity in it is appropriately estimated, and it is assimilated to structures of thinking... which give us the means of understanding.
>
> (1979, p. 8)

Stenhouse was concerned to transform teaching in the state educational system from a system in which the great majority of children experienced their teacher as *an authority* on the content of education to one in which the teacher was *in authority* with respect to the process of *education* and the maintenance of procedures that are consistent with his or her pedagogical aim as an educator. This involved inquiry in particular contexts into how to effect such a transformation in practice.

He cast the problem in a form that turned it into an agenda for *educational* research:

> The problem is how to design a practicable pattern of teaching which maintains authority, leadership and the responsibility of the teacher, but does not carry the message that such authority is the warrant of knowledge.
>
> (1979, p. 7)

The major task of educational research is to show how teaching and learning can be made more *educational*. For Stenhouse, such research produced *actionable evidence* as a basis for teaching, but included evidence of a rather different kind to that envisaged by Hargreaves. It is evidence that is relevant to the problem of how to make the concrete activities of teaching and learning more *ethically consistent* with the criteria that define what it means to become educated (e.g. those cited by Peters). Evidence that is relevant to simply making teaching and learning a more effective and efficient process for the production of specific learning outputs is not sufficient as a basis for inducting students into the deep structures of knowledge. Indeed, the ethical requirements of the latter may impose limits on the strategies the teacher employs to secure specific instructional or training outputs.

Educational research of the kind Stenhouse envisages, as a basis for teaching, implies a similar stance from the teacher to the one he describes in relation to his or her subject matter:

> Just as research in history or literature or chemistry can provide a basis for teaching those subjects, so educational research can provide a basis for teaching and learning about teaching. Professional skill and understanding can be the subject of doubt, that is of knowledge, and hence of research.
>
> (1979, p. 18)

Stenhouse's view of educational research implies *doing* research as an integral part of the role of the teacher, just as a teacher who *uses* research into their subject as a basis for teaching implies that s(he) *does* research into the subject *through* teaching it. In this respect, both dimensions of research-based teaching are similarly conceptualised in terms of their relationship to educational practice. Neither implies that research, whether it be in history or education, can only be carried out by 'insiders' who are actively engaged in educational practice. However, for Stenhouse *educational* research does imply that 'outsiders' engaged in such research need to collaborate with educational practitioners. His reasons for this are clearly stated. *Educational* research is a form of *action research*, and this means that:

> real classrooms have to be our laboratories, and they are in the command of teachers, not of researchers...the research act must conform to the obligations of the professional context. This is what we mean by action research. It is a pattern of research in which experimental or research acts cannot be exempted from the demand for justification by professional as well as by research criteria. The teacher cannot learn by inquiry without undertaking that the pupils learn too; the physician cannot experiment without attempting to heal. ...Such a view of educational research declares that the theory or insights created in collaboration by professional researchers and professional teachers, is always provisional, always to be taught in a spirit of inquiry, and always to be tested and modified by professional practice.
>
> (1979, p. 20)

Stenhouse would agree with Hargreaves about the limitations of an 'enlightenment model' of educational research. He argues (1979, p. 18) against 'the received doctrine' that 'has been at the core of education for teaching' since the 1950s; namely, that it should be based 'in the findings of research in the "contributory disciplines" of philosophy, psychology and sociology'. Stenhouse proposes an alternative to the constituent disciplines approach, which was 'to treat education itself – teaching, learning, running schools and educational systems – as the subject of research' (see also Elliott, 1978). In this respect, Hargreaves appears to echo Stenhouse in a common aspiration for educational research to directly inform the concrete activities of education rather than studying them for the contribution they can make to the development of theory within a particular discipline. However, as I have indicated, their ideas about what constitutes *actionable evidence* from research are somewhat different.

Stenhouse claims that his alternative proposal does not imply a neglect of the disciplines, because research in education draws eclectically upon them, particularly with respect to 'methods of inquiry and analysis together with such concepts as have utility for a theory of education'. In relation to the very last point, I have attempted to show how Stenhouse's idea of 'research-based teaching' is informed by Peters's theory of education as a process. What distinguishes his idea from Hargreaves's idea of 'evidence-based teaching' is that 'what counts as evidence' is not simply evidence about the instrumental effectiveness of the strategies employed to secure certain learning outcomes, but evidence about the extent to which teaching strategies are ethically consistent with *educational* ends. What characterises Stenhouse's view of educational research is its focus on the problems of realising a form of teaching in particular contexts of professional practice. He writes:

> The problems selected for inquiry are selected because of their importance as educational problems; that is, for their significance in the context of professional practice. Research and development guided by such problems will contribute primarily to the understanding of educational action through the construction of theory of education or a tradition of understanding. Only secondarily will research in this mode contribute to philosophy, psychology or sociology.
>
> (1979, p. 19)

Here Stenhouse is alluding to the inseparability of developing a theoretical understanding of educational action and doing educational research into the practical problems of education. If educational research focuses on the problems which arise in trying to realise a form of *educational* practice, then it will pose questions both about which actions in the context are constitutive of such a practice and about the educational criteria employed in deciding this. Educational research, on Stenhouse's account, is a process which involves the joint development of educational practice and theory in interaction.

[...]

Concluding remarks

In this chapter, David Hargreaves' ideas, about the nature of 'evidence-based practice' and the future direction for educational research, have been explored in the light of the linked work of Richard Peters, on the aims of education, and of Lawrence Stenhouse, on curriculum design and 'research-based teaching'. This has involved revisiting a body of once influential thinking about the nature of education and educational research respectively. If the tone of this article, with respect to this work, has been expository rather than critical, it can be justified in terms of the need to produce a largely descriptive account of a neglected system of thought. It then becomes accessible to further critique and development. Educational theory should be dynamic rather than static.

Central to both Peters' and Stenhouse's work is a view about the relationship between educational aims and processes, which is neglected in Hargreaves' account of the role of educational research in informing educational practice. The explanation appears to lie in Hargreaves' unquestioning commitment to an outcomes-based view of education. I have tried to show how Stenhouse drew on Peters's educational theory to construct a comprehensive view of *educational* research as 'research-based teaching'.

[...]

What is lacking in the contemporary discourse about the future direction and practical utility of educational research is any consideration of the contribution of educational and curriculum theory to conceptualising its aims and processes. The current discourse is uninformed by any theory about the nature of *educational* practice, and therefore excludes any consideration of the implications of such a theory for educational research. In rectifying this situation, we could make a beginning by revisiting the work of Richard Peters and Lawrence Stenhouse. This article is a contribution to that 'beginning'. In drawing attention to work that shaped 'a new direction' for both teaching and learning *and* educational research in the recent past, I have tried to demonstrate that its potential, as a resource to draw on in conceptualising links for the future, has not yet been exhausted.

References

Bloom, B.S. (Ed.) (1956) *Taxonomy of Educational Objectives I. Cognitive Domain* (London, Longmans).

Bloom, B.S. (1971) Mastery learning, in: J.H. Block (Ed.) *Mastery Learning: theory and practice* (New York, Holt, Rinehart & Winston).

Ebbutt, D. and Elliott, J. (Eds) (1985) *Issues in Teaching for Understanding* (London, Longmans/Schools Curriculum Development Committee [SCDC]).

Elliott, J. (1976–1977) 'Developing Hypotheses about classrooms from teachers' practical constructs: an account of the work of the Ford Teaching Project', *Interchange*, 7(2). Toronto, OISE.

Elliott, J. (1978) Classroom Research: science or commonsense, in: R. McAleese and D. Hamilton (Eds) *Understanding Classroom Life* (Slough, National Foundation for Educational Research).

Elliott, J. (1988) The state v education: the challenge for teachers, in: H. Simons (Ed.) *The National Curriculum*, pp. 46–62 (London, British Educational Research Association).

Elliott, J. (1989) Teacher evaluation and teaching as a moral science, in: M.L.Holly and C.S. McLouchlin (Eds) *Perspectives on Teacher Professional Development* (London, Falmer Press).

Elliott, J. (1991) *Action Research for Educational Change* (Buckingham, Open University Press).

Elliott, J. (1998) *The Curriculum Experiment: meeting the challenge of social change* (Buckingham, Open University Press).

Elliott, J. (2000) Revising the National Curriculum: a comment on the Secretary of State's proposals, *Journal of Education Policy*, 15, p. 248.

Elliott, J. and MacDonald, B. (Eds) (1975) *People in Classrooms*, CARE Occasional Publications no. 2 (Norwich, University of East Anglia).

Ford Teaching Project (1974) *Implementing the Principles of Inquiry/Discovery Teaching* (Norwich, Ford Teaching Project Publications, University of East Anglia).

Hammersley, M. (1997) Educational research and teaching: a response to David Hargreaves's TTA Lecture, *British Educational Research Journal*, 23, pp. 141–161.

Hargreaves, D. (1996) Teaching as a research-based profession: possibilities and prospects, Teacher Training Agency Annual Lecture (London, Teacher Training Agency).

Hargreaves, D. (1997) In defence of research for evidence-based teaching: a rejoinder to Martyn Hammersley, *British Educational Research Journal*, 23, pp. 405–419.

Hargreaves, D. (1999) *Revitalizing educational research: lessons from the past and proposals for the future*, Cambridge Journal of Education, 29, pp. 239–249.

MacIntyre, A. (1981) *After Virtue: a study in moral theory*, 2nd edn 1985, pp. 88–108 (London, Duckworth).

Peters, R.S. (1966) *Ethics and Education*, pp. 23–45 (London, Allen & Unwin).

Peters, R.S. (1973) Aims of education – a conceptual inquiry, in: R.S. Peters (Ed.) *The Philosophy of Education*, Oxford Readings in Philosophy, pp. 11–57 (Oxford, Oxford University Press).

Stenhouse, L. (1970a) Some limitations of the use of objectives in curriculum research and planning, *Paedagogica Europaea*, 6, pp. 73–83.

Stenhouse, L. (1970b) The Humanities Curriculum Project: the rationale, *Theory into Practice*, 10, pp. 154–162.

Stenhouse, L. (1975) *An Introduction to Curriculum Research and Development* (London, Heineman).

Stenhouse, L. (1977) *Problems and Effects of Teaching about Race Relations*, a report to the Social Science Research Council on Project HR 2001/1 (Lodged in the British Library).

Stenhouse, L. (1979) 'Research as a Basis for Teaching', Inaugural Lecture at the University of East Anglia, Norwich. Subsequently published in L. Stenhouse (1983) *Authority, Education and Emancipation* (London, Heinemann).

Stenhouse, L., Verma, G., Wild, R. and Nixon, J. (1979) *Problems and Effects of Teaching about Race Relations* (London, Ward Lock).

CHAPTER 9

USING RESEARCH TO IMPROVE PRACTICE

The notion of evidence-based practice

International Handbook on the Continuing Professional Development of Teachers
(eds) C. Day and J. Sachs, Open University Press: Maidenhead, 2004

Introduction

Within the UK the Teacher Training Agency (TTA) played a major role, during the final years of the twentieth century, in constructing a new discourse about the professional development of teachers. Central to this discourse is the idea of *teaching as an evidence-based profession*. In this respect the agency initiated schemes to provide grants to teachers for carrying out small-scale research projects, and disseminated the findings of selected research studies they undertook for Masters degrees and PhDs. It established a National Teachers Panel to represent the voice of teachers as users of educational research. From 1997 the agency funded four pilot research consortia to promote teachers' engagement with research in Leeds, Manchester, Newcastle and Norwich. The consortia consisted of partnerships between schools, local education authorities, and higher education institutions. The broad focus of each consortium was on pedagogical practice in classrooms, and the strategic goal that under-pinned this focus was that of raising the educational achievements of students.

From the TTA's perspective (see TTA, 1998) too little educational research in the recent past had focused on teaching and learning in schools, or involved teachers in utilising and disseminating its findings. It argued that educational research "has avoided this and tackled less challenging aspects of the educational system." The agency was quite explicit about its aspiration to exercise more influence over the funding of educational research, and to ensure that it became focused on pedagogy. It claimed to have influenced the deployment of substantial Higher Education Funding Council funds to establish the 'Teaching and Learning' Research Initiative (see TTA, 1998) under the administration of the Economic and Social Research Council (ESRC). Indeed, the National Teachers Panel became involved in reviewing, on behalf of the 'users' of research, proposals to the ESRC 'Teaching and Learning' programme from university-based researchers.

More recently the task of reshaping educational research to provide a basis for the development of teaching as an evidence-based practice has been taken up directly by the Department for Education and Skills (DFES), following the publication of the Hillier Report (1998) into the state of educational research within the UK. The crisis in the UK surrounding teacher recruitment and supply also led to the DFES asking the TTA to focus on this as its core business, while the department took more responsibility for steering initiatives linked to the Continuing Professional Development of Teachers (CPD). The Teacher Research Grant Scheme was re-created as the DFES Best Practice Scholarships, and the Research Consortia laid the foundations for the Networked Learning Communities Initiative administered through the National College for School Leadership (NCSL).

There are two broad interpretations of UK government initiatives to promote teaching as an evidence-based profession. The first interpretation (I shall refer to the second later) is that they are simply trying to ensure that educational research produces findings that are relevant and useful to teachers in their efforts to improve classroom practice. This, of course, implies greater regulatory control over how educational knowledge is constructed and used, but control that can be justified in terms of constructing a knowledge-base to empower teachers as professionals. Although such an interpretation has been widely espoused within the TTA and the DFES, it will be endorsed by many teachers who dismiss educational research as high on theory and low on practicality.

Indeed, many academic educational researchers in the UK, Europe and USA over the past thirty years, including this author, have expressed concern about the fact that teachers rarely use the findings of research *on* education to inform their practice. We tended to argue that in order to engage teachers *with* research it was necessary to engage them *in* a form of research that addressed and sought to ameliorate the practical problems they experienced in their particular contexts of action (see, e.g., Stenhouse, 1975, 1979; Elliott, 1978, 1991; Carr and Kemmis, 1986). It was out of this internal critique of the credibility and relevance of much educational research for teachers that the practitioner action research movement emerged, with its emphasis on teachers as active participants working alongside academic researchers to actively construct useful knowledge (see, e.g., Elliott and Adelman (Eds), 1974; Elliott and MacDonald (Eds), 1975; Elliott, 1976–77; Ebbutt and Elliott (Eds), 1985; Hustler and Cuff (Eds), 1986; Sanger, 1989; Hollingsworth and Sockett (Eds), 1994; O'Hanlon (Ed.), 1996; Altrichter, 1997; Hollingsworth (Ed.), 1997; Somekh, 2000; Day *et al.* (Eds), 2002; Elliott and Zamorski, 2002; O'Hanlon, 2002). Such collaboration implied that teachers not only engaged in the activities of gathering, analysing and interpreting evidence but had a voice in what counted as credible and relevant evidence to gather in the first place.

However, in recent years some educational researchers in the UK, notably David Hargreaves (1996, 1997, 1999) and David Reynolds (1998), have argued for a reshaping of educational research to provide more useful and relevant evidence to teachers in a form that neither presumes (a) that teachers need to do research in order to use it, nor (b) that what counts as relevant and useful evidence is sufficiently contestable for teachers to have a say about. For these academics the problem of developing teaching as an evidence-based practice is one of reshaping educational research to produce the right kind of knowledge, and then ensuring that it is easily accessible to teachers.

For Hargreaves, priority should be given in educational research to the production of evidence that yields actionable knowledge of 'what works', which he defines in a purely instrumental sense. He argues that:

> research should provide decisive and conclusive evidence that if teachers do X rather than Y in their professional practice, there will be a significant and enduring improvement in outcome.
>
> (1997, p. 412)

Such evidence will largely be couched in terms of statistical probabilities gathered through experimental trials.

The discourse of evidence-based practice promoted by various government initiatives is often perceived to stem from rationales for a reinstatement of a quantitative paradigm of educational research provided by David Hargreaves and David Reynolds at their Annual Lectures to the TTA in 1996 and 1998 respectively, rather than from rationales for teachers' engagement *in* research provided by Stenhouse (1975, 1979) and other like-minded academics in the field of education. Hargreaves is one of the main architects of the government sponsored National Educational Research Forum established after the publication of the Hillier Report. Also, the establishment at the Institute of Education in the University of London of a national co-ordinating centre for the production of systematic reviews of educational research (EPPI-Centre) to facilitate evidence-based policy and practice is likely to reinforce the future dominance of quantitative experimental studies of the kind advocated by Hargreaves and Reynolds (see Hammersley, 2002; Oakley, A., 2000, 2002).

In spite of the role of academics like Hargreaves and Reynolds in shaping the terms of the discourse of evidence-based practice, two rather different 'trajectories of meaning' are circulating in the UK policy context. Another but less dominant trajectory implies that, in order to use research, teachers need to be engaged *in* researching their own practices within their particular action contexts. This does not mean that the only useful research evidence for teachers is that which they generate. It does, however, imply that in order to make good use of evidence it must be deemed credible to teachers as a basis for researching their own situated practices. It further implies that such credibility will depend on the extent to which teachers are able to exercise a significant measure of control over methodology through their active participation in designing educational research projects and programmes, e.g. in relation to what is to count as useful and relevant evidence about their practices. The more dominant 'trajectory of meaning' at the present time does not imply that teachers as a profession should be actively engaged in research at the level of their own classrooms and schools. However, it does sanction the idea of more 'user' involvement in the design of 'practically relevant' research projects and programmes, although this appears to fall short of giving teachers a significant voice on questions of research methodology.

Hargreaves' definition of what counts as relevant and useful evidence for teachers appears to positively feed a second broad interpretation of government initiatives as an attempt to co-opt teachers into a strictly instrumental view of practically relevant educational knowledge, and thereby disconnect it from fundamental questions about the ends of education in the wider society (see Elliott and Doherty, 2001; Elliott, 2002). This second interpretation will tend to be associated with academic critiques of Hargreaves' account of evidence-based practice (e.g., Hammersley, 1997; Lomax, 1999; Elliott and Doherty, 2001; Elliott, 2002).

It would be a mistake, however, to view government policy initiatives as unambiguously reflecting one 'trajectory of meaning' for evidence-based practice to the exclusion of the other. Although the policy discourse tends to be dominated by the framing provided by academic consultants like Hargreaves and Reynolds, the policy initiatives in practice embody conflictual tendencies at the heart of which stand the issues surrounding teachers' engagement with research, as outlined above.

The DFES 'Best Practice Scholarships' endorse teachers' engagement in researching their own practices while, at the same time, appearing to require a measure of compliance to a procedural framework that makes presumptions about what constitutes relevant and useful evidence, e.g., in terms of the significance of standardised measures of learning outcomes. The TTA Research Consortium Initiative in practice embodied a tension between the two trajectories of meaning referred to. This created space for lively debates about the conceptualisation of the process of engaging teachers with research evidence. The issues have now been inherited by the Networked Learning Communities Initiative.

It could be argued that the conflicting 'trajectories of meaning' embedded in the implementation of policies to effect evidence-based teaching, have very different sources, such that the 'dominant' trajectory stems from the policy context while the counter-oppositional position stems from the contexts of implementation: the collaborating school and higher education systems. In the experience of this author, as the co-ordinator of one of the former TTA Consortia, this is an over simplified explanation. The two 'trajectories of meaning' at tension with each other appeared to be constructed and sustained through networks of affiliation that cut across so-called 'interest groups'; schoolteachers, LEA officials, HE-based researchers, and government officials (see Elliott, 1999). How then do we best understand the practical intentions which underpin policy initiatives to promote evidence-based practice?

1   As an attempt to empower teachers by giving them more access to relevant and useful evidence about their practices, and by implication to limit the epistemic control exercised by much HE-based educational research.

2   As an attempt to disempower teachers by controlling their thinking about what is to count as relevant and useful evidence, and thereby restricting their access to knowledge of a particular kind; namely, to knowledge that is instrumentally useful as a basis for driving-up externally defined standards.

This author is of the view that these initiatives embody both intentions and are sustained at tension with each other through their respective interpersonal networks of affiliation that cut across 'interest groups' (see Brennan and Noffke, 2000). This is not to deny that one intentionality dominates the policy context but, as policy interacts with practice, spaces are opened up in both the policy and implementation contexts for the other intentionality to gain a measure of leverage, and thereby render the discourse of evidence-based practice inherently unstable.

It was the spaces created by the tension within the discourse itself that enabled the TTA Research Consortia to explore the issues surrounding the problem of engaging teachers with research. What follows is an examination of these issues in the context of the Norwich Area Schools Consortium (NASC).

Engaging teachers *in* and *with* research: the experience of NASC

Teachers researching the issue: what counts as credible evidence?

The overall focus of the Norwich Area Research Consortium was on the 'pedagogical dimensions of student disaffection from learning'. This focus shaped the kind of evidence that was considered to be relevant; namely evidence about the relationship between disaffection as a phenomenon that teachers encountered in their classrooms on a daily basis and the pedagogical strategies they employed. Moreover, following discussions with headteachers before the research got underway 'disaffection' was broadly defined as 'disengagement from learning' to include the 'quietly disaffected' in addition to students who manifested their disaffection more obviously through disrupting lessons and truanting.

This broad definition raised issues early on in the project about what counted as evidence of disaffection from learning and the validity of teachers' inferences from patterns of student behaviour in classroom settings. If disaffection is to be entertained as a possible outcome of the operation of pedagogical factors, or even a partial one inasmuch as other factors are also implicated, then what evidence can be trusted as a basis for identifying it? Can it be operationally defined in terms of an agreed set of behavioural indicators? What about the quietly disaffected whose condition is not obvious to their teachers, and who in behavioural terms appear to be playing the learning game? On what reliable evidential basis can one identify such students?

Given this context, some of the Phase 1 research projects initiated by teachers within their schools addressed these methodological issues quite explicitly. Those engaged in such projects were sometimes reluctant to regard them as anything more than exploratory investigations, or even to call them 'research'. They tended to use different approaches to exploring the question 'what counts as credible evidence?' Two examples will be provided below (for detailed accounts of some of the NASC research studies see Elliott and Zamorski, 2002).

Example One. Staff in one school embarked on a piece of survey research in an attempt to discover an agreed set of behavioural indicators as a basis for selecting a research sample of disengaged students (see Gutteridge, 2002). They discovered a lack of any high level of agreement on the majority of the indicators listed in the questionnaire and concluded that disengagement from learning manifested itself behaviourally in different ways for different students and was bound strongly to particular curriculum and teaching contexts. Interestingly this project was initiated at a meeting when a teacher circulated a list of personal behavioural indicators he tacitly employed to intuitively identify a disaffected student. The list generated considerable discussion in which other teachers produced counter instances and conflicting behavioural evidence. As a result the teacher, who was the overall co-ordinator for research in the school, circulated his list to all members of staff, asking them to reflect about the behavioural indicators they tacitly employed and to add any not included on his list. The final list was then used as a basis for constructing the questionnaire.

Example Two. In another school, teachers embarked on a study of students they called RHINOs (Really Here In Name Only) based on an intuitive belief that significant numbers of underachieving students were quietly coasting through lessons 'invisible' to their teachers (see Oakley, J., 2002). In undertaking this study, they soon encountered the problem of what counted as credible or trustworthy evidence for identifying these 'quietly disaffected' students. They discovered, from interviewing teachers, that annual assessments of students' achievements in relation to estimates of their potential were unreliable as a basis for identifying underachievement and possible RHINOs. The teachers concluded that a combination of observational evidence, which focused on the classroom behaviour of particular individual students, combined with in-depth follow-up interviews with them, generated the credible evidence for identifying RHINOs. They also concluded, on the basis of their observations and interviews, that the existence of RHINOs appeared to be linked to poor learning environments in particular classroom settings. This study tended to confirm the intuitive beliefs which it was set up to test, and had school-wide implications for identifying under-achievers and improving the quality of learning environments in classrooms.

Evidence and intuition

Both the above examples illustrate a form of hypothesis-testing which originates from teachers reflecting about the evidential basis of their intuitive judgments, and then seeking to test their judgments against systematically gathered evidence. In this context, evidence is perceived to be credible by teachers if it informs and educates, rather than simply displaces, their intuitions.

This does not imply that evidence only becomes credible if it confirms teachers' intuitive beliefs (prejudices). The outcomes can be counter-intuitive as the following example demonstrates.

Modern Foreign Language (MFL) teachers in one school were experiencing significant numbers of disruptive students in their lessons and frequent absenteeism from them. They believed that the major cause of their problem lay in parental attitudes to the value of learning a modern foreign language. Disaffection from their lessons was a parentally condoned phenomenon. The teachers decided on reflection to turn their intuitive belief into a research hypothesis and test it through a survey of parental attitudes to MFL. The outcome of the research was counter-intuitive. The majority of the parents surveyed expressed a positive attitude to their children learning a modern foreign language. As a result the teachers began to focus their attention on factors operating inside their classroom.

The proposition that teachers do not have to have their beliefs confirmed in order to find research evidence credible is highly consistent with Kennedy's US study (1999) of the ways teachers evaluate different kinds of research evidence. When presented with examples of different genres of research '*only a small fraction of teachers said that either of these studies was persuasive because their own experiences reinforced the study's findings*'. Kennedy found that most of the research that teachers found persuasive and relevant to their practice also provoked new thinking on their part.

The role of teachers in determining what counts as evidence about their practices

Kennedy's study is also relevant to the issue, long debated within the educational research community, about whether teachers need to do research in order to meaningfully engage with it. The study appears to confirm the view that teachers can meaningfully engage with research without necessarily having to do research as some methodologists have tended to argue. An initial reading would suggest that teachers' engagement in research is not a necessary condition for evidence to become credible in their eyes, although it may be the case that in certain contexts teachers are more likely to find evidence credible if they are involved in its generation. Such involvement can range from fully participative studies, such as those cited in the above examples, through collaborative research between outsider researchers and teachers, to 'outsider research' that consults teachers at particular points. Research projects in NASC varied in these respects.

The following is an example of research led by an outsider (see Doherty and Elliott, 1999; Doherty, 2001, 2002) but which engaged teachers in the process at particular points. It is cited at this point to further illuminate the relationship between teachers' intuitive beliefs and their perceptions of what constitutes 'credible evidence'. It suggests that for teachers to find externally generated evidence credible and trustworthy they may need a context which enables them to examine it in the light of their own reflections about the evidential basis of their intuitive judgments.

In one school all the staff met for half a day to consider questionnaire evidence of students' classroom and school experiences. Three groups of students had collaborated with a UEA researcher in designing this questionnaire. The researcher invited the teachers to discuss and challenge '*the main findings*' contained in three summary reports in the light of their own experience. In responding, teachers drew on the evidential basis of their own intuitive judgments and rendered them increasingly explicit, as well as recalling research they were familiar with that either confirmed or challenged the findings reported. By the end of the meeting, staff had collectively assembled clusters of evidence around the main findings from the questionnaire which generated further questions to be addressed and hypotheses to be tested through research in the school and its classrooms. In retrospect the researcher used the phrase '*data poles*' to describe the function the reports of the questionnaire findings he introduced into the meeting unintentionally served. In doing so he found himself drawing an analogy with the functions of 'poles' in directing the flow of radioactivity in a nuclear reactor. By the end of the meeting his reports had become somewhat dispensable, he argued, because in the process the teachers provisionalised and problematised the evidence they contained in the light of their experience and other research evidence they were aware of. In this way the evidence contained in the reports was incorporated into a 'wider evidence framework' constructed through the discussion, and now owned collectively by the staff as a common stock of professional knowledge.

Evidence only appeared to become credible to the teachers cited in the example above through contexts of reflection that enabled them to claim ownership over it, in the sense of making it part of the 'frame of reference' they employed in their everyday professional judgments. If this point is generalisable beyond the school depicted above then it suggests that, in teachers' encounters with evidence, there may need to be:

> an examination of the implications of evidence for action in an open and equal forum, as a precursor to the collection of evidence or accompanying the suggestion of changes in practice based upon it.
>
> (Doherty and Elliott, 1999)

Such a forum would not simply provide a context for disseminating research findings to a passive audience. It would be integral to a research process that actively engages teachers in knowledge creation. Through it teachers are enabled to define what counts as credible and useful/relevant evidence rather than having it defined for them.

Kennedy's interview study may also be understood on a 'second reading' as providing a context in which teachers do not simply engage with evidence but, in doing so, become engaged in researching their own practice. She presents her findings as if their validity is independent of the context she creates for teachers to engage with the research they are asked to read. She assumes that teachers' judgments that a particular piece of research is plausible and relevant do not mirror qualities that are inherent in the study itself. I would argue that they are the outcome of an inquiry the teachers undertake within the context of her study into the connection between the evidence presented and their own teaching practices. In this sense teachers' engagement with research does indeed depend on them researching their practice, at least in a minimal sense. It is not a matter of teachers straightforwardly *applying* the findings from other people's research to their own practices. This would presume that the credibility and usefulness of such findings had been independently established prior to teachers engaging with them. One wonders how many of Kennedy's teachers would have come to value some of the studies they read if she had not provided a context that enabled them to use them as a resource for inquiring into their practices.

The discussion of the possible implications of the example of outsider-led research described above suggests that the distinction between engaging teachers *with* and *in* research may pose a false dichotomy. Its usefulness presumes a context in which universities have traditionally exercised hierarchical and bureaucratic control over what is to count as knowledge about educational practice in schools. As Hollingsworth and Sockett (1994, Ch. 1) summarise this legacy "Scientific conclusions are discovered by university researchers, tested in the Heraclitan fire of the refereed journal, and handed down to efficient classroom technicians". It is only in a context where teachers are being expected to passively implement the findings of outsider research that the contrast between engaging teachers *in* and *with* research has much point.

Since the TTA's initiative in establishing four research consortia can be interpreted as an attempt to reconstitute the relationship between universities and schools in a form that gives teachers greater control over what is to count as knowledge about their practices, then the example of outsider-led research in NASC, cited above, may itself constitute some evidence of its effectiveness in this respect (as also would the Phase 2 cross-school research on 'Rewards and Sanctions' and 'Classroom Management', since it was in many respects led by UEA-based researchers). However, as described earlier, the idea of evidence-based practice that underpins the rationale for the TTA consortia itself became the subject of debate within the educational research community (see Hargreaves, 1996, 1997; Hammersley, 1997; Reynolds, 1998; Elliott, 1999, 2002; Elliott and Doherty, 2001). One strand of this debate has been the issue of whether the idea is being used to legitimate the erosion rather than strengthening of teachers' judgments as a basis for action in classrooms. In this context there may still be some point in drawing a distinction between teachers' engagement *in* and *with* research to counteract a tendency to interpret the latter as a passive stance to evidence.

Evidence, context, and the complexity of teaching

Although the student questionnaire, referred to earlier, was constructed by the students themselves with the support of an external researcher, this also involved detailed discussions with key members of staff in the school to ensure that teachers' concerns were also being addressed. Much of the evidence generated by educational research is ignored because it fails to match teachers' concerns. Again Kennedy's study (1999) is illuminating in this respect. She found that what makes evidence credible or plausible to teachers is that it helps them to make sense of the complex triangular relationship between teaching, learning and subject matter in their classrooms. Different genres of research – experiments, surveys, case studies and narratives – can be of equal value if they help teachers deepen their understanding of the complexity of this relationship. If they fail to address this concern, teachers find little value in them. The studies which teachers found to be of little value '*each addressed only one or another corner of the triangle connecting teachers, subject matter, and learners'*. The provision of student performance data was not viewed by teachers as particularly useful. They found it difficult to interpret *'without more knowledge of what these students' teachers were doing'*.

This may explain why teachers involved in NASC displayed less interest in externally generated data sets that focused exclusively on student performance. They found it difficult to use this data to make sense of the complexities of life in their classrooms. Giving teachers more control over the design of research generally and the questions it asks may increase the possibility that the complexity of teaching and learning as they experience it is addressed. This is very well exemplified by Zamorski and Haydn (2002) in their account of teachers' participation in the design of NASC's cross-school 'classroom management' research at the beginning of Phase 2 of the programme.

In the course of their Phase 1 investigations, many teachers became more aware of disaffection as a context-bound phenomenon which manifested itself in particular learning environments rather than others. They also became more aware of the variety of ways in which different students manifested their disaffection behaviourally in the same learning environment.

> I find every student is so different, and what one person is manifesting can be a very obvious thing, just an attitude where they are not going to work... with other students it can be so different... even as simple as trying to get you into conversation about something completely outside the subject and in that sense trying to distract you from teaching them because they are trying to avoid work.
>
> (teacher researcher)

The Phase 1 projects, and the reports on them, revealed the value teachers perceived in gathering evidence of students' perceptions and interpretations of life in classrooms, either through interviews or questionnaire surveys or both. Observational evidence was also important but, alone, was generally not regarded as sufficient. Participating teachers tended to attribute great importance to understanding the reasons why individual students became disaffected from learning in particular lessons. When asked what kind of evidence they found useful the following responses were not untypical:

> Listening to them telling us why they are disaffected if we could do that. Finding the reasons why they are disaffected.

> ...talking to children. The amount of insight we got...in half an hour...You would think 'Well, this person is underachieving, why...? They were shy initially, but once you hit upon the key issue. The key issues were different for everyone...we got loads and loads of stuff...lesson observations have been good but all that has been able to confirm is 'Yes, this is a (quietly) disaffected child and they behave in this way. The patterns in which they behave are quite similar...The reasons behind the behaviours are all unique. That's what you need to know. You can identify the fact that that child is underachieving but [need] to find out why.

> I have been happy with what I have done because the part of research that I was involved in was with one of my year 10 English groups and it has improved my rapport with them, it has improved my understanding of them.

> I think it has made them feel valued and I think it will probably lead to an improvement in their grades. But I think that's a side thing. I think that has come out of talking to them. I think it's like any good teacher. If we had more time to talk to pupils we would get better results and because we allocate a time to talk to them because of the research I think that is paying off. In terms of ideas about RHINOs I think it does raise issues – it has made me look a bit more at what is happening.

Some teachers, including the last one quoted, were ambiguous about whether the evidence elicited by talking to individual children and the insights they gained as a result constituted proper research. They saw such evidence-gathering activity as an integral component of 'good teaching' rather than something that was confined to a separate activity called research with its own distinctive aims and purposes. It is interesting that the last teacher quoted saw the value of the insights he gained and its pay-off for his teaching as spin-offs from the research rather than part of its central purpose. The reason for this appears to lie in the belief that proper research should yield generalisable findings about the relationship between teaching and learning, that have clear practical implications. While the teacher in question valued the insights he personally gained from talking to individual children, he was less certain that he had produced any useful 'research outcomes'.

> I'm a bit afraid of generalising...I would generalise about boys being more likely to be RHINOs and teachers being wary of confrontation and therefore enabling this to go on. .... I wouldn't say that arising out of the research I had thought 'Gosh, if I did this, this would be better'.

However, in talking to individual students and asking them why they experienced disaffection in particular learning environments, other teachers began to question the value of research aimed at discovering pedagogical solutions that could be generalised to populations of students.

> ...the other thing I did was talk to pupils in general about their learning and I think what I found was...they are all individually very different...it's very easy to come up with general strategies...we are sort of throwing strategies at whole class situations or whole school situations whereas what we really should be looking at is smaller events and individual pupils...there's never a dialogue about learning or teaching or why they don't learn.

From this perspective, credible research evidence emerged from the detailed study of particular cases. Given sufficient time the tension between the two perspectives on what counted as credible research evidence might have got resolved within the consortium. Signs of a move in this direction were present at Phase 2 in the work of the 'classroom management' group (see Zamorski and Haydn, 2002) as it designed a qualitative study to run in parallel with a cross-school survey of student perceptions of teachers and teaching.

Whereas the survey offered the group a prospect of generalisation through aggregating data across classroom, subject and school contexts the qualitative study offered them a prospect of generalisation through the comparison of individual cases of disaffection (Glaser and Strauss, 1967). By designing an interview study that would enable them to compare and contrast the experiences of individual disaffected students in relation to their different classroom, subject, and school contexts, the group acknowledged the possibility of accumulating evidence from particular cases as a different basis for generalisation to that provided by the survey. It is unfortunate that the period of NASC funding terminated and we were unable to establish a context in which the relative value of the two sets of findings could be fully discussed with teachers throughout the consortium. It may well have gone a long way to resolving the tension between the two perspectives on credible research evidence that emerged in the course of the programme.

Teachers who talked to students in order to discover why they were disaffected in particular learning environments, became increasingly reluctant to view the relationship between pedagogy and 'disaffection' as a straightforward linear relationship between cause and effect. The relationship came to be viewed as a very context-bound and complex affair. Pedagogy was viewed as only one category of factors configuring with others to shape learning environments. For example the following were considered to be significant components of these configurations: personality characteristics; the climate of expectations in the home and the community as well as the school generally; peer relationships and cultures outside lessons; gender differences.

> ...because I'm a mathematician I expected to see certain patterns that you would say 'Oh, yes. I can understand why that happens.' It has given certain patterns but not the ones I was expecting. So in that sense (the research) has actually opened up the way I see the exclusion room...the students are being a problem not for obvious reasons...There's more to it than the person whose teaching them or the subject they are doing. It seemed to be a lot wider than that.
>
> ...it depends where the survey starts and finishes. One of the things we might argue for this school is that our parents are not largely very ambitious for the children...So I think in a sense some of the disengagement of the kids is a social thing, I would argue a lot of it is social. But we are not actually doing research on that.

Some teachers, like the above, came to feel that exploring the relationship between pedagogy and disaffection should not restrict the evidence gathered to pedagogical factors. They did not imply that as pedagogues they were powerless to effect changes in their students' levels of engagement and motivation; only that in order to do so they needed to understand how the pedagogical factors interacted with other factors to shape these levels. This emerged as an issue for teachers in a policy context where they felt that they alone were being held to account for the educational destinies of their students, and that the influence of wider social factors on students' attainment levels was being played down. Perhaps many teachers engaged in NASC had always intuitively experienced the relationship between teaching and learning as a complex affair, as Kennedy's study would suggest. In which case, the interview evidence made teachers more consciously aware of this complexity, and gave them the confidence to articulate what they already knew and to resist a policy-driven discourse that oversimplified the relationship. At this point we would like to point out that, although some teachers may have initially feared that the TTA would reinforce such a discourse, their fears diminished in the course of time, particularly during Phase 2 when the particular TTA link-officer for NASC in post at this time reassured teachers that they were not expected to assume a straightforward linear relationship between teaching and learning.

The status of evidence that raises more questions than answers

An increasingly conscious awareness of the complexity and context-bound nature of the phenomenon they were investigating made busy teachers anxious about drawing valid conclusions from the evidence they had gathered. They experienced a tension between the process they were engaged in and the expectation that '*proper research*' yielded clear and firm conclusions. The origins of this expectation is a matter for speculation, but it appeared to stem from a dominant conception of science embedded in our culture and transmitted through the educational system, including higher education. Given this expectation about what 'proper research' entails, the problem for the NASC teachers was that the evidence they gathered kept raising more questions than answers. A number of Phase 1 reports failed to generate 'findings' within the time set for their submission (summer 1999) but pointed to an ongoing process of question-posing. As one teacher commented:

> Certainly I would like to see people encouraged to carry it on because I think from what I have read most people would say they had made a start but they hadn't actually finished. Everything you do raises more questions.

In fact a number of teachers began to value this kind of inquiry for its own sake as a process of continuous reflection on their practice. Engagement in such 'reflective inquiry' became a source of professional satisfaction for these teachers, inasmuch as it moved them beyond a narrowly instrumentalist and reactive view of their practice.

The perception that 'proper research', regardless of its scale, produced evidence to support the drawing of firm conclusions, was sometimes seen to be reinforced by remarks made by some senior staff and colleagues in their schools, or by academics or TTA consultants. For example:

> The great difficulty is...feeling secure that you have the evidence to support what you believe to be happening, to be able to demonstrate to others that it is...rigorous research...I am not even bothered with rigour to be truthful...the fact of the matter is that (the project) has involved inquiry, it has involved an assessment of the evidence and people have written up, albeit tentatively, what their findings have been. Some smart academic may say well that is rubbish isn't it?...that they have done the same thing and much better. My answer to that is 'So what?' I think process is arguably more important than the product and I think we should not underestimate the value of the process.
>
> (Headteacher)

The headteacher here appears to be saying that engaging teachers in a dynamic process of evidence gathering which promotes reflection about teaching is more valuable than being able to produce an end-product in the form of a set of validated findings. If the evidence teachers gather in the process provokes thinking about their practice that is sufficient. Another headteacher came to a similar view when he explained how long it had taken him to see the potential of NASC for achieving a cultural change in the way all his teachers think about their practice. He no longer saw teachers' engagement in the process of research as something whose value simply depended on being able to demonstrate the validity of its findings to others not so engaged. This last headteacher subsequently began to explore ways of engaging all his staff in exploratory research within their classrooms. Strategies in this respect are still evolving in the school nearly a year after the consortium funding from the TTA ceased.

Experience within NASC suggests that the adoption of a whole school approach to engaging teachers in the kind of reflective question-posing inquiry referred to above presented practical problems for some school managers. These are somewhat different from the problems posed by a 'research and disseminate' approach that attempts to engage all teachers with research evidence generated within the school by either outsider researchers or a small group of staff or a mixture of both. It appears to be more difficult for a large number of teachers in a school, compared with a small group, to sustain engagement in a process that involves time-consuming observations and interviews with students in their own and each other's classrooms. Academic staff of the University were available to assist teachers with this kind of data-gathering, and a small number of teachers made use of this support. Given the fact that OFSTED (Office for Standards in Education) inspections coincided with the NASC programme in a number of schools, there was an understandable reluctance on the part of many teachers to open their classrooms to more external observation, even from their peers. Some headteachers and senior staff confronted realities in their staff-rooms and their school that made a 'research and disseminate' approach attractive, inasmuch as it avoided pressurising staff to commit time to a process that risked any further lowering of confidence and morale while, at the same time, providing opportunities for all staff to reflect about evidence and its implications for their practice. Although the majority of NASC schools adopted this approach to engaging teachers with research, at least three schools also evolved strategies for fostering amongst their staff a research stance that was integral to their teaching.

Ideographic and nomothetic conceptions of credible evidence

In the context of school-based research into student disaffection many NASC teachers were concerned that evidence was credible to their professional colleagues within and beyond their school. 'Disaffection' was viewed as a problem all teachers had to handle on a daily basis. Most of those engaged in Phase 1 projects felt an obligation to report their work to other teachers within their school, and across the consortium as a whole.

A tension emerged between ideographic and nomothetic conceptions of credible and useful evidence. The former conception attributes value to the study of particular cases while the latter attributes value to the study of populations. Evidence gathered from the ideographic study of particular cases had obvious value for those engaged with the case, but for them its value to others was less obvious. On the other hand, evidence gathered for the purpose of generalising to populations appeared to many teachers to possess plausibility and relevance to others. Some of the Phase 1 projects largely adopted a case study approach to evidence gathering, while others veered towards aggregating data based on questionnaire and structured interview surveys. Some attempted a mixed mode approach with a view to creating fruitful links between the two kinds of evidence.

The reader may feel that a false dichotomy emerged in the context of NASC. If this is so, it is a dichotomy that is well explored and represented in the methodological literature of the social sciences. In the NASC context it constituted a creative tension that enabled many teachers to explore and discuss possible links between the two kinds of evidence, as happened in the Phase 2 'classroom management project'.

Interestingly the Phase 1 research report that appears to have had the greatest impact on teachers across the consortium was unambiguously ideographic; namely, the case studies of RHINOs (see Oakley, J., 2002). It even influenced the successful submission of a research proposal to the ESRC on the 'Invisible Child' in the Mathematics classroom. This might be viewed as quite consistent with the claims of certain case study methodologists (see, e.g., Stake, 1995) that ideographic accounts are 'naturalistically generalisable', in the sense that it is the readers who do the generalising, by discovering similarities between the case(s) depicted and those they have direct experience of.

Cross-school research and the drift in favour of nomothetic methods

Phase 2 of the NASC programme involved a shift away from the Phase 1 projects, generated by individual and small groups of teachers within their schools, towards a small number of cross-school projects on topics which emerged from the sharing of ideas and issues across the Phase 1 projects. Each cross-school project was collaboratively planned by teachers and academic staff members at UEA. Interestingly, the two largest cross-school projects tended to prioritise the gathering and statistical analysis of questionnaire data about teachers' and students' perceptions of events and situations, although in some schools this data was supplemented by case data gathered through classroom observation and interviewing.

The teachers involved in the Phase 2 projects were not primarily concerned with the credibility of their evidence to academic researchers as such, but they did see the latter as an important source of technical expertise to draw on in the production of 'credible' survey evidence. They felt that to make evidence credible to teachers across the consortium, it should consist of aggregated data capable of yielding generalisable findings.

The majority of teachers involved in the cross-school Phase 2 projects were happy to be engaged in research with respect to defining both the research agenda – the questions to be addressed – and the kind of evidence worth gathering. They were more hesitant when it came to claiming ownership over the processes of gathering and analysing evidence, and expected much of this to be carried out by the 'experts' from the university. One academic research mentor related the following episode:

> One afternoon when we were trying to get the cross-school projects in place, I felt that in the last half an hour, some of the teachers were looking to me to just do a questionnaire and give it to them. In the end we worked it out together over about three meetings and a pilot, and I'm sure that this was a much better approach.

The reason for this dependence may appear to be obvious. Teachers did not see themselves to possess the necessary technical skills and did not connect them with the skills of the good teacher. These perspectives, however, stemmed from what has now become a dominant view about the nature of 'credible research evidence'. Nomothetic survey evidence was presumed to be more credible to colleagues across the consortium as a whole, because it promises to yield tidier and more generalisable findings than ideographic case study evidence. This preference, in the context of cross-school research, for gathering quantifiable evidence about teachers' and students' perceptions of life in classrooms resulted in a greater dependency on the academic staff of the university than was apparent with many of the Phase 1 case study projects initiated in particular schools. It may have also been reinforced by teachers' experience of the time-consuming nature of qualitative case study research, and their anxiety and doubt about the adequacy of their evidence as a basis for producing firm and clear conclusions.

The knowledge and skills involved in designing surveys and analysing survey data were not perceived by teachers initially to be an integral part of their role. Whereas a number of the participating teachers in Phase 1 did perceive the knowledge and skills involved in gathering and analysing ideographic evidence as integral to being a good teacher, they were hesitant about regarding such activities as 'proper research'.

The view of the relationship between teaching and research that tended to shape the cross-school research was reinforced by professional norms which worked against teachers collaborating to gather qualitative data about particular cases of teaching and learning, e.g., by observing each other's lessons and interviewing the students involved about their interpretations of events. Teachers displayed, with some exceptions, a reluctance to embark on data-gathering activities in each other's classrooms. They feared that their colleagues would experience such activities as intrusions into their professional domain, particularly in a climate where they carry overtones of inspection and performance appraisal and threaten to drain trust out of professional relationships.

The development of a proposed code of practice for collaborative classroom research, aimed at maintaining trust, was not generally sufficient to overcome this fear. Ideographic research methods involve more than technical expertise. They involve the exercise of very high levels of interpersonal skill and ethical competence in face to face situations. Many teachers not only lacked confidence in relation to this personal dimension of qualitative research, but needed to be convinced that the time invested in developing the necessary research skills would have sufficient pay-off for their own teaching, given what is demanded of them. For example, the teachers engaged in the Phase 1 projects did not make full use of the funds available to buy themselves out of teaching duties for periods to engage in peer-observation activities. This was because they feared that reduced continuity of contact might jeopardise the exam and test results of their students, for which they would be held accountable.

Given the above constraints on the use of case study research methods by teachers, it should not surprise us to find some teacher-researchers preferring survey methods as their primary means for generating 'credible research evidence', in spite of the attempts of UEA-based co-ordinators and mentors during both phases of the programme to get teachers to appreciate the relative strengths and limitations of each approach. Many teachers did develop some appreciation of these. Nevertheless, in the circumstances depicted above and given the pressures of time that mounted during Phase 2, the use of surveys appeared to offer teachers the prospect of producing a set of reasonably tidy and useful findings, even if the evidence provided only partial insights into how and why particular students became disaffected in their particular learning environments.

The retreat from qualitative methods at Phase 2 may well prove to be only a temporary stage in teachers learning to do research. The time and trouble involved in doing qualitative research, and concerns about generalisability, may only provide a partial explanation for a shift towards survey-based research. There were, for example, signs at Phase 2 of some teachers beginning to broaden their research expertise to include quantitative methods and becoming more independent of the UEA team in this respect. They developed skills with the help of UEA mentors in working the SPSS computerised data analysis package.

At some future stage of the consortium, if it proves sustainable in some form, many teachers might well develop a deeper understanding of the pros and cons of different approaches to research. This began to be evident, as indicated earlier, in the work of the group of teachers involved in the cross-school 'classroom management' project. The UEA-based project co-ordinator and its mentor were able to demonstrate to the teachers involved the potential in using the analysis of qualitative data as a basis for questionnaire design. The group struggled to accommodate the insights they had gained into the complexity of teaching from the qualitative analysis into the framing of the questions for the survey. They then went on to help with the design of a parallel qualitative study, subsequently carried out by the project co-ordinator, to complement the survey evidence. It was unfortunate that there was not sufficient time for the teachers to become involved in the production of a synthesis analysis of the two data sets.

Beyond the battle between paradigms

In spite of the tensions and issues noted above, a very noticeable feature of the NASC project has been the developing confidence of teachers in handling different kinds of research evidence. Initially, teachers were tentative, even defensive, about their ability to go 'beyond the known'. Later, they became more at ease, and developed a much broader view about what research was, and what it was for. This was arguably an outcome of the rich mixture of the personnel involved in NASC: professional researchers (some with international reputations), teacher educators who were comparatively new to educational research, full-time doctoral students, and teachers with varying degrees of research experience. This involvement of people with several different layers and levels of research expertise helped to broaden and question views of what constituted credible and relevant evidence, and what research was for.

Teachers in the NASC did not only find evidence about their own practices and classroom situations credible and relevant. Both case study evidence gathered in others classrooms and decontextualised survey evidence became credible and relevant, albeit for different reasons, inasmuch as both provoked thought about the complexities of teaching and learning in their own classrooms. This supports Kennedy's finding that research evidence of very different kinds, whether case studies or surveys or even experimental studies, can provoke such thinking. This is because teachers are able to forge analogies between such studies and their own practices.

What counts as credible and relevant evidence is ultimately defined by the teachers who engage with research and not by the genre in which the research is carried out. Although the distinctive features of each genre may appeal to different ways of knowing and understanding teaching and learning situations, Kennedy found that teachers do not attribute monolithic importance to any one set of characteristics. This was confirmed by our experience, in the context of NASC, of engaging teachers *in* and *with* research. It is an experience that offers a challenge to both quantitative and qualitative educational researchers who presume that what constitutes 'useful' evidence can be defined independently of teachers.

Learning how to handle the complexity of 'life in classrooms' as a focus for CPD: implications for educational research and policy

Standards-driven educational reform over the past decade and a half in the UK has encouraged teachers to view pedagogy as the construction of *rationally* or *logically* ordered learning environments. Such reform has shaped pedagogy in terms of learning requirements that stem from 'social and economic needs' as these are defined by policy-makers, and are cast in the form of standardised and measurable intended learning outcomes (see Hinchliffe, 2001, p. 31). *Standards-driven reform* has also shaped educational research as a source of means-end rules (encapsulated in a particular concept of 'evidence') for rationally ordering the learning environment to produce such outcomes. It involves the construction of a clockwork world characterised by repetition and predictability. The learning environment is viewed as a closed and linear system governed by the laws of cause and effect. Such a system leaves little space for the 'personal', for the cultivation of the individual learner as a unique centre of consciousness with a distinctive point of view, endowed with particular talents and abilities, and possessing particular characteristics. Seen in this light it is not surprising to find that current pedagogical practice in schools tends to neglect the complexity of classroom life, and fails to meet the needs of individual learners. The counter-productive side effect of a pedagogy shaped by *standards-driven* educational reform is wide-spread disaffection from learning. The experience of the NASC project suggests that many teachers understand this, implicitly if not explicitly.

What is required as a future focus for the professional development of teachers in the UK, and other countries that have embraced a similar reform ideology, is a shift in the policy context towards providing better support for teachers to develop their pedagogical practice in a form that acknowledges the complexity of teaching and learning. I have argued (see Elliott 2003, and Chapter to following) that such development will involve the creation of more *aesthetically ordered* learning environments that accommodate the diverse needs of individual learners and the personal dimension of learning in specific classroom situations. Such environments are dynamic complex systems characterised by a large measure of unpredictability with respect to learning outcomes, a high degree of conscious self-monitoring on the part of the teacher and learners, and spaces for conversation and dialogue about the process of teaching and learning. Their creation is a matter of *personal artistry* on the part of teachers rather than the application of a uniform control technology of teaching derived from the research findings of 'teacher effectiveness' research.

If one views *educational* change in terms of an intelligent response to the pedagogical problems and challenges that confront teachers in handling the complexity of life in their classrooms, then one might describe it as *pedagogically-driven reform*. This view of educational reform stands in marked contrast to the *standards-driven reform* movement that has tended to shape pedagogy in educational institutions according to a change agenda which ignores this complexity and views the ideal learning environment as a simple, stable, linear system that behaves in quite predictable ways.

Pedagogically-driven change depends upon the capacity of teachers to progressively deepen their understanding of the complex situations they face in attempting to create high quality learning environments that meet the diverse learning needs of their learners. Such *situational understanding* (see Elliott, 1993) is developed not so much in advance of their practical interventions but in conjunction with them. Understanding informs action and action informs understanding. This is the process by which teachers develop their practical knowledge of how to create *aesthetically ordered* learning environments, and is often depicted as a form of action research in which 'action' is an integral part of the research and 'research' an integral part of the action. As indicated earlier in this paper such a process provides a context for utilising research 'evidence' generated outside the particular action situation.

As a mode of knowledge construction and utilisation in a pedagogical context action research cannot be dissociated from the creative activity of constructing an educationally worthwhile learning environment for learners. It will therefore mirror the form of such activity and can be depicted as an *aesthetically organized* construction of practical/educational knowledge, in which the teacher selects, assembles, and synthesizes a diversity of inquiry devices (together with different kinds of externally generated evidence) in terms of his/her judgements about their appropriateness to the pedagogical situation.

[. . .]

If learning how to handle the complexity of teaching and learning is to become the focus for CPD it implies a radical re-thinking of the relationship between pedagogy, research and educational policy. This paper has hopefully contributed to re-thinking the triangle, particularly with respect to the relation between pedagogy and research. With respect to policy it implies a shift away from a *standards-driven* and socially engineered model of change towards supporting a *pedagogically-driven* model that gives space for teachers to exercise artistry in their teaching. This will involve re-casting national curriculum frameworks in forms that permit teachers to respond more flexibly to the diversity and complexity of the learning needs that exist in their classrooms. Such re-casting will imply more focus on the process of teaching and learning, and take the form of frameworks couched in terms of principles and criteria rather than specific learning outcomes. Their main purpose will be to guide rather than prescribe the development of school-based programmes. . . . (see Elliott, 1998).

A shift of emphasis in the model of change shaping policy will also involve developing an integrated model of professional *accountability* and *development* (see Elliott, 1989). Such a model will place a higher trust in teachers with less emphasis on the production of standardised and measurable learning outcomes and more emphasis on the responsibility of teachers to construct learning environments that challenge, engage and motivate all pupils. Such an emphasis would require teachers to elicit feed-back from their peers and their students on a continuous basis, and to regularly produce reflective reviews of their attempts to improve the quality of teaching and learning in their classrooms (see O'Hanlon, 2003). These would function as a contribution to the development of pedagogical scholarship within the teaching profession. . . .

References

Altrichter, H. (1997) Practitioners, Higher Education and Government Initiatives in the Development of Action Research: the case of Austria, in Hollingsworth, S. (Ed.) *International Action Research: A Casebook for Educational Reform*, Falmer Press: London, Ch. 3.

Brennan, M. and Noffke, S. (2000) Social Change and the Individual: changing patterns of community and the challenge of schooling, in Altrichter, H. and Elliott, J. (Eds) *Images of Educational Change*, Open University Press: Milton Keynes, Ch. 5.

Carr, W. and Kemmis, S. (1986) *Becoming Critical: Education, Knowledge and Action Research*, Falmer Press: Lewes.

Day, C., Elliott, J., Somekh, B. and Winter, R. (Eds) (2002) *Theory and Practice in Action Research*, Symposium Books: Oxford.

Doherty, P. (2001) *The Curriculum Dimensions of Student Disaffection: A single site case study*, unpublished PhD Thesis University of East Anglia: Norwich, UK.

Doherty, P. (2002) Engaging Pupils in Researching Disaffection within a School, in Elliott, J. and Zamorski, B. (Eds) (2002) *Teachers Research Disaffection*, a special number of Pedagogy, Culture and Schooling devoted to collaborative research within the Norwich Area Consortium.

Doherty, P. and Elliott, J. (1999) Engaging teachers in and with research: the relationship between evidence, context and use. *Presentation to the Annual Conference of the British Educational Research Association (BERA)*, University of Sussex, Brighton. University of East Anglia: Norwich, Mimeo.

Ebbutt, D. and Elliott, J. (Eds) (1985) *Issues in Teaching for Understanding*, Longmans/ Schools Curriculum Development Committee (SCDC).

Elliott, J. (1976–77) Developing hypotheses about Interchange, Classrooms from Teachers' Vol. 7, No. 2, Practical Constructs: An Account of the work of the Ford Teaching Project.

Elliott, J. (1978) Classroom Research: Science or Commonsense? in McAleese, R. and Hamilton, D. (Eds), N.F.E.R.

Elliott, J. (1989) Teacher Evaluation and Teaching as a Moral Science in Holly, M.L. and McLoughlin, C.S. (Eds) *Perspectives on Teacher Professional Development*, The Falmer Press: London & New York.

Elliott, J. (1991) *Action Research for Educational Change*, Open University Press: Milton Keynes, esp. Ch. 3.

Elliott, J. (1993) Three Perspectives on Coherence and Continuity in Teacher Education, in Elliott, J. (Ed.) *Reconstructing Teacher Education*, The Falmer Press: London. Ch. 1.

Elliott, J. (1998) *The Curriculum Experiment: Meeting the Challenge of Social Change*, Open University Press: Milton Keynes, Ch. 3.

Elliott, J. (1999) Evidence-based practice, action research and the professional development of teachers, *Goldsmiths Journal of Education*, Vol. 2, No. 1, July.

Elliott, J. (2002) Making Evidence-based Practice Educational, *British Educational Research Journal*, Vol. 27, No. 5, Dec.

Elliott, J. (2003) Re-thinking Pedagogy as the Aesthetic Ordering of Learning Experiences, Invited paper for the Annual Conference of the Philosophy of Education Society (UK), New College Oxford, April.

Elliott, J. and Adelman, C. (1974) (Eds) *Ford Teaching Project Reports and Documents*, CARE, University of East Anglia: Norwich.

Elliott, J. and Doherty, P. (2001) Restructuring Educational Research for the 'Third Way', in Fielding, M. (Ed.) *Taking Education Really Seriously: Four Years' Hard Labour*, Routledge Falmer: London, Ch. 16.

Elliott, J. and MacDonald, B. (Eds) (1975) *People in Classrooms*, CARE Occasional Publications No. 2, University of East Anglia: Norwich.

Elliott, J. and Zamorski, B. (Eds) (2002) *Teachers Research Disaffection*, a special number of *Pedagogy, Culture and Schooling* devoted to collaborative research within the Norwich Area Consortium.

Glaser, B. and Strauss, A. (1967) *The Discovery of Grounded Theory: Strategies for Qualitative Research*, Chicago: Aldine; London: Weidenfeld & Nicholson.

Gutteridge, D. (2002) Identifying the Disaffected, in Elliott, J. and Zamorski, B. (Eds) *Teachers Research Disaffection*, a special number of *Pedagogy, Culture and Schooling* devoted to collaborative research within the Norwich Area Consortium.

Hammersley, M. (1997) Educational Research and Teaching: a response to David Hargreaves TTA Lecture, *British Educational Research Journal*, Vol. 23, No. 1.

Hammersley, M. (2002) On 'Systematic Reviews' of Research Literatures: a 'narrative' response to Evans & Benfield, *British Educational Research Journal*, Vol. 27, No. 5, Dec.

Hargreaves, D. (1996) Teaching as a Research-based Profession: possibilities and prospects, *Teacher Training Agency Annual Lecture*, Teacher Training Agency: London.

Hargreaves, D. (1997) In Defence of Research for Evidence-based Teaching: a rejoinder to Martyn Hammersley, *British Educational Research Journal*, Vol. 23, No. 4.

Hargreaves, D. (1999) Revitalising Educational Research: lessons from the past and proposals for the future, *Cambridge Journal of Education*, Vol. 29, No. 2.

Hillier, J., Pearson, R., Anderson, A. and Tampkin, P. (1998) *Excellence in Research on Schools*, Research Report 74, Department for Education and Employment, UK.

Hinchliffe, G. (2001) Education or Pedagogy? In *Journal of Philosophy of Education*, Vol. 35, Issue 1.

Hollingsworth, S. (Ed.) (1997) *International Action Research: A Casebook for Educational Reform*, Falmer Press: London & Washington DC.

Hollingsworth, S. and Sockett, H. (Eds) (1994) *Teacher Research and Educational Reform: Ninety-third Yearbook of the National Society for the Study of Education*. Part 1, esp. Ch. 1, University of Chicago Press: Illinois.

Hustler, D., Cassidy, T. and Cuff, T. (Eds) (1986) *Action Research in Classrooms and Schools*, Allen & Unwin: Boston & Sydney, esp. General Introduction.

Kennedy, M. (1999) A Test of Some Common Contentions about Educational Research, *American Educational Research Journal*, Vol. 36, No. 3, pp. 511–541.

Lomax, P. (1999) Working Together for Educative Community through Research, *Research Intelligence*, No. 68.

Oakley, A. (2000) *Experiments In Knowing: Gender And Methods In The Social Sciences*, Polity Press: Cambridge.

Oakley, A. (2002) Making Evidence-based Practice Educational: a rejoinder to John Elliott, *British Educational Research Journal*, Vol. 27, No. 5, Dec.

Oakley, J. (2002) RHINOS – a tale of collaboration between teachers within a school to identify the passively disaffected, in Elliott, J. and Zamorski, B. (Eds) *Teachers Research Disaffection*, a special number of *Pedagogy, Culture and Schooling* devoted to collaborative research within the Norwich Area Consortium.

O'Hanlon, C. (Ed.) (1996) *Professional Development through Action Research in Educational Settings*, Falmer Press: London.

O'Hanlon, C. (2002) Reflection and Action in Research: is there a moral responsibility to act? In Day, Elliott, Somekh and Winter (Eds) (2002) *Theory and Practice in Action Research*, Symposium Books: Oxford, pp. 111–121.

O'Hanlon, C. (2003) Educational Inclusion as Action Research, Maidenhead: Open University Press.

Reynolds, D. (1998) *Teacher Effectiveness*, TTA Corporate Plan Launch 1998–2001, Teacher Training Agency: London.

Sanger, J. (Ed.) (1989) *The Teaching, Handling Information and Learning Project*, Library and Information Research Report 67. British Library: London.

Somekh, B. (2000) Changing Conceptions of Action Research, in Altrichter and Elliott (Eds) *Images of Educational Change*, Open University Press: Milton Keynes, Ch. 9.

Stake, R.E. (1995) *The Art of Case Study Research*, Sage Publications: London & New Delhi.

Stenhouse, L. (1975) *An Introduction to Curriculum Research and Development*, Heinemann: London, Chs 9 and 10.

Stenhouse, L. (1979) Using Research Means Doing Research, in Dahl, H., Lysne, A. and Rand, P. (Eds) *Spotlight on Educational Problems*, University of Oslo Press: Oslo, pp. 71–82.

Teacher Training Agency (1998) *Promoting Teaching as a Research and Evidence-Based Profession*, Corporate Plan Launch 1998–2001, Teacher Training Agency: London.

Zamorski, B. and Haydn, T. (2002) Exploring the Relationship between Classroom Management and Pupil Disaffection: an account of across-school collaborative research, in Elliott, J. and Zamorski, B. (Eds) *Teachers Research Disaffection*, a special number of *Pedagogy, Culture and Schooling* devoted to collaborative research within the Norwich Area Consortium.

CHAPTER 10

RETHINKING PEDAGOGY AS THE AESTHETIC ORDERING OF LEARNING EXPERIENCES

Presented at the UK Philosophy of Education Annual Conference, New College, Oxford, April 2003

Pedagogy as 'classroom management': the transition from chaos to cosmos

The role of the teacher as a classroom manager is increasingly regarded as a central feature of the teacher's role. Viewed in these terms pedagogy involves the construction and maintenance of an ordered world in the classroom to effect learning. It presupposes a movement from chaos to cosmos, from a disordered rather random state of affairs to an ordered one that is governed by a teacher. Underpinning this vision of the teacher's role as a classroom manager is the fear of children as the bearers of chaos. It is assumed that if the teacher leaves them to their own devices and desires the result will be chaos and disorder. Children cannot be trusted to supply their own motivation for learning and to create their own learning agendas through their interactions with their teachers and each other. An ordered learning environment has to be brought into being by an external force: the teacher. 'Pedagogy' when conceived in these terms necessarily entails the existence of a hierarchical power relation between teachers and students, and therefore a disjunction between the maker of order and those who benefit from it.

Another assumption underpinning an understanding of pedagogy as a movement from chaos to order is that the power wielded by the teacher as a *manager of learning* is not arbitrary but in some sense 'rational'. The pedagogical ordering of students' learning experiences is grounded in certain normative rules and principles that can be appealed to by the teacher to justify his(her) classroom management strategies. The teacher constructs order by applying to the given situation in his(her) classroom some antecedent pattern of relatedness. In other words the rules and principles that guide the pedagogical construction of the learning environment 'transcend' the particularities of the given situation. The particular characteristics of individual students and indeed of the teacher – background history, social background and ethnicity, talents and abilities – are only deemed pedagogically significant if they need to be taken into account in determining a learning environment according to a pre-determined pattern of relatedness. One of the devices employed in pre-determining such patterns is to categorise students in terms of fixed ability characteristics.

A teacher can construct order in the classroom non-pedagogically. For it to take the form of a pedagogically constructed order, the world of the classroom must take the form of a *learning* environment. This is why the current emphasis on the acquisition of *behaviour management skills* by teachers can gloss over the fact that such skills may have less to do with constructing the conditions for learning, and more to do with constructing the conditions of their own survival. The exercise of such skills may simply constitute a device for warding off the fear of chaos.

This glossing over of the distinction between the 'management of learning' and 'behaviour management' in classrooms has considerable significance for the way teachers view and categorise individuals in their classroom. It is often assumed that 'disruptive students', those who appear to continually threaten chaos in the classroom, are the disengaged/disaffected from learning and that 'well-behaved' students whose behaviour poses no such threat are motivated to learn. Such assumptions have been convincingly challenged by Norwich secondary school teachers who have researched 'student disaffection' in the context of their own classrooms (see Brown and Fletcher, 2002; Oakley *et al.*, 2002; Boddington and Larner, 2000). Brown and Fletcher (pp. 169–192) discovered that in Modern Foreign Language classes students assumed to be disaffected from these subjects were in fact disruptively engaged in learning, and Oakley and his colleagues (pp. 193–208) identified students who were skilful at rendering themselves invisible to their teachers in the classroom but were 'really here in name only' (RHINOs). In evaluating 'curriculum enrichment' programmes that took students outside the classroom and school for part of the week, Boddington and Larner concluded that the programmes helped to improve school attendance and reduce disruptive conduct in 'core subject' lessons without resulting in commensurate improvements in learning, as measured against the learning targets set for these students. Learning to manage behaviour and avoid chaos in classrooms must therefore not be confused with the pedagogical construction of an orderly classroom environment. The latter brings into being and sustains an ordered world in the classroom for the purpose of learning.

[. . .]

The 'evidence-based practice' movement holds that a science of what works is the basis of effective pedagogical practice aimed at the construction of effective learning environments. From the standpoint of such a science the ordered world of the classroom is viewed as a linear order characterised by repetition and predictable outcomes. Its role is to reveal pedagogical pathways to improving learning outcomes for students. In order to fulfil this role desired learning outcomes must be specified in standardised measurable terms. Evidence-based teaching promises to provide teachers with a 'rational' and 'logical' foundation for the 'pedagogical' construction of order from chaos. In doing so it renders them accountable for the learning outcomes of their students in exchange for releasing them from the fear of chaos. But what if there is nothing to fear? What if students are not as dangerous as they are led to believe? What if one can become a good teacher by courageously positioning oneself on the edge of chaos rather than attempting to transform it into a pedagogically rational order? Then the exchange that pedagogy currently involves – *accountability* for *survival* – may appear to be open to question. I will now begin to explore the possibility that 'pedagogy' can be re-thought in different terms to those I have outlined above.

Pedagogy and education

Geoffrey Hinchliffe (2001) argues that *pedagogy* and *education* are quite distinct concepts. He contrasts them in the following terms:

> Whereas the former (pedagogy) has specific objectives, the latter (education) is underpinned by the idea that the outcome of education is open (like a good

conversation) – (and) must be left, in part, to the interaction between learners and teacher. Construed as education, the results of learning can never be measured according to a common standard. But construed as pedagogy, those results must be measurable because the whole point of learning is to equip people for specified social, political and educational requirements.

(p. 31)

For Hinchliffe a learning environment that is entirely pedagogically ordered is not an educative one, for the individual student is expected to comply with learning requirements that stem from the needs of society and have been defined for the class as a whole, rather than those which flow from his or her own personal learning agenda and needs. One of my own persistent frustrations as a school student was that my own personal learning agenda rarely coincided with what teachers were trying to get 'the class' to learn.

Hinchliffe's account of pedagogy is not unlike the one I outlined earlier. It involves the construction of a clockwork world characterised by repetition and predictability. Such a learning environment is a closed and linear system governed by the laws of cause and effect. It appears to leave little space for the 'personal', for the cultivation of the individual as a unique centre of consciousness with a distinctive point of view, endowed with particular talents and abilities, and possessing particular characteristics.

From Hinchliffe's perspective, the construction of a learning environment that caters for the particular needs of individuals conceived as persons, as opposed to their needs as potential occupants of a social or economic role, is the task of the educator rather than the pedagogue. He argues that:

the very things that education is supposed to produce – critical awareness, creativity, an imaginative response – simply do not count for anything very much from the standpoint of pedagogical considerations and, indeed, may well count against the student.

(p. 33)

His account of education implies the construction of a learning environment that does not structure learning along predetermined trajectories but is highly interactive and inter-personal, and therefore dynamic and open to a diversity of learning outcomes. It suggests that education is not a disordered and random process but closer to the edge of chaos than pedagogy. Hinchliffe's account also implies a distinction between a learning environment that caters for the personal development of individuals and one which equips them for their roles and positions in society. This distinction fundamentally underpins his contrasting conceptions of 'education' and 'pedagogy'. I shall return to it in due course, particularly when I examine the relationship between 'personal' and 'social development' in Confucian thought. If it can be challenged and shown to be a culturally relative distinction, then this opens the way to asking whether we can in some sense change pedagogical practice to make it more educative, as opposed to seeing as necessarily distinct from educational practice.

Interesting Hinchliffe likens 'education' to 'conversation'. This echoes the centrality of discussion-based inquiry in classrooms in the thought of the curriculum theorist, Lawrence Stenhouse (1971, 1975), and his 'process model' of curriculum development. For Stenhouse (1975, Ch. 7) the teacher's role was to create a learning environment that took the form of an open-ended and reflective discussion as opposed to being structured in terms of instructional objectives. It is an environment that enables students to freely express their own ideas, and to develop them further as they interact with and build on each others ideas. The learning experiences of students in such an environment are not ordered in terms of a pre-specification of desired learning outcomes but in terms of the discussion as it dynamically and unpredictably unfolds. The learning outcomes cannot be specified in advance of this process and they will not be the same for all. The discussion-based classroom yields differentiated learning outcomes. Stenhouse was an articulate critic of the exclusive use of the objectives model for planning the learning experiences of students in many curriculum areas (1975, Ch. 6). He argued that it distorted the nature of knowledge by treating the concepts that structured it as having fixed meanings and not being open to further questioning.

Archbishop Rowan Williams, in his book *Lost Icons* (2000, Chs 1 and 2), also argues for the creation of more 'conversational space' in our educational institutions to counterbalance an educational system driven by 'vocational' concerns that emphasise the acquisition of knowledge and skills required for an individual to succeed in the competitive environment of the labour market. Learning in such a system will be primarily motivated by a need to achieve competitive edge over one's rivals. Our present system, Williams argues, is oriented towards the production of individuals as 'economic subjects', as atomistic systems of desire, which can only be satisfied through competition with others. From the standpoint of the 'economic subject' others are always perceived as a potential threat to "my interests," although "I may co-operate with you to satisfy your desires if you can help to satisfy mine." Economic subjects engage in *relations of exchange* with others as a means of satisfying their interests and desires.

Williams's account of the dominant 'pedagogical' orientation operating in our educational system depicts the construction of a learning environment in which competitiveness supplies the major motivation for learning. It implies that those who refuse or lose the desire to compete get labelled as the 'disaffected' from learning and threaten to take teachers back into chaos.

According to Williams, the danger of an educational system that only impresses on students their duty to perform 'competitively' by meeting the learning requirements of the job market is that "other kinds of learning that occur through particular sorts of process" become eroded. The sorts of process that he has in mind as under threat are the "disciplines of conversation." He sees these to lie at the heart of the process of education.

> A good educational institution would be one in which conversation flourished – that is, one where activities were fostered that drew students away from competition as a norm.
>
> (p. 89)

[. . .]

According to Williams, it is through their participation in conversational activities that individuals break through into a recognition of the common good, of the things "they can only value or enjoy together." Williams argues that this is not a matter of discovering answers to the question 'What do we have in common?' by way of shared interests, background history, ideological stance or attitudes, in relation to some state of affairs that exists outside and independently of the conversational process itself. It is rather a matter of each participant discovering that their interest is bound up, not with the 'out-there' states of affairs the conversation may be about, but with the continuance of the conversational relationship and the shared sense of enjoyment and well-being that accompanies it. This does not depend on the participants needing to be assured of their sameness with respect to some external factor. From Williams's point of view, consensus about the things 'out-there' is not a condition for continuing the conversation, as Stenhouse (1971, 1975, Ch. 7) echoed when he argued that the teacher should 'protect divergence' and the expression of minority viewpoints in discussions about controversial issues in classrooms.

Williams suggests that conversation provides a necessary context for the development of individuals who acknowledge "that someone else's welfare is constitutive of my own." It is through the 'disciplines of conversation' that individuals experience a kind of non-competitive communion with others and forge bonds of charity that transcend the conflicts of interest and desire that attend their relationships with each other as 'economic subjects'.

What then do individuals learn through an engagement in activities which promote conversation that they could not learn through an engagement in activities structured by externally imposed learning requirements. Williams argues (p. 93) that they learn to question a picture of themselves and others they have been "encouraged to think obvious and natural by countless pressures." It is a picture of an "atomistic system of desires confronting other such systems," i.e. a robust, primitive, individual self "seeking its fortune in a hostile world and fighting off its competitors." Activities which promote conversation enable a "questioning appropriation of selfhood" in which individuals continuously revise their accounts of their 'natural' needs and desires. For Williams, such activities are the medium in which individuals develop themselves in communion with each other. 'Self-cultivation' is neither a solitary or closed process and in these respects differs markedly from a learning process conditioned by a picture of the self as an economic subject.

Hinchliffe, Stenhouse and Williams in many respects share similar conceptions of an educative learning environment, and each share overlapping conceptions of a learning environment that stands in opposition to education. The latter appear to be very congruent with prevailing conceptions of pedagogy as the construction of rational order in classrooms. However, for both Williams and Stenhouse, learning environments that create space for conversation have a social and political as well as a personal dimension. For Williams, conversation provides the context in which individuals break through into a mutual recognition of their common humanity and form bonds of 'charity'. In doing so, they transcend their merely private and sectional interests. This implies that the creation of conversational space in learning environments constitutes a preparation for citizenship in what Williams (p. 86) calls a "more than liberal" society. Such a society is more than a tolerant society, the outcome of political activity aimed at balancing and accommodating conflicting interests. It is a society that also embraces the virtue of 'charity', the outcome of activities in society that promote conversation. ...

Stenhouse's Humanities Project can also be read as an attempt to prepare students for their social role as citizens. It created space within classrooms for sustained and disciplined conversation about issues that the non-charitable world of politics habitually deals with, issues that arouse conflicts of interest and desire, and indeed feelings of obstinacy on the part of students. By learning to participate in such conversation, students were challenged to question themselves and their attitudes to others, to stand back from a vision of themselves as members of a particular interest group, whether defined in terms of opinions, gender, social class, language, national identity, or race, and to discover the joy of being together as human beings. It is this charitable outlook towards each other, that sees the other as not simply the bearer of some sectional interest, which enriches students' understandings of the situations, events and issues that characterise the realm of human affairs, and constitutes a major source of motivation, beyond self-interest, for their active and responsible engagement in it.

[. . .]

How do we characterise the kind of order implicit in an educational process that has conversation at its centre? What implications does this have for the role of the teacher? In attempting to explore these questions, I will draw on two overlapping perspectives that are currently challenging many assumptions about 'systems' that are embedded in western thought. One, which I will dwell on very briefly, is 'complexity theory' and the other, which I will explore more fully is 'Confucian thought'.

The learning environment as a complex, aesthetic order

From the standpoint of 'complexity theory' (see Lewin, 1993) a learning environment that provides conversational space is a complex, dynamic, non-linear system whose components interact with each other in quite unpredictable ways. The conditions of such a system are constantly changing to render its outcomes unpredictable. They make the system to appear to be never far from the edge of chaos. If we view learning environments in these terms, then the role of the teacher is to stand at the edge of chaos shaping the conditions of learning by responding to situations as they arise, rather than attempting to render the possibility of chaos remote by imposing a linear and rational form of order in the classroom. When we view learning environments in terms of complexity theory, then using research to establish initial conditions that enable teachers to predict learning outcomes, along the lines suggested by such advocates of 'evidence-based teaching' as Hargreaves (1996, 1997, 1999) and Reynolds (1998), will appear to be counter-productive. When learning environments constitute complex, dynamic and non-linear systems they are, I will argue, best characterised as *aesthetic orderings of experience*.

Hall and Ames (1987, pp. 132–133) identify issues surrounding the interpretation of *praxis*, construed as the ordering of individual and social behaviour, that have arisen within Western thought. There is the dominant Platonic and idealist conception "which characterise praxis as activity in accordance with the normative principles of knowledge." In this conception *theoria* is separated out from *praxis* and the latter understood almost entirely in terms of the former. Hall and Ames argue that this is both cause and consequence of a belief in a normative dimension that transcends the concrete particulars of every day sense experience. Such a belief underpins an interpretation of *praxis* as the making of a 'rational' or 'logical' order.

Hall and Ames compare the Platonic and idealist conception of *praxis* with existentialist and pragmatist rejoinders and argue that they still contain a transcendent normative dimension. In the existential tradition it is the power and influence of heroic individuals who shape our understandings of the world, and they provide normative measures for assessing human thinking and conduct. The pragmatic tradition defines *praxis* "as actions stimulated by problematic situations from which guiding principles may be abstracted" (p. 132). The basis for such abstraction, Hall and Ames argue, lies in the scientific method elaborated by Pierce, Dewey and, to a lesser extent, Mead.

The implication of Hall and Ames account of the issues surrounding the interpretation of *praxis* in Western thought is that they have largely revolved around the origins and nature of the normative principles of knowledge that are to govern the way human experience ought to be ordered in society. None of the main rejoinders to the Platonic and idealist conception fundamentally question the transcendent dimension of order. Nor do they question a disjunction between the makers of order and those who benefit from it. However, Hall and Ames also identify an interpretation of *praxis* "that has not been exploited in our tradition" and that challenges a view of order as pre-determined by transcendental principles and based on a presumed disjunction between the makers of order and those who enjoy its benefits. They are referring to a conception of *praxis* as *aesthesis* (p. 133) construed in terms of aesthetic creativity. At one level Hall and Ames point out that *aesthesis* can simply be understood as "perceiving the external world through the senses." However, the related term, in Ancient Greek, *Aisthetikos* carries the sense of "being preoccupied"; a distinctive form of human consciousness that cannot be reduced to a mere "animal consciousness" of the sensory world as 'pleasantness'. Qualified in this way Hall and Ames argue that *aesthesis* connects *theoria and praxis* in a novel form. They believe this connection was made quite specific by John Ruskin, when he described *theoria* "as the perception of beauty regarded as a moral faculty," in contrast with *aesthesis* regarded as a form of mere 'animal consciousness'.

Hall and Ames (1987, pp. 132–138) contrast the vision of *rational* or *logical order* that is implicit in the dominant Western interpretations of *praxis* with the vision of *aesthetic order* that they believe to be particularly evidenced in Confucian thought.

> To the extent that our social interactions are limited by appeal to a pre-established pattern of relatedness, be it political, religious or cultural, and to the extent that we conform to or express this pattern as containing habits, customs, rules, or laws determinative of our conduct, we are constituted as a 'rational' or 'logical' order.

On the other hand:

> to the degree that we interact without obligatory recourse to rule or ideal or principle, and to the extent that the various orders which characterize our modes of togetherness are functions of the insistent particularities whose uniquenesses comprise the orders, we are authors of an aesthetic composition.

Whereas from the perspective of *rational* or *logical order* one attends to the manner in which the different elements constituting the order conform to a given pattern or set of formal relations, from the perspective of *aesthetic order* one attends to the manner in which the elements that compose it "constitute themselves and their relation to each other in such a way as to permit of no substitutions" (p. 134). The first perspective involves abstracting from the particular and unique characteristics of each of the elements by ordering them into a uniform pattern. It is indifferent to the elements in themselves. Each element therefore is replaceable by any other element that can be made to fit the pattern. The second perspective involves acknowledging the particular and unique characteristics of each element yet ordering them into a harmonious whole. Elements which do not comprise the order fail to meet the conditions for the harmony achieved and cannot be substituted for those that do. Hall and Ames point out that an understanding of orders

> as functions of the particular, idiosyncratic items which in fact comprise them provides a much more complex conception of order than that of rational orderdness.
>
> (p. 137)

They contend however that the creation of *aesthetic orders*, as well as the making of rational ones, involves abstraction, but in a different form. Whereas the latter abstracts from "actuality", the former abstracts from "possibility" (p. 135). The maker of *rational order* abstracts from the concrete particularities of individual elements in the context of action, whereas the maker of *aesthetic order* imagines a possible composition in which these elements in all their particularity and uniqueness are brought into a harmonious relation with each other. *Theoria* establishes the initial conditions for the production of *rational order* by those who make it. However, in the making of *aesthetic order* it is generated in the acts of creative artistry that constitute the *praxis* itself.

Hall and Ames argue that the concepts of *aesthetic* and *rational* order are inversely related. The more uniformity of behaviour and pattern regularity is evidenced in the system the more aesthetic disorder is likely to prevail; a situation in which the celebration of the particularity and uniqueness of individuals is suppressed by the system. The greater the disclosure of the particularity and uniqueness of the elements in the system, the greater the degree of rational disorder; a situation marked by a lack of uniformity and pattern regularity. In other words from the standpoint of one who desires rational order, aesthetic order looks like 'chaos'.

Hall and Ames suggest that what we normally call order is a mixture of the two varieties which stand in tension with each other, and that the value of distinguishing them alerts us to contrary tendencies in the production and maintenance of order.

The aesthetic perspective throws light on Rowan Williams's call for a social order that is more than based on liberal-democratic principles. As Hall and Ames point out:

> Concepts of "human nature," "human rights," "equality under the law," and so forth, signal the resort to logical or rational orderdness.
>
> (p. 137)

In articulating the 'charitable bonds' created in complex conversational activities, Williams appears to be adopting an aesthetic perspective on the relationship between persons and society. Hall and Ames argue that aesthetic enjoyment involves extending our understanding of what human beings *need* beyond "the strictly economic interpretation" (p. 133). In pinpointing the 'social joy' made in conversational activities, Williams is also engaged in enlarging our understanding of human needs.

Rethinking the pedagogical role of the teacher as the creator of aesthetic order

The distinction between the two varieties of order also throws light on the concepts of education employed by Hinchliffe, Stenhouse and Williams. They appear to presuppose an aesthetically ordered learning environment and the desirability of creating such environments to counterbalance a current tendency in the educational system to stress the production and maintenance of rationally ordered learning environments in terms of 'classroom management'.

For Hinchliffe, the latter is a matter of *pedagogical praxis* which he unambiguously demarcates from *educational praxis*. However, he does so on the grounds that education focuses on the development of individuals as persons as opposed to meeting the external requirements of society. For Hall and Ames the concept of aesthetic order explains "why there is no disjunction between the need of individuals for personal cultivation and the needs of society as a whole in the thinking of Confucius. They are mutually dependent. A harmonious social order for Confucius depends on the fullest disclosure of the unique capacities of the individuals that compose it. This in turn depends on reciprocating acts of deference on the part of individuals" (see Hall and Ames, p. 137) in which they mutually acknowledge each others distinctive contribution to the whole by virtue of their different dispositions, talents and points of view. Such an order does not presume uniformity of conduct based on agreed norms. Hall and Ames contend that from the perspective of Confucius, the self-cultivation of the individual is always in relation to others, not by subordinating their individuality to an agreed vision of the good, but by accommodating a plurality of points of view in the development of their own distinctive and unique outlook on life.

> The process of person making entails both the taking in of other selves to build a self, and the application of one's own personal judgment (yi). And personal judgement is refined and developed in appropriating the meanings and values of other persons and taking them in as one's own.
>
> (p. 118)

Self-cultivation is a personal ordering of the self that also takes an aesthetic form and in doing so participates in the creation of a harmonious social order. Hence the creation of personal and social order are coextensive. This has important implications for how we might characterise the creation of aesthetically ordered learning environments. Hinchliffe's distinction between a *pedagogical* and *educational* ordering of learning experiences collapses. An aesthetically ordered learning environment would provide conditions for students to meet the learning requirements of a society based on harmonious relations, as opposed to relations governed entirely by consensual norms, but these are also the conditions for the development of individual selves in all their particularity and uniqueness.

Another important implication is that the disjunction between the teacher as the maker of learning environments and the learners who benefit from them dissolves. It does so partly because the creation of aesthetic social orders involves the active collaboration of the individuals that compose it. It requires them to actively engage in a process of person making that discloses and expresses their particularity and uniqueness.

As we have seen, Hinchliffe characterises 'pedagogy' in terms of a praxis that orders learning experiences according to some pre-ordained pattern of activities that transcends the concrete particularities the teacher confronts in any given classroom situation. Underpinning such a characterisation is a disjunction between teaching and learning. It is the role of the teacher to order the learning experiences of students and the role of the latter to benefit as a learner from the experiences provided. Of course there is room for different interpretations of pedagogy within this common framework of assumptions. Conceived in idealist terms 'pedagogy' will seek to make a learning environment in which students' experiences are structured by the forms of knowledge that disclose the things that are constituted by truth, goodness, and beauty. Conceived in existentialist terms it will make a learning environment in which students experience the power and influence of heroic individuals. Conceived in pragmatist terms it will make a learning environment in which students inquire into problematic situations and abstract from them principles to guide problem-solving activities. Neither of these conceptions fundamentally calls the disjunction between teaching and learning into question. However, the aesthetic perspective of Confucius does just this, as I shall now demonstrate with reference to his characterisation of teaching and learning.

In aesthetically ordering learning experiences for students, the teacher's dependence on having the active co-operation of his or her students is well-illustrated by Confucius, when talking about his primary criterion as a teacher for engaging students in the educational process:

> In instructing students, I do not open the way for them until they are struggling for clarity; I do not elaborate for them until they have given it their best effort. If I give a student one corner and he does not return with the other three, I will not go over it again.
>
> (Quoted from the Analects 7/8 by
> Hall and Ames p. 146)

This is the depiction of a teacher who in a sense stands at the edge of chaos, but declines to see his students as fearful objects, as members of the masses that need to be managed and controlled. Hall and Ames point out that for Confucius education, conceived as *edification*, is a process that enables individuals to emerge from the masses by cultivating their different and distinctive dispositions. They explain:

> Edification permits one to move from the indeterminate masses to the expression of one's particularity and, ultimately to the expression of one's authoritative humanity.
>
> (p. 146)

This movement though is a voluntary one and not coerced or controlled, as Confucius illustrates in the above account of his role as a teacher. In an aesthetically ordered learning environment the students are receptive to teaching but far from submissive in their stance towards it. Indeed the teacher will welcome his(her) 'knowledge' being challenged and questioned by students for, as we shall see, his(her) authority does not reside in having reached a point of mastery over the subject-matter. The teacher, in creating an aesthetically ordered learning environment, pursues harmony with students rather than agreement. As Hall and Ames (p. 165) point out Confucius described the *exemplary person* as one who pursued harmony among differences rather than agreement, implying that there is no harmony in agreement. They refer to his admonishment to his disciples "to qualify even the instruction of their teacher with their own insights" (p. 48). This stands in contrast with the teacher engaged in the production of a rationally ordered learning environment where learning is conceived as submission to learning requirements imposed by the teacher. From the standpoint of Confucius teaching is a matter of *artistry* rather than *management*.

The aesthetic perspective of Confucius therefore also challenges the disjunction between teaching and learning with respect to the teacher being prepared to learn from his students. The role of the teacher, according to Confucius, is not simply to transmit the cultural tradition but also to engage students in the creative process of adapting and extending its meanings to "maximise the possibilities of their own circumstances" (see Hall and Ames, p. 47). This entails the teacher being receptive to insights introduced by his(her) students. Students' learning feeds back into the teacher's own understanding of the cultural legacy (s)he is responsible for transmitting. Hence, for Confucius, the transmission of the cultural tradition is not a one way process. It requires the teacher also to become engaged as a learner in the creative process of extending and adapting the cultural meanings presented to their students as objects of learning.

It is at this point that Confucius' concepts of the *exemplary person* and the *authoritative person* are helpful in understanding the authority of the teacher as the creator of aesthetically ordered learning environments. Hall and Ames suggest that these are overlapping concepts picking out specific aspects of the general project of personal growth. As such the characteristics of a commitment to learning, self-cultivation, and personal refinement are held in common (p. 188). The *exemplary person* is one who "serves as the primary agent of socio-political ordering" but s(he) can only do this by virtue of his(her) role as a model of self-cultivation (p. 189). Such a model is the *authoritative person*: one who engages as a learner in the process of cultivating his(her) humanity through his(her) relations with others.

In the light of these concepts, one can argue that the artistry the teacher displays in creating aesthetically ordered learning environments is the achievement of an *exemplary person*. However, such artistry is coextensive with the artistry the teacher displays in cultivating a personally ordered self in the process by 'taking in' and 'learning from' the other selves they engage with; namely, their students. In teaching students, the teacher must be involved in cultivating his(her) own humanity because it is in doing so that his(her) authority as a teacher resides. The authority consists in being a model or exemplar of the process of self-cultivation. It is the authority of the *authoritative person*.

Hall and Ames argue that the authoritative person is not the same as the charismatic person gifted with a message derived from some source beyond him(her)self. The former signifies the actualisation of a novel mode of being and in doing so provides a model for others who seek to realize their authoritative humanity. They point out that one cannot imitate such a model "in any literal or formal sense and still achieve the sort of originative thinking and acting associated with the authoritative person" (p. 178). The dynamics of modelling in the thinking of Confucius "require both deference and personal creativity" (p. 178). Imitating the model provided by an *authoritative person* is a matter of re-enacting the "functions, processes, actions and events" such a person signifies to be meaningful and appropriate ways of aesthetically ordering ones 'self'. However, this is not a matter of replication but of the re-presentation of the model in a novel form "that is a function of the unique particularity of the imitating being" (p. 179).

To what extent then can we characterise a teacher's aesthetic ordering of his(her) students' learning experiences in terms of the dynamics of modelling depicted in the thinking of Confucius? I will explore this question in relation to a paper by Chris Amirault entitled *The Good Teacher, The Good Student* (1995, pp. 64–78). It is an account of his relationship with his best student during his first year as a College Instructor and Graduate Student. Shannon, his student, was in his writing courses. One day she came to his office to discuss a paper he had found disappointing and she had been struggling to rewrite in the light of his comments. She informed him that she had been struggling to "figure out what you wanted me to write" and couldn't do it. Then she realised that "what I needed to do was to figure out what I wanted to write." He was thrilled that she had learned "what I most wanted as a teacher was for my students to figure out what they most wanted as students." As a result of the discussion that followed with Shannon, he felt he had broken through into a dialogical and student-centred model of teaching, from narcissistically positioning the student where he wanted her to be to pedagogically positioning himself selflessly at a point where the student wanted to be as a learner. He felt that he and Shannon had repositioned themselves in the pedagogical relationship and broken through the boundary between 'teacher' and 'student' to become a teacher-student and student-teacher respectively in line with Freire's radical pedagogy (1990).

However, a week later, Shannon appeared once more in Amirault's office to inform him that she had wanted to be a college professor. He was horrified and suddenly convinced that whatever good teaching was, he wasn't doing it. He assumed that Shannon was saying that she wanted to become exactly what he wanted to become, a college professor in English. His new found student-centred pedagogical strategies appeared to be a fiction masking the fact that "my best student was merely a reproduction of myself" (p. 74). He comes to understand his relationship to Shannon in terms of the reproductive function of education depicted by Bourdieu and Passeron (1970). He writes:

> As the "object of all his care and attention, the "gifted pupil" embodies the teacher's narcissistic desire for reproduction (of himself as a model pupil), and at the same time confirms the institutional pedagogy within which both are constructed.
>
> (p. 71)

However, over time after many conversations about his meetings with Shannon he suddenly realised that she had simply declared she wanted to be a college professor. His subsequent urgings that she consider disciplines other than English were based on the assumption that she wanted to become an English professor.

He came to acknowledge that his disavowal was in fact trying to deflect, not so much her identification with him but rather his identification with her, for "after all – I want to be a college professor someday too" (p. 75). In doing so he was faced with the paradoxical nature of his pedagogy: which appeared to function reproductively and yet at the same time acknowledged that Shannon's agenda for learning was *different* to his own.

In Confucian terms Shannon treated her teacher as an authoritative person and appropriated him as a model for developing her own particularity. Amirault concluded that his "pedagogy has more to do with my investments and identifications than with anything else" yet he goes on "to deny that real teaching and learning took place between Shannon and me would be to deny the possibility of pedagogy" (p. 77). I would put it another way. It would be to deny the possibility of an *educative pedagogy*, for what Amirault's study of his teaching demonstrates is the possibility of infusing the public institutional roles of teachers and learners with a personal and educative dimension that breaks through the boundaries between them. It is at the points of 'break through' that the artistry of the teacher in the aesthetic ordering of learning experiences is evidenced.

References

Amirault, C. (1995) The Good Teacher, The Good Student in Gallop, J. (Ed.). *Pedagogy: The question of impersonation*, Indiana University Press: Bloomington and Indianapolis.

Boddington, D. and Larner, M. (2000) Curriculum Enrichment at Key Stage Four, NASC Papers, CARE/UEA: Norwich, Mimeo.

Bourdieu, P. and Passeron, J.-C. (1970) *Reproduction in Education, Society, and Culture*, Sage: London.

Brown, K. and Fletcher, A. (2002) Disaffection or Disruptive Engagement? A Collaborative Inquiry into Pupils' Behaviour and their perceptions of their Learning in Modern Language Lessons, *Pedagogy, Culture and Society*, Vol. 10, No. 10.

Freire, P. (1990) *Pedagogy of the Oppressed*, Continuum: New York.

Hall, D.L. and Ames, R.T. (1987) *Thinking Through Confucius*, State University of New York Press: Albany, NewYork.

Hargreaves, D. (1996) Teaching as a research-based profession: possibilities and prospects, *Teacher Training Agency Annual Lecture*. Teacher Training Agency: London.

Hargreaves, D. (1997) In Defence of Research for Evidence-based Teaching: a rejoinder to Martyn Hammersley, *British Educational Research Journal*, Vol. 23, No. 4.

Hargreaves, D. (1999) Revitalising Educational Research: Lessons from the past and proposals for the future, *Cambridge Journal of Education*, Vol. 29, No. 2.

Hinchliffe, G. (2001) Education or Pedagogy? in *Journal of Philosophy of Education*, Vol. 35, Issue 1.

Lewin, R. (1993) *Complexity: Life at the edge of chaos*, Phoenix Books: London.

Oakley, J. (assisted by others) (2002) RHINOs: A research project about the quietly disaffected, *Pedagogy, Culture and Society*, Vol. 10, No. 10.

Reynolds, D. (1998) Teacher Effectiveness, *Teacher Training Agency Corporate Plan Launch 1998–2001*, Teacher Training Agency: London.

Stenhouse, L. (1971) The Humanities Project: The Rationale, *Theory into Practice*, No. 10.

Stenhouse, L. (1975) *An Introduction to Curriculum Research and Development*, Heinemann Educational: London.

Williams, R. (2000) *Lost Icons: Reflections on cultural bereavement*, T&T Clark: Edinburgh & New York.

PART 5

RESOLVING THE DUALISM OF THEORY AND PRACTICE

CHAPTER 11

DOING ACTION RESEARCH – DOING PRACTICAL PHILOSOPHY

What the academy does with an antagonistic view of educational enquiry?

Prospero, Vol. 6, Nos 3 and 4, pp. 82–100

The discourse surrounding the idea of educational action research: distortions and subversions

In various past writings I have argued that action research is a *moral/practical science* and that educational research is best viewed as a form of action research directed towards the moral/practical ends of education rather than the discovery of disinterested facts about education (see Elliott 1980, 1983, 1987, 1989, 1991, 1996).

Although I partly formulated the idea of educational action research as a moral science to make my own practice of action research with teachers intelligible to myself, I also did it to provoke my academic readers and disturb their assumptions about the nature of scientific enquiry in general and the nature of educational enquiry in particular; namely, that it is directed towards the discovery of empirical facts about the world rather than towards moral or practical ends. I wanted to challenge that contemporary academic culture which is characterised, as Alaisdair MacIntyre (1990, p. 217) has pointed out, by the professionalisation, specialisation and fragmentation of inquiries and the exclusion of questions about moral, as well as theological, truth from the academic arena to the private sphere. The challenge hasn't worked too well. I underestimated the capacity of the academic culture to, in MacIntyre's words (p. 219), "dissolve antagonism and emasculate hostility" by admitting the counter-doctrine "only in reduced and distorted versions, so that it becomes an ineffective contender for intellectual and moral allegiance."

I will provide two examples of contemporary academia operating on claims about educational action research. One, provided by Martin Hammersley (1995), adopts a conventional liberal academic standpoint towards educational inquiry, while the other provided by Maggie MacLure (1995, see also Stronach and MacLure, 1997) adopts a post-modern standpoint. Interestingly these apparently different standpoints produce a similar account of the idea of action research although their critique of it significantly differs.

Hammersley (1995), in a reply to Pat D'arcy's response to his critique of action-research theory (1993), explains:

> I am arguing against those who criticise conventional research and promote action research on the grounds that the latter unifies educational theory and practice. Very few teachers are committed to this view, in my experience, but

some academics are. An example is John Elliott – What he sees as replacing academic research is, of course, action research by educational practitioners – The message is rarely spelt out so bluntly, but it is implicit in many of the arguments used to justify teacher research, as I showed in my article.

(p. 118)

As Hammersley points out to his protagonist he is not against action research as such but a certain idea of it, one particularly articulated by myself. Why? Because it denies the importance of *clearly distinguishing* different types of educational research, a denial which according to Hammersley could result in action research, what he calls *practical problem-solving research*, becoming devalued. It seems Hammersley assumes that treating action research as equivalent in function to *academic research* in the field of education implies judging it according to the criteria and standards of the latter, from which standpoint it will probably be found wanting. Here Hammersley appears to lose the point of me redefining *educational research as action research*. Such a redefinition from my standpoint implies a radical shift in the criteria and standards for judging the quality of educational research. This standpoint asserts that what makes research *educational* is not simply a particular kind of subject matter but the type of ends towards which it is explicitly directed; ends which in the broader sense of the term can be called *moral*. The idea of educational research as a form of action research which unifies theory and practice is rooted in a particular vision of educational research as a form of moral inquiry.

In his original critique of the idea of the 'Teacher as Researcher' (1993) Hammersley defends conventional educational research against the criticisms of those who advocate collaborative and practitioner research. First, he counters a perceived criticism that conventional research is irrelevant to the practical concerns of teachers. He does so on the grounds that "sound practice cannot amount to the straightforward *application* of theoretical knowledge" (p. 430). It depends as much on judgement and experience, if not more so. The fact that conventional research does not meet the expectation that it yields solutions to practical problems does not, Hammersley argues, warrant the accusation that it is irrelevant. The findings of conventional research may be "relevant and useful to teachers without providing them with solutions to their problems." This argument is again based on a misunderstanding of what some advocates of teachers action research, such as myself, expect from educational research. We would agree with Hammersley's point that 'relevance' should not be confused with the provision of problem-solutions. Our critique of conventional research in the field of education is based on the view that it is not informed by a well-articulated theory of education, as opposed to theories derived from particular academic disciplines. Much of it neglects the question 'what makes educational research *educational*?' (see Elliott, 2002). Such research might be characterised as *research on education* rather than *educational research* (see Elliott, 1978). This categorisation does not amount to an accusation of irrelevance. It may well inform teachers understanding and judgements in classrooms and schools. What the distinction does is highlight the special significance of a form of research which requires the active engagement of teachers because it is conditioned by *educational values*.

It may be the case that the realisation of such values, conceived as *educational ends*, are not a matter of practical concern to many teachers. However, the central relevance for some advocates of action research, of research directed towards the realisation of such ends needs to be understood in a certain context. It is a context in which teachers are actively engaged in curricular reforms, with the intention of transforming the quality of students' learning experiences in schools. In a context of curriculum change notions like 'inquiry/discovery learning' emerged as conceptions of *educational ends* and came to characterise the practical concerns of teachers.

Hammersley is aware of the change context from which the advocacy of teachers action research emerged, pointing out that advocates tend to criticise traditional 'knowledge transmission' teaching methods as well as conventional educational research. He appreciates that such criticism is intended to pave the way for an alternative conception of pedagogical aims based on a different epistemology. He is also aware that this alternative conception implies a form of pedagogy which, "is closer in nature to research" (p. 436). Why then does he appear to misunderstand the critiques of conventional modes of research produced by the advocates of action research? One explanation is that he is concerned to accommodate action research as a mode of educational knowledge production without disrupting the status quo.

As Hammersley illustrates in his reply to D'Arcy, academic educational researchers need not be opposed to action research so long as it is seen as one type of educational research amongst others within the academic canon of the liberal university; namely, *practical problem-solving*. What does this imply about the sort of activity it is? I would suggest that first it implies that action research is a relatively small scale activity which focuses on practical problems that emerge in highly localised settings and therefore is not in the business of producing highly generalisable knowledge. Second, it implies that the knowledge products of action research constitute forms of *instrumental knowledge* i.e. knowledge about practical problem-solving strategies. Third, it implies that action research non-contentiously fits into a *hierarchy of modes of knowledge production* and that the view that it stands in an oppositional relation to them is erroneous.

Regardless of the oppositional idea of action research, that I and some other academics may have articulated, when one examines how action research is currently shaping up in the academy it looks very much the sort of practical problem-solving activity depicted above (see Elliott, MacLure and Sarland, 1997). Action research has established its niche in the contemporary liberal university, largely in the context of post-graduate courses supporting practitioner professional development. It operates at a fairly lowly level in the research hierarchy at the border between research and teaching. However, its instrumentalist conception of knowledge enables universities to successfully market their professional development courses as a means of improving performativity in the work-place, e.g. classrooms and schools. The admission of action research into the academy has therefore been secured at a price, its value being associated with its marketability as a professional development process rather than with mainstream educational research.

The value of action research for the academy at a time when vocationally orientated post-graduate provision is expanding appears to reside in its appeal as a source of practically useful knowledge. It is not however viewed as a source of high status theoretical knowledge. Practical problem-solving is not assumed to involve addressing theoretical questions about the conceptual schemes embodied in a practice and which shape the ways problems are constituted in the consciousness of practitioners. When action research is viewed solely in terms of practical problem-solving what counts as useful academic knowledge is not something which challenges and destabilises the action-frames of practitioners within the work-place, but rather something which is constituted and shaped by them. Although Hammersley expresses a concern that action research will become discredited if it is judged against the same standards as conventional research, his construction of the idea as *practical problem solving* effectively discredits it as an alternative and, indeed antagonistic, vision of educational enquiry.

MacLure's (1995) post-modern deconstruction of the claims of action research as a counter-oppositional idea imply a similar reading to Hammersley's. A post-modern reading she writes "might be interested in how the claims of action research often rest on an opposition between practice and theory, that privileges the former." As an idea action research is understood to privilege practical knowledge in opposition to theoretical knowledge and therefore provides an example of the binary oppositions which have characterised the logic of western thought for over 200 years. Such oppositions constitute attempts to create an orderly world by privileging "one of the pair as more important/basic/central/deep/stable than the other." In subduing meaning and excluding chaos through such binary oppositions our thinking about nature, society, and self has been underpinned by the foundational principles of modernity, which MacLure identifies as "the decideability of truth, the inevitability of progress, the triumph of reason, the possibility of a universal moral code, the objectivity of science, the forward march of history, the existence of the singular, autonomous self." She explains how, from a post-modern standpoint, these principles are about making the world more controllable, predictable and manageable and therefore link the very structure of western thought with oppression; thus echoing the Nietzschean view that our major categories of thinking mask a generalised 'will to power'.

MacLure argues that in privileging practice in opposition to theory claims about action research ascribe a special, presumably epistemological, status "to *experience*, with its connotations of authenticity, directness, naturalness, immediacy, relevance, life-as-it-is-lived" and counterpoises it with claims about the "remoteness and abstraction of research/theory/policy/positivism." The epistemological claims made for practitioner experience thereby derive their power from the critique of theory and conventional modes of knowledge production. Moreover, MacLure argues that a post-modern reading of the claims for action research would "register the continuing appeal to/of the *self* (of the 'practitioner') as a singular, knowable, perfectible entity." On the basis of the claims made for action research, she concludes that, it appears to be "a very modernist sort of enterprise."

The 'thesis' is further refined and developed by MacLure (see Stronach and MacLure 1997, Ch. 7) in a deconstruction of *life history* interviews carried out with 10 academic advocates of action research, including myself. She claims that these narratives, stories of the transition from teacher to academic/action researcher:

> embody, in an almost literal sense, the engagement with boundaries that are addressed within action research itself: between theory and practice; between the personal and professional; between the organisational culture of the school and the academy; between 'insider' and 'outsider' perspectives; between the sacred languages of science, scholarship or research, and the mundane dialectics of practice and everyday experience.

For Maclure the *exit* from teaching, from the primary ground of practice, and the *entry* into the academy, generated accounts which attempted to reconcile 'the love of teaching' with suppressed longings for 'the intellectual life'; hence, the commitment to action research as a resolution to the boundary problems posed by the transition. Such accounts, she argues, depict transitions as solutions to the boundary problems experienced in *exits and entrances*. They constitute *theories of the self*, in the form of narratives which offer coherent explanations of the present in terms of the past by presenting at their core a *singular self* "discoverable through reflection," and which, in spite of being "pushed in different directions, or into somewhat different shapes" by external events, persists over time.

For MacLure, theories of action research tend to be concerned with resolving the binary opposition between *theory* and *practice*, and in doing so to provide a rationalisation for *exits* from the primary field of practice and *entrances* into the academy. The intellectual project MacLure argues is underpinned by the existential project which revolves around the notion of a singular and continuous self moving towards a state of perfection through a series of transitional experiences that enable it "to triumph over the adversity of contradiction (between values and practice, between real and false consciousness etc.)."

In her 1995 paper MacLure claimed that the resolution of the intellectual project tended to involve privileging *practice* over *theory*, but this is qualified in her 1997 book with Stronach. Here the resolution consists of either "reversing the poles of the traditional dichotomies – or by seeking reconciliations, in which the interests of those who previously lived antagonistically on opposite sides of the boundary will find a new space in which their differences can be resolved or dissolved." The latter kind of resolution tends to get interpreted by Stronach and MacLure as a form of colonisation of the primary field of practice by the academy, in order to render practice subordinate to its theoretical concerns. In a section of their analyses of the life histories of academic action researchers entitled 'Interviews with the vampires' they endorse Couture's (1994) characterisation of action research as the work of 'Dracula', the university, "feeding off the virgin souls (selves) of teachers who offer themselves up in the name of reflective practice."

Stronach and MacLure argue that whichever form of resolution to the theory-practice dichotomy is adopted "in order to tell these smooth stories of the self" it involves *forgetting* the paradoxes and self-contradictions in which we are caught up, both existentially and intellectually. The academic action researcher *forgets* about:

> the impossibility and necessity of leaving the 'island', or the Garden, of teaching, and the discomforts of being 'haunted' thereafter by the spectre of practice. About the way the poles of the 'inside' – 'outside' dualism reverse themselves, valorizing first one term, then the other, in a movement which is never fully or finally arrested.

From their post-modern perspective we should abandon all futile attempts to resolve and transcend dichotomies, even by attempting to dissolve them through a 'unifying theory' of the relation between theory and practice, and resist all resolutions to the problem of getting safely across the boundaries by accepting a life of risk and uncertainty and giving up any hope for a happy ending. For Stronach and MacLure the only alternative to a modernist version of action research would be one which problematises its own clear-cut distinctions and categories – 'experience', 'practice', 'self' – viewing them as a 'site of struggle' between different discourses, criss-crossed by different 'regimes of truth' (see also Somekh, 2000, pp. 116–117).

From my standpoint Stronach and MacLure provide us with a rather distorted account of the claims made for action research by myself and some other action research 'theorists' (e.g. Winter, 1991). In characterising action research as a moral or practical science I did not see this as either an attempt to reverse the poles of the traditional dichotomies by privileging practice over theory or as a 'Dracula' like attempt to colonise the primary field of practice in the service of academe. I am aware that MacLure (with Stronach) would argue that she is unmasking a 'will to power' in this latter respect that the academic action researcher will not be aware of. In reply, as one of the 'vampires' interviewed in the study referred to, I would simply point out that I publicly deconstructed some academic discourses about action research in similar terms to Couture within the same journal volume (see Elliott, 1994), and have long argued (see Elliott, 1987, 1991) that the idea of the teacher as action researcher originated within the field of practice rather than the academy. At its best the academy has articulated a logic (theory of theory and practice) embedded in certain kinds of innovatory practices which were self-initiated by teachers. At its worst the academy has distorted and domesticated that logic to serve its own interests.

For some action research theorists, like myself, the task has been to explicate the theory of theory and practice tacitly embedded in innovatory practices initiated by teachers, and to safeguard it against possible distortion and domestication from the bipolar thinking endemic within the academy. In doing so we saw ourselves to be articulating a *unifying theory* which 'dissolved' the binary opposition between theory and practice. However, from MacLure and Stronach's post-modern perspective it is impossible to construct a *unifying theory* which abandons binary thought. Therefore, those academics who claim they have are denying a hidden 'will to power'.

Since neither subordinating theory to practice nor vice versa transgresses and destabilises the fundamental norms which underpin the culture of academe, both 'readings' of action research conveniently provide the post-modern analyst with an object to demolish. They are 'readings' constructed with 'destruction' in mind. In describing the production of the life history narratives, MacLure confesses her own complicity as one of the interviewers in the production process. She admits that she and her co-researcher shaped responses by the kinds of questions posed; questions which expected responses to be framed by modernist assumptions and which were sometimes challenged by the interviewees. We appear to have a situation in which a postmodernist researcher colludes, albeit unwittingly at the time, in manipulating the responses of interviewees to elicit accounts she can adopt an oppositional stance towards. Later I shall argue that post-modern analysts tend to reduce all stances that are antagonistic to their own position to a single antagonism; namely, that of modernism. MacLure, with disarming honesty, appears to lend support to the argument when she comments:

> it could be argued that our reading above of the interviews is equally guilty (or certainly not innocent) of consuming the alterality of the individual stories in order to produce a singularly postmodern account.

However, I would extend this argument in her case to include a reductionism which, on her own admission, appears to have operated prior to 'the reading' of the interviews in the very process of interviewing itself.

MacLure's own bipolar thinking, the tendency to reduce all inquiry to either 'modern' or 'post-modern' thinking prevents her, I shall argue, from acknowledging a point of view on action research which is neither modern nor post-modern. Just as Hammersley's conventional assumptions about the nature of educational enquiry (which MacLure would undoubtedly interpret as habits of mind which stem from the structures of modernist thought) blind him to the view of action research I and others have attempted to articulate, so the assumptions which underpin MacLure's post-modernist stance blind her to it. How can we explain this blindness of both the modern and post-modern points of view to a third perspective on the nature of educational inquiry.

Alaisdair MacIntyre and versions of moral enquiry

MacIntyre suggests a possible explanation in *Three Rival Versions of Moral Enquiry* (1990). In comparing two of the rival views, which he characterises as the *encyclopaedic* and *genealogic*, he argues that in each the other is always a shadowy presence, for each:

> contains within itself a more or less spelled-out representation of the other, indeed cannot dispense with such a representation as a counterpart to its representation of itself to itself. From the standpoint of the encyclopaedist the genealogist is reproducing familiar irrationalist themes and theses; so the genealogists perspectivism is characteristically understood as merely one more version of relativism, open to refutation by the arguments used by Socrates against Protagoras. From the standpoint of the genealogist the encyclopaedist is inescapably imprisoned within metaphors unrecognised as metaphors. And from both standpoints any attempt – to produce a characterisation of this antagonism from some external, third vantage point is doomed to failure; there is no idiom neutral between the encyclopaedist's affirmations and distinctions and the genealogist's subversions.
>
> (p. 43)

Before revisiting contemporary 'academic' critiques of action research, let's look at MacIntyre's characterisation of these different standpoints. MacIntyre uses the term 'encyclopaedic' to characterise an organisation of knowledge shaped by a post-enlightenment conception of *rationality* which it was the task of philosophy to articulate and justify; namely, as *impersonal, impartial, disinterested, uniting, and universal*. It is this conception of rationality that underpins the habits of mind, such as a belief in theoretical reason as the key to human emancipation and social progress, which MacLure sees it as the task of postmodernism to undo. The encyclopaedic standpoint therefore appears to be the same standpoint as the one post-modern thinkers have tended to call *modernity*. Its conception of rationality applies as much to reasoning about our moral conduct, *the right* and *the good*, and the *obligations* and *duties* they entail, as to reasoning about the empirical world in pursuit of *truths* about it.

MacIntyre argues that the encyclopaedic organisation of knowledge has been convincingly subverted by *genealogy*, a form of enquiry into the psychological and social formation of knowledge originated by Nietzsche in the 19th century and continued through the 20th century by post-structuralist and post-modern thinkers such as Foucault, Deleuze and Derrida. The genealogist deconstructs thought and language – about truth, knowledge, duty and right – governed by an encyclopaedic conception of rationality. Given post modernist thinkers, such as MacLure, set themselves a similar task we will be quite justified in characterising their enquiries as *genealogy*.

Genealogical deconstruction, according to MacIntyre, has four aspects; psychological, epistemological, historical and literary. First, psychologically what encyclopaedic rationality takes to be fixed and binding about truth, duty, right etc., is an "unrecognised motivation serving an unacknowledged purpose" which Nietzsche came to characterise as *the will to power*. Genealogical deconstruction not only unmasks such rationality as possessing oppressive intent but imputes lack of self-knowledge to those who give it their allegiance. Second, this lack of self-knowledge has an epistemological implication. It sustains a blindness to the multiplicity of perspectives from which the world can be viewed, and the idioms in which it can be represented and the fact that there is no single reality they are about. Genealogical deconstruction is explicitly at odds with encyclopaedic rationality, inasmuch as it is open to rival and antagonistic conceptual schemes. MacLure's characterisation of a post-modern version of action research as a 'site of struggle' between different discourses, criss-crossed by different 'regimes of truth', is an expression of such a commitment to openness.

Third, the genealogical deconstruction of encyclopaedic rationality involves exhibiting the *historical genesis* of "the psychological and social formations in which the will to power is distorted into and concealed by the will to truth" (p. 39). Thus as a genealogist of 19th century morality Nietzsche:

> traced both socially and conceptually how rancour and resentment on the part of the inferior destroyed the aristocratic nobility of archaic heroes and substituted a priestly set of values in which a concern for purity and impurity provided a disguise for malice and hate.
>
> (pp. 39–40)

Fourth, the genre of the genealogists text was intended to differ markedly from the conventional academic text of the encyclopaedist which strives to establish a warranted certainty and fixity of belief in the form of a thesis. From the genealogical standpoint the thesis expresses a passive, reactive and repressed self which nevertheless represses, behind a mask of objectivity. 'Insights' are therefore to be represented within the genealogical genre as expressions of an active, energised self, open to ambiguity of meaning and the play of forces between contrary 'regimes of truth'. Such 'insights' constitute personal, creative, and dynamic interpretative acts expressed in the form of aphorisms, poems and prophetic utterances, which convey no fixed meanings, but are being continuously superseded as mere moments in the development of the enquiry. Such a genre is deeply subversive to the encyclopaedic conventions governing academic text production in universities.

MacIntyre asks whether the genealogical project, conceived in terms of the aspects referred to above, has succeeded or failed in its own terms, noting that its narratives from Nietzsche to Foucault can be read as a continuing tendency for their authors to "relapse and collapse" into encyclopaedia; psychologically, epistemologically and methodologically. He argues that it is difficult *not* to read Nietzsche's *Zur Genealogy der Moral* as yet one more magisterial academic treatise, "better and more stylishly written indeed than the books of Hermann Cohen, of Ranke or of Harnack – , but deploying arguments and appealing to sources in the same way and constrained by the same standards of factual accuracy and no more obviously polemical against rival views" (p. 44).

MacIntyre considers the genealogist's answer to such an apparent relapse into the conventional academic genre of the thesis, that the thesis should not be read in isolation from what precedes and follows it, abstracted from the movement of the author's thinking over time. Read in context it will be understood as a temporary stance, the putting on of a mask for the purpose of addressing a particular audience. The relapse into the encyclopaedic genre is more apparent than real, the genealogist will argue in defence of either a particular narrative or of the genealogical project as a whole. MacIntyre sees a problem with this line of defence.

> For the genealogist who has put the academic stance in question by writing and publishing his or her book is addressing whom? Someone presumably to and with whom he not only puts in question the objects of his critique, but to whom he opens up in turn the possibility of in turn putting the genealogist in question, either in respect of particular theses or in respect of his or her overall project. Yet this cannot be done without adopting a certain fixity of stance, a staying in place, a commitment to defend and to respond to and, if necessary, to yield.
>
> (p. 45)

The act of writing for a particular audience, MacIntyre contends, presupposes a self which has "enough fixity and continuity" (of purpose) to enter into those relationships "constitutive of the acts of reading-as-one-who-has-been-written-for and of writing-as-one-who-is-to-be-read." Hence, MacIntyre concludes, in the context of the discourse surrounding the genealogical narrative, the genealogist has to assume a self which cannot be dissolved into masks and moments but is persistent and substantial. The problem for the genealogical project becomes one of how to resolve the paradox:

> The problem – is how to combine the fixity of particular stances, exhibited in the use of standard genres of speech and writing, with the mobility of transition from stance to stance, how to assume the contours of a given mask and then to discard it for another, without ever assenting to the metaphysical fiction of a face which has its own finally true and undiscardable representation, –. Can it be done?
>
> (p. 47)

If the genealogist's self is nothing more than the genealogist makes of it then, MacIntyre suggests the project as a whole as opposed to particular enquiries within it, has failed.

In seeking an answer to this question MacIntyre turns to Foucault who consciously attempted to carry through the genealogical project. MacIntyre argues that no attempt to carry it through "is likely to be more impressive," either in terms of systematic implementation, erudition or honesty, than Foucault's. Yet, he concludes, Foucault increasingly regressed, during his 15 years at the College de France, into academic mode, culminating in "the plain academic style of the *Histoire de la Sexualite* and the even plainer explanations – offered in that wearisome multitude of interviews in which the academic deference evident in the questions is never rejected by Foucault in his answers" (p. 53). Those features of the essentially temporary stances which mark the genealogist's historical disclosures – ironic distance, unmasking and self-masking – are, MacIntyre argues, entirely absent in the 'final Foucault' who largely abandons the project by escaping its central paradox.

For MacIntyre the question of the place of the genealogist within the genealogical project raises a further question. In evaluating the development of the strategies employed by a genealogist, such as Foucault, he argues that we have to recognise the part played by 'logic' in his or her thought; the identification of contradictions, appeals to evidence, the practical reasoning exhibited in the actions through which the genealogical project progresses or fails to progress, and the genealogist's self-evaluations of their success and failure. All of this presupposes standards of rationality which are independent "of the particular stages and moments of the temporary strategies through which the genealogist moves his or her overall projects forwards and which need to be acknowledged if the genealogist is to find his or her actions and utterances intelligible" (p. 55) let alone intelligible to others. Hence, once more MacIntyre concludes that "genealogy requires beliefs and allegiances of a kind precluded by the genealogical stance" (p. 55). It therefore has to demonstrate that it has the internal resources to answer two questions:

> Can the genealogical narrative find any place within itself for the genealogist? And can genealogy, as a systematic project, be made intelligible to the geneal-ogist, as well as others, without some at least tacit recognition being accorded to just those standards and allegiances which it is its avowed aim to disrupt and subvert?
>
> (p. 55)

If the genealogical project discovers that it has no resources for furnishing positive answers to these questions then its "relapse and collapse" into encyclopaedia become inevitable and real rather than apparent, showing that it cannot finally emancipate itself from the 'shadowy presence' it defined itself against.

The genealogist's paradox within the post-modern critique of action research

I would argue that MacLure's analysis of the claims of action research reveals this tendency for genealogy to collapse and relapse into encyclopaedic mode. She doesn't problematise her categorisations of the claims for action research, or perhaps even present them as a temporary mask, because they are shaped by the shadowy presence of the encyclopaedic standpoint and the habits of mind with which it is associated. In other words MacLure appears intent on fixing meaning and this is evidenced in the conventional academic style in which she writes. In which case she may also be concealing from her readers and herself a motivation to suppress rival interpretations of action research. Again the shadowy presence of the ency-clopaedic standpoint assists this suppression by blinding her to a view of action research as a moral science which is incommensurable with both the encyclopaedic and genealogical standpoints. In the light of MacIntyre's account of two rival and antagonistic standpoints and their relationship it is possible to read MacLure's post-modern critique as an example of the collapse and relapse of genealogical enquiry into the encyclopaedic mode.

MacLure (1997) fully acknowledges the paradoxical nature of much post-modern critique, including her own. She writes:

> Yes, it's impossible not to sit on that branch that has already been sawn off – on some value position, or commitment, or principle. Yes, every attempt to characterise postmodernism (including this one) uses, while it abuses, the logics of causality and rationality that were the target of deconstruction in the first place. – A postmodern rejoinder would be to refuse the dare to jump one way or the other, the invitation to solve an insoluble paradox. To accept would be to rejoin the modernist community of binary choosers.
>
> (p. 113)

It is interesting to look at the assumptions which underpin this passage. First MacLure assumes that it is possible for the postmodernist to sustain the paradoxical nature of its stance. This in turn assumes, as MacIntyre has pointed out, the possibility of 'self-masking', the adoption of temporary stances which are continuously discarded and never become fixed positions. He questions from his own reading of the major post-modern thinkers who have attempted to carry the genealogical project forward whether they have managed to sustain the paradox and avoid the collapse and relapse into the encyclopaedic mode, arguing for example, in the case of Foucault, that he virtually abandoned it. In other words we may question whether the genealogical paradox is sustainable and this is something that MacLure refuses to do by not problematising the category of *a sustainable paradox* which she deploys to defend the use of modernist logic by post-modern thinkers, including herself.

Second, MacLure assumes that that there is no solution to the paradox except to jump one way or another and thereby relapse into the binary choices which shape modernist thinking. She does not entertain the possibility of a third standpoint which may resolve the genealogical paradox that post-modern enquiry is caught up in without relapsing into modernist ways of thinking.

This blindness to a third position, which stems in my view from an unacknowledged relapse into habits of mind which underpinned the encyclopaedic organisation of knowledge, accounts for her inability to comprehend the claims of action research in any other terms than those which reflect the structures of modernist thought.

Since I argued earlier that MacLure's interpretation of the claims of action research fits Hammersley's interpretation of the idea as *practical problem-solving*, and suggested that the latter constituted a distorted version reproduced from within the liberal academic culture, we may ask the question of how that culture relates to an encyclopaedic conception of rationality?

The 'absent presence' in the contemporary academy

MacIntyre believes that the possibility of the collapse and relapse of genealogy, and by implication of post-modernist enquiry, into encyclopaedic rationality should not be something that the surviving adherents of the encyclopaedic mode of moral enquiry should take comfort in, for two reasons. First, the genealogist's deconstruction of encyclopaedic rationality at work in the fields of morality and religion – manifesting itself in the construction of ethics and theology as scientific disciplines – retain their cogency independently of the fate of the genealogical project. He argues that it has at least succeeded in impugning moral, theological, and metaphysical inquiry as part of the unified view of knowledge the encyclopaedist attempted to construct, evidenced by the marginalisation, within the contemporary liberal university, of ethics and theology as academic disciplines, and the transformation of philosophy from metaphysics (conceived as the discipline which unified the whole of Knowledge) to a method/technique of linguistic analysis. With the genealogical discrediting of these 'disciplines' as sciences the encyclopaedic *tree of knowledge*, with its vision of knowledge as a unified whole, capturing and mirroring the order of the cosmos, collapsed. The university curriculum and its associated forms of enquiry have become a collection of fragmented specialisms.

According to MacIntyre, the outcome of such fragmentation and professionalisation of knowledge is the cultural irrelevance of the contemporary university. This is because it has lost any conception of an *educated public*. With the collapse of a unified account of all knowledge went the idea of publicly shared standards of reasoning against which claims to knowledge could be debated and justified in the wider society. For purposes of communication, the facts emanating from the specialised enquiries of the university are abstracted from the context of their production. Their meaning and significance is left to 'the readers' to interpret for themselves.

For MacIntyre, the latter-day advocate of an encyclopaedic view of a moral science can take little comfort at the relapse of the genealogist into modes of thinking they would recognise, because whatever the defects in the genealogical treatment of the incommensurability of rival standpoints, these do nothing to lessen the existence and significance of that incommensurability. The transformation of the moral enquirer, from a participant in an enterprise shared by all rational beings, into an engaged partisan of a standpoint at war with its rivals, is evidenced in the diversity and fragmentation of the moral standpoints and types of moral discourse abroad in society. Since these antagonistic moral discourses have no place within the contemporary university curriculum of fragmented and specialised enquiries there is no way in which the latter can mediate a conversation between them.

In the light of the above one can perhaps begin to understand why an account of action research as a moral science is, within the contemporary liberal academic culture, an unintelligible one and therefore something Hammersley cannot acknowledge. I say "begin to understand," because surely Hammersley's treatment of action research, the way he categorises it so unproblematically and thereby tames and domesticates it by hierarchalising it in terms of his construct of a *tree of educational knowledge*, is evidence of encyclopaedic habits of mind at work. MacLure might well interpret Hammersley's conception of action research, as *practical problem-solving*, to be an example of the bipolar thinking of the modernist inasmuch as it implies a contrast between theoretical and practical knowledge. However, the tendency for post-modern deconstruction itself to relapse into such habits as fixing categories unproblematically and formulating knowledge claims on the basis of them in the form of *theses* is also evidence of the persistence of encyclopaedic rationality.

We have a situation within the contemporary culture of the university in which there is little room, thanks to the genealogists, for an encyclopaedic view of knowledge as a unified whole and a vision of moral enquiry as an integral part of that whole. However, within this culture the habits of mind and modes of thinking which underpinned the 'architecture' still operate. Modes of academic practice, such as the lecture and journal article, which only make sense in terms of an encyclopaedic conception of knowledge continue to survive and persist within the fragmented and specialised academic cultures of the contemporary university, and with them the structures of reasoning they presuppose. In spite of its successes the genealogical project has not eradicated these cultural practices within the university. It is therefore a mistake, as MacIntyre argues, to infer that contemporary academia has become hospitable to genealogical voices, in spite of the fact that they now occupy "professorial chairs with an apparent ease." Active participation in conventional academic practices, like lectures and the production of journal articles, ensures that such voices are neutralised, and that their activity is treated as a non-antagonistic sub-discipline.

It was characteristic of the *liberal academy* informed by an encyclopaedic conception of knowledge that it took for granted the belief that all rational persons will conceptualise data in one and the same way. This assumption in the post-encyclopaedic university still persists. The 19th century genealogists, according to MacIntyre, eroded this assumption in the fields of moral and theological enquiry but left unfinished business to complete in other fields. The encyclopaedic conception of rationality and its associated habits of mind still lingers on in the contemporary academy, in spite of the 20th century post-modern deconstructions of the ways this conception structures 'knowledge' and culture in a variety of fields, including the natural sciences. Hence, Kuhn showed, in *The Structure of Scientific Revolutions*, that in the domain of the physical sciences "there is no way of identifying, characterising, or classifying data in ways that are relevant to the purposes of theoretical enquiry except in terms of some prior theoretical or doctrinal commitment" (p. 17). His work has still to make a significant impact on the assumptions which actually underpin the practice and teaching of scientific enquiry in the university. If it had we would have moved into a post-liberal academy which acknowledges scientific enquiry as a domain in which incommensurable and antagonistic standpoints need to be accommodated and discussed. Such a post-liberal academy would find room again for moral inquiry, but this time conceived as open to rival and antagonistic standpoints.

The fact that Hammersley and MacLure, from their apparently different standpoints, are blind to a conception of educational action research as a moral science is surely an indication that we cannot as yet characterise the academy as a post-liberal one. Inasmuch as their thinking is still shaped by beliefs and habits of mind once associated with an encyclopaedic conception of knowledge, they cannot acknowledge a moral science paradigm which is incommensurable with either of their apparently differing standpoints. It is to this third paradigm of moral enquiry that I shall now turn, in an attempt to locate educational action research in a paradigm of enquiry which has nevertheless found little room for expression in the post-enlightenment culture of the liberal academy.

Educational enquiry from the standpoint of *tradition*

MacIntyre calls this paradigm the standpoint of *tradition* in contrast to those of *encyclopaedia* and *genealogy*. Such a standpoint is reflected in a strand of thinking that runs from Socrates, through Aristotle and Augustine, to Aquinas. Its view of reason differs from the views of both the encyclopaedic and genealogical standpoints. For the encyclopaedist the essence of reason is that its operation does not depend on any prior commitment and allegiance to a particular set of moral or religious beliefs and customs. From this standpoint, as MacIntyre points out, the *objectivity of reason* is inseparable from *its freedom* from the partialities, the particular traditions, which bind people together as members of particular moral or religious communities. It is this account of reason that the genealogist/postmodernist deconstructs and unmasks as an expression of the *will to power*. Both the encyclopaedist and the genealogist would agree, argues MacIntyre, that the issue at stake between them can be framed as follows:

> *Either* reason is – impersonal, universal, and disinterested *or* it is the unwittingly representative of particular interests, masking their drive to power by its false pretensions to neutrality and disinterestedness.

> (p. 59)

He goes on to point out that this way of defining what is at issue:

> conceals the possibility that reason can only move towards the being genuinely universal and impartial insofar as it is neither neutral nor disinterested, that membership in a particular type of moral community, one from which fundamental dissent has to be excluded, is a condition for genuinely rational enquiry and more especially for moral and theological enquiry.
>
> (pp. 59–60)

What is concealed is the possibility represented by the standpoint of *tradition*, the possibility of transcending the bipolar categories in which post-enlightenment and modernist thought has constructed the issue of reason. From the standpoint of *tradition* any rational enquiry into the nature of the human good, and one might include here the nature of *educational goods*, presupposes the possession of certain virtues which are acquired as a result of having made a commitment to, and been initiated into, a particular moral practice and the beliefs and customs (tradition) which constitute it. In other words, moral enquiry presupposes a prior commitment to make oneself into a particular kind of person by acquiring certain virtues, which are deemed within the tradition to be conditions for knowing the truth about the human good (see MacIntyre pp. 60–61). The acquisition of such virtues by the novice involves submission to the authority of a teacher, acknowledged by the moral community to have acquired the requisite moral and intellectual habits. In this authority-dependent context the novitiate learns what mental and moral habits s(he) is expected to cultivate and to begin to recognise what it is about them which make them virtues. Such a process of initiation is from the standpoint of *tradition* a precondition of being able to engage later in self-directed moral enquiry.

As Macintyre points out the conception of *rational teaching authority* is in conflict with both encyclopaedic knowledge and genealogy. From the former standpoint the development of rationality involves emancipation of the individual "from the tutelage of authority," while from the standpoint of the latter the exercise of such authority is viewed as the operation of "a subjugating power which has to be resisted" (p. 64).

The apparent paradox in a conception of moral enquiry as embedded in tradition – that we can only move towards a knowledge of the human good generally, and our own good in particular, if we have already been taught on the basis of authority something of what that good consists of – stems, according to MacIntyre, from the form in which standards of achievement are justified in any practical craft; namely, historically. He writes:

> The participant in a craft is rational qua participant in so far as he or she conforms to the best standards of reason discovered so far, and the rationality in which he or she thus shares is always, therefore, unlike the rationality of the encyclopaedic mode, understood as a historically situated rationality, even if one which aims at a timeless formulation of its own standards which would be their final and perfected form through a series of successive reformulations, past and yet to come.
>
> (p. 65)

What then motivates the participants in a moral practice to problematise the standards of rationality it embodies, to embark on a new enquiry into how best to categorise its moral ends and the virtues necessary for enacting them? The answer, for MacIntyre, resides in the necessity to continuously reinterpret the tradition and the standards it embodies in response to social change. Old virtues have to be enacted in new ways "and rules extended to cover new contingencies." In circumstances of change, he argues, "we are forced back to a reconsideration of first principles and how they apply to particulars" (p. 129).

Given the practical context of moral enquiry the aims of such enquiry are both theoretical and practical. The question of 'what is good for human beings in general?' cannot be answered independently of the question 'what is good for me, given the person I am, in these particular circumstances?' The answer to the practical question will consist of a particular interpretation of what is judged to be the best answer to date to the theoretical question. It involves interpreting its practical significance 'for me and my situation'. Answers to practical questions constitute concrete practical embodiments of answers to theoretical questions. From the standpoint of *tradition* the moral life is a life which actualises, under particular psychological and socio-historical conditions, universal conceptions of the human good. Moral practices embody moral theories. This is why we cannot produce narrative descriptions of such practices without revealing the moral theories they embody, and why we cannot describe the practical means of realising certain moral ends independently of any reference to those ends.

However, as MacIntyre points out, from the standpoint of tradition our universal concepts of the human good are only fully intelligible in terms of their practical embodiments. We are only in a position to evaluate and debate a universal moral concept, to understand what it amounts to, if we know "what type of enacted narrative would be the embodiment, in the actions and transactions of actual social life, of this particular theory?" (p. 80). Such knowledge is provided by answers to the practical question cited above. This is why, from the standpoint of tradition, one cannot segregate theoretical philosophical enquiry into what is good for human beings universally from enquiry as a form of practical problem-solving. From the standpoint of *tradition* moral enquiry or *science* consists of *doing philosophy*. This is not simply a matter of reflecting about universal moral ends independently of the means of achieving them, since the latter consists of enacting narratives which embody such ends. *Doing philosophy* also involves *undertaking practical experiments* as part and parcel of the philosophical task of justifying a moral theory. It requires what such a theory amounts to in practice to be debated and evaluated.

The relationship between the conception of moral enquiry outlined above and an account of *educational action research* as a form of moral enquiry should at this point become clearer. From the standpoint of *tradition* educational enquiry emerges in a context where members of a particular community of *educators* are seeking ways of reconstructing their traditional practice in response to social change, and in doing so to develop themselves as practitioners of the craft of teaching. Part of that enquiry is the philosophical task of reformulating a theory of education about the universal goods which characterise its ends. (In doing so they will need to enter into a conversation with past educational thinkers through engagement with their texts.)

From the standpoint of *tradition*, educational goods are internal to the process of education rather than extrinsic consequences. The philosophical task is therefore appropriately a task for those who have 'inside' experience of education as a practical craft. It certainly cannot be accomplished independently of that practice. This is because it also involves seeking answers to the practical question of how an educational theory can be enacted in the contemporary lives of educational practitioners, including that of the theorist, given their particular biographies and circumstances. Doing philosophy in the context of educational enquiry, viewed as a form of moral enquiry, therefore involves doing action research as a means of evaluating and testing the practical validity and intelligibility of a universal educational theory. On this view action research does not privilege practice in relation to theory; rather it witnesses to the unity of theory and practice.

Educational action research as the practical enquiry dimension of a moral educational science is not simply an activity that follows after the independent philosophical development of an educational theory. In testing a theoretical stance, by enacting it in particular circumstances, action research can reveal ambiguities in that stance and thereby problematise it in ways that prompt further theoretical reflection. It ensures that theoretical stances do not become permanently fixed and remain open to the complexities of action in particular situations. This is precisely what MacLure argued a post-modern version of educational action research would do.

From the standpoint of *tradition* the claims to truth which emerge from theoretical and practical enquiry in education are justified on the grounds that they represent, not final answers to the theoretical and practical questions addressed, but more comprehensive answers than those previously achieved. This often involves addressing ambiguities and tensions in current practices that stem from unresolved issues presented by the theoretical stances they embody, e.g. between subject-centred and child-centred theories of education. From the standpoint of *tradition*, in order to advance educational theory and practice, an educational moral science grounded in action research must acknowledge that educational practice is 'criss-crossed by different regimes of truth'. Again, according to MacLure, educational action research could only do this if it operated from a post-modern standpoint.

The conjoint development of educational theory and practice through an educational moral science will display discontinuities with the intellectual and practical achievements of the past. In doing so, however, such development will also display continuity with past theory and practice. Although the claims to truth of such a science are always acknowledged to be provisional they do assume an epistemological *stance* which transcends *relativism* and *subjectivism*. Such claims imply an advance on existing theoretical and practical knowledge in the form of a movement towards both a fuller understanding of and a better realisation of an ideal for education, which although never fully comprehended and realised is necessary to posit as an end-in-view.

Towards a reconstruction of contemporary discourse about the nature of educational enquiry

I have attempted to show that an account of educational action research articulated from the standpoint of *tradition* is not vulnerable to the kind of post-modern critique of action research provided by MacLure, in which the claims of some contemporary action research theorists, like myself, are distorted by being represented as examples of modernist thought structures. The question then arises as to which of these rival standpoints, that are in many respects incommensurate with each other, offer the best basis for reconstructing educational enquiry in the post-modern and post-liberal academy? Which standpoint can summon up the intellectual and moral resources to free educational enquiry from the inheritance of an *encyclopaedic view of scientific rationality*? What seems reasonably clear to me is that the most productive discourse about the nature of educational enquiry in the future will transcend the debate between modernists and postmodernists.

The most productive antagonism that has to be established and accommodated, both inside and outside the academy, will be the encounter between the post-modern (genealogical) standpoint and the standpoint of *tradition* that has been so eloquently rearticulated in the context of contemporary thought by MacIntyre. From the latter standpoint the challenge to post-modernism, as the inheritor of *genealogy*, is whether it can emancipate itself from constantly defining itself against the standpoint it is trying to overcome. As I have tried to show with respect to MacLure's critique of action research it is paradoxically this tendency to engage in a form of bipolar thinking that blinds the post-modern analyst to a standpoint that cannot be understood in terms of the contrasts and distinctions s(he) employs. If the genealogical standpoint of the post-modern thinker fails by its own standards to escape the thought structures that characterise the standpoint it has so effectively discredited, and MacIntyre believes that it is too early as yet to draw such a conclusion, then it is vulnerable to being overcome by a third standpoint which can show that it has the resources to accommodate much of its critique of post-enlightenment rationality, while not being caught up irrevocably in its shadow. It is therefore important that the philosophical task of elaborating an account of educational enquiry from the standpoint of *tradition*, in which action research plays a central role, proceeds by means of an antagonistic critique of the genealogical standpoint represented by post-modern thinkers in the field of education. Such a critique should provide little comfort for those researchers who continue to reproduce encyclopaedic habits of thinking within the academy. It will involve, following MacIntyre's question of whether one can construct from the standpoint of *tradition* a *genealogy of genealogical thinking*, not only identifying the defects and limitations of the rival point of view, such as I have attempted in this paper, but also explaining them.

What might such a *genealogical deconstruction of genealogy* look like from the standpoint of *tradition*. MacIntyre perhaps points the way with his example of where a genealogy of Nietzsche's genealogising might begin:

> The answer: with what Aquinas says about the roots of intellectual blindness in moral error, with the misdirection of the intellect by the will and by the corruption of the will by the sin of pride – where Nietzsche saw the individual will as a fiction, as part of a mistaken psychology which conceals from view the impersonal will to power, the Thomist can elaborate out of materials provided in the *Summa* an account of the will to power as an intellectual fiction disguising the corruption of the will. The activity of unmasking is itself to be understood from the Thomist standpoint as a mask of pride.
>
> (p. 147)

If this is anything to go by a genealogy of post-modern genealogising in the field of education will be very antagonistic indeed. This poses the question of whether contemporary academia and its conventional ways of sustaining discourse can accommodate such an antagonistic stance. At the same time we should be aware that such antagonism has a constructive dimension because a genealogist of post-modern genealogising, operating from the standpoint of *tradition*, will also show how what is true and insightful in the rival account can be incorporated into his or her own theoretical and practical enquiries.

[. . .]

References

Couture, J.-C. (1994) Dracula as Action Researcher, *Educational Action Research Journal*, 2(1), pp. 127–132.

Elliott, J. (1978) Classroom Research: Science or Commonsense, in McAleese, R. and Hamilton, D. (Eds) *Understanding Classroom Life*, NFER Publishing Co: Windsor, Berks.

—— (1980) Educational Action-research, in *Research, Policy and Practice* (Eds) John and Stanley Nisbet, Kogan Page: London, Ch. 18.

—— (1983) Self-evaluation: professional development and accountability, in *Changing Schools – Changing Curriculum* (Ed.) Galton, M. and Moon, R., Harper and Row: London, Ch. 15.

—— (1987) Educational Theory, Practical Philosophy and Action Research, in *British Journal of Educational Studies*, 25(2), pp. 149–160.

—— (1989) Teacher Evaluation and Teaching as a Moral Science, in *Perspectives on Teacher Professional Development* (Eds) Holly, M.L. and McLoughlin, C.S., Falmer Press: London and New York.

—— (1991) *Action Research for Educational Change*, Open University Press: Milton Keynes and Philadelphia.

—— (1996) Curriculum Study in *A Guide to Educational Research* (Ed.) Gordon, P., Woburn Press: London and Portland, OR; Ch. 11.

—— (2002) Making Evidence-based Practice Educational, *British Educational Research Journal*, Vol. 27, No. 5.

Elliott, J., MacLure, M. and Sarland, C. (1997) *Teachers as Researchers in the context of award bearing courses and degrees*, ESRC Report (Ref.R000235294).

Hammersley, M. (1993) On the Teacher as Researcher, *Educational Action Research Journal*, 1(3), pp. 425–446.

—— (1995) 'Playing Aunt Sally: an open letter to Pat D'Arcy', *Educational Action Research Journal*, 3(1).

MacIntyre, A. (1990) *Three Rival Versions of Moral Enquiry*, Duckworth: London, esp. Chs 2, 3, 6, 9, and 10.

MacLure, M. (1995) Postmodernism: a postscript, *Educational Action Research*, 3(1), pp. 105–126.

Somekh, B. (2000) Changing conceptions of action research, (Eds) Altrichter, H. and Elliot, J., *Images of Educational Change*. Buckingham: Open University Press.

Stronach, I. and MacLure, M. (1997) *Educational Research Undone – The Postmodern Embrace*, Open University Press: Buckingham.

CHAPTER 12

THE STRUGGLE TO REDEFINE THE RELATIONSHIP BETWEEN 'KNOWLEDGE' AND 'ACTION' IN THE ACADEMY

Some reflections on action research

Educar, No. 34, 2004, pp. 11–26, Universitat Autònoma de Barcelona

Action research and the theory-practice relationship

Action-research might be defined as '*the Study of a social situation with a view to improving the quality of action within it.*

(Elliott, 1991, p. 69)

This definition appeared in my book '*Action Research for Educational Change*' (1991) and is widely cited in books and papers on action research. Rather than feeling pleased about this, I find myself annoyed and irritated. Why? Because I feel that the authors neglect my attempts to redefine the relationship between theory and practice in terms of the idea of action research. At times they appear to be using my definition to place a tight boundary between action research aimed at the improvement of practice and research aimed at the construction of theory. The drawing of such a tight boundary is often based on the assumption that the practical knowledge which stems from action research is non-theoretical in character because its value is entirely instrumental to the task of improving practice as a means to an end. Such an assumption implies that the pursuit of practical knowledge through action research is for the sake of practical goals that can be defined independently and in advance of the action research process, whereas research aimed at the construction of theory is the pursuit of knowledge for its own sake. Conceived in such instrumental terms, practical knowledge has no value in itself, and is set against theoretical knowledge regarded by those who pursue it as valuable in itself. My own work was being selectively appropriated to legitimate a conception of action research which privileged practice over theory, whereas I had seen it as an attempt to redefine the relationship between theory and practice in a way which dissolved the dualism.

[. . .]

Earlier in '*Action Research for Educational Change*', I am more explicit about the relationship between the practical aim of action research and the production of knowledge.

> The fundamental aim of action research is to improve practice rather than to produce knowledge. The production and utilisation of knowledge is subordinate to, and conditioned by, this fundamental aim.

(p. 49)

As I shall explain more fully later, I was trying to signify *the primacy of the practical standpoint* as a context for knowledge generation. I was saying that in the process of action research the intention to produce knowledge cannot be separated from the intention to improve practice. However, I see now that my words can be read as *a privileging of practice over theory*. Just as to privilege theory over practice implies the exclusion of the practical standpoint, so to privilege practice over theory excludes the theoretical standpoint.

Research that privileges practice over theory does not dissolve the theory-practice dualism by linking theory to practice. It simply excludes the theoretical standpoint. In doing so, it is shaped by the same assumptions which shape forms of educational research that privilege theory over practice; namely, that 'theory' consists of generalisable representations of events that are generated through inquiries that are dissociated from the practical intentions of human agents. In failing to challenge these assumptions, much of what counts as action research in the field of education fails to dissolve the dualism between theory and practice. It simply sets up a tension inside the academy with those forms of educational research that privilege 'theory'. Educational action research is pitted against educational science, and as such confined to a lowly status in the academic hierarchy of knowledge as a minor 'sub-discipline' in the field of educational research (see Elliott, Maclure and Sarland 1996).

The shared assumptions outlined above positively shape the conduct of educational (science) whereas they negatively shape the conduct of educational action research. They effectively exclude action research from the domain of public knowledge and confine it to the domain of private knowledge. In terms of these assumptions, public knowledge is defined from a standpoint which privileges theory over practices. From this standpoint, what counts as public knowledge is determined by considerations concerning the validity and truth of theoretical propositions rather than considerations concerning their practical usefulness. The latter may be important to address but they are extrinsic to the activities of knowledge production. In the UK, educational researchers are being asked to address the relevance of their research to potential users before they design it, and to play a more active role in disseminating their findings to the public. Although researchers may regard such considerations as important they are viewed as quite distinct from methodological considerations about the conduct of the research itself.

What counts as public knowledge generally determines what gets published. Academics who wish to support action research with teachers and other professional practitioners (e.g. nurses and social workers) tend in the main to publish accounts of the research process and methodology. The knowledge outcomes are often not deemed to be of sufficient status to report and find acceptance in prestigious academic publications. Academic action researchers tend to find themselves marginal players in the educational research establishment. Most of them go along with this. They compensate by identifying with communities of practitioners and may acquire the status of 'big fish' in the small action research pool inside the academy, but they leave the domain of educational research essentially intact and unchallenged.

Currently the most influential challenge to this domain inside the academy is stemming from the ideas of post-structuralist thinkers like Derrida, Lacan, Lyotard and Foucault (see Belsey, 2002). From the perspective of post-structuralist educational researchers, such as Stronach and MacLure (1997), inasmuch as the idea of action research privileges practice over theory it is trapped in the patterns of dualistic thinking that characterise the western tradition of enlightenment thought established by the philosophy of Descartes. I will now examine the post-structuralist challenge to enlightenment thinking with a view to asking what its implications are for the theory-practice problem and the idea of action research as a resolution of this problem.

The post-structuralist challenge and the theory-practice relationship

It is often assumed that theorising is a mental activity and action a physical activity. In this mind-body dualism resides the problem of theory and practice. From a theoretical standpoint the 'self' is a thinking subject that construes the world as an object of contemplation rather than an object of change. Descartes' 'Cogito ergo sum' (1968) established 'the self' as a substance whose essence is thinking and therefore the primacy of the theoretical over the practical standpoint. From the standpoint of the 'Cogito', reasons for action have their source outside the context of the practical affairs of everyday life in the contemplative knowledge of the 'thinking subject'. Such knowledge can therefore be applied to practice but not derived from it. The 'Cogito' has defined the relationship between theory and practice in the western enlightenment tradition and shaped the process of knowledge production within the academy. In doing so it challenged traditional authority on matters of belief and constituted a declaration of independence. As the Scottish philosopher John Macmurray (1957, p. 75) explained, if to think is my essential nature then "I have the right and the duty to think for myself, and to refuse to accept any authority other than my own reason as a guarantor of truth." This logic was radically challenged by Macmurray himself as well as by the post-structuralist and post-modern thinkers on the European continent during the latter half of the 20th Century.

Post-structuralist thinkers elaborated on the work of Saussure (1916, trans 1974) and brought the idea of the substantial self whose essence is thinking into question, and along with it the idea of reason as a guarantor of truth. According to Saussure, 'meanings' such as theories about the world do not originate from a 'thinking self'. The latter is a product of the meanings individuals learn from their culture, and that originate in its symbolic systems or discourses. The words and other symbols that make-up a language do not refer to meanings that exist outside the language itself. They neither represent an objective order of things in the world nor the ideas of a thinker that exists independently of their use within the culture. Meaning resides in the sign, not beyond it. It is differential rather than referential (see Belsey, 2002, p. 10) in the sense that it is culturally differentiated and has no existence beyond the words and symbols that signify it.

Post-structuralist thought deconstructed a conception of theoretical knowledge as the product of a thinking subject, construed as the 'essential self', contemplating independently existing objects in the external world. If the thinking subject is the effect of learning the trajectories of meaning embedded in the symbolic systems of the culture, then it does not exist as an unconditioned consciousness. The subject is decentered as the origin of thought. It thinks only what it is permitted to think within the culture it is conditioned by. The world it 'knows' is therefore a culturally differentiated one rather than an objective world that exists independently of the knower. One cannot even talk intelligibly of the decentered subject possessing *personal knowledge* for this presupposes a culturally unconditioned consciousness or 'self'. If the objects of knowledge are culturally differentiated and the knower is the effect of culture, then individuals are not in a position to construct purely personal knowledge. What they believe is always what their culture permits. Poststructuralism, through its method of deconstruction, dissolves the binary opposition enshrined in Descartes' *Cogito* between "the knowing subject in here and the objects of its knowledge out there" (see Belsey, 2000, pp. 72–73).

Foucault in particular pointed out the implications of this decentered vision of the subject for the way power operates in society (see 1979a,b). Learning and maintaining the ways of thinking about the world differentiated by the culture, its theoretical and normative discourses, involves submission to the authorities responsible for their transmission and maintenance. For Foucault all social relations connecting the individual to social institutions are relations of power. Power is not a thing some individuals have and others do not, that can be gained or lost. Rather it defines the relation between all individuals and their culture, including those authorities who are responsible for the transmission and maintenance of that culture. The latter exert power in their relations with others by virtue of their own compliance to the culturally differentiated meanings circulating within the society. According to Foucault, this relational conception of power implies the possibility of resistance. Individuals can always refuse to conform, although usually at a price, and create *reverse discourses* to maintain their resistance to the dominant ones operating in the society. Power relations are a site of struggle and conflict. One might indeed interpret the action research movement in such Foucaultian terms as a reverse discourse of resistance to the prevailing discourse of research in the academy; namely one which privileges theoretical knowledge over practice.

From the post-structuralist perspective, 'theories' are not a rational foundation for ordering practical affairs. In learning to apply them to our practices, we are not grounding those practices in objective truths about the objects of our experience, but securing their compliance with culturally differentiated systems of meaning that tell us what to think about what we are doing. Theoretical discourses, understood as systems of culturally differentiated meanings circulating in society, constitute resources for exerting epistemic sovereignty over our practical thinking. The increasingly policy-driven 'evidence-based practice' movement in the UK (see Hargreaves, 1997) that holds professional practitioners (e.g. doctors, nurses, social workers and teachers) accountable for the extent to which they ground their practices in research evidence, is an attempt by the state to get them to base their practical judgements and decisions on the generalisable representations of good practice that are produced by research. From a post-structuralist point of view this movement can be interpreted as an indirect and 'soft' attempt to exert a form of epistemic sovereignty over the practical thinking of practitioners in the guise of fostering rational practices.

If, in applying theory to practice, social practitioners such as teachers are managing their own compliance with culturally determined systems of meaning, how are we to understand the practices shaped by this process? Descartes' 'Cogito' assumes a sharp division between mind and body. Whereas the thinking and reasoning mind is the essence of the self, the body is simply an organism it possesses (see Belsey, 2000, p. 66). When left to respond to its environment on the basis of its own physiological make-up, the movements of the body are entirely independent of the reasoning activities of the mind. However, the thinking and reasoning mind can exert a measure of control over the physical movements of the body as a means of achieving practical ends that transcend the survival needs of the organism. From the standpoint of the 'Cogito', the physical movements of the body (behaviour) are transformed into the practices of a human agent (actions) by the capacity of the mind to impose some form of rational order on them. The post-structuralist challenge to the 'Cogito' nullifies this account of social practices as the effect of rational human agents on the movements of the body and construes social practices as reactions on the part of the human organisms to stimuli in the cultural environment, motivated by their survival needs. Such reactions will involve consciousness but it will take a different form from consciousness conceived in terms of an agent having reasons for action. As Macmurray (1957, p. 167) points out, conscious reactions to environmental stimuli stem from motives connected to the organisms survival needs, rather than reasons for action. The initiative for such behaviour lies with the stimulus as opposed to a human agent, whereas the initiative for action lies with an agent who determines it in the light of their knowledge. From the perspective of post-structuralist theory, social practices are conceived in terms of adaptive responses on the part of human organisms to cultural stimuli rather than in terms of self-initiated actions. Viewed in such terms, the activity of applying theory to practice depicts not so much the process by which human agents rationally determine their actions in the world, as the process by which human organisms consciously adapt their behaviour in response to cultural stimuli.

The post-structuralist challenge, as I have argued, acknowledges the possibility of resistance to the cultural conditioning it depicts. Human beings can inhibit the tendency to adapt to their cultural environment in the required ways but only at the risk of their survival. They can transgress and disrupt hegemonic discourses and even establish *reverse discourses*. However, might such resistances be simply interpreted as negative reactions to cultural stimuli – failures on the part of certain human organisms to adapt appropriately to the prevailing hegemonic discourses within the cultural environment – rather than forming a basis for free action? I shall return to this question a little later.

Hannah Arendt and the philosophy of action

It is interesting to look at the view of social practice implicit in post-modern deconstructions of the prevailing discourses in western societies in the light of Hannah Arendt's account of the *The Human Condition* (1958). As Canovan (1974, p. 54) points out, Arendt focuses her philosophy on describing and evaluating the various forms of human activity, rather than focusing, like most western philosophers have done, on evaluating the products of human thought. Human activity she claimed had not been sufficiently thought about and "its modes not clearly articulated" (Canovan, p. 54). I would argue that such philosophical neglect also extends to post-structuralist thinkers. Their deconstructions of western enlightenment thought appear to leave us with a view of social practices as forms of cultural conditioning, but they are less than clear about the extent to which alternative modes of activity are possible.

Arendt distinguishes three basic modes of human activity: *Labour, Work and Action*. 'Labour' is activity dictated by what is required to sustain life. It is basically life lived under the domination of biological necessity, although Arendt reluctantly acknowledges that in the modern world what is experienced as necessary to sustain life has been extended to cover the consumption of material goods that go beyond the basic necessities of living (see Coulter, 2002, p. 195). Activities of labour involve endless repetition. They are not directed to some end determined by an agent. They focus on means rather than ends. If labour has an 'end' it is simply the perpetuation of life, the successful adaptation of human organisms to their environment, in an endless cycle. The post-structuralist perspective on social practices in western societies appears to render them predominantly activities of 'Labour' in the Arendtian sense of this term.

'Work', according to Arendt, involves the creation of enduring objects or arte-facts for use rather than consumption to satisfy basic needs (see Canovan, 1974, p. 56; Coulter, 2002, p. 197). Unlike 'Labour' such activities have a beginning and a finite ending consciously determined by the workers themselves. Moreover, workers deploy their particular talents and abilities to create their 'works'. 'Work', in the Arendtian sense of the term, calls forth the generative capacities of human beings and, in doing so, as Canavan (1974, p. 56) points out, "is characteristically human as labour is not." From an Arendtian perspective theories or ideas can be regarded as the products of human work. They form part of a cultural environ-ment that human beings create for themselves. Once created, cultural artefacts like theories and ideas stand over against human beings to define their world. Post-structuralist theory only leaves space for conceiving culture as that which stands over against human beings. From this point of view 'the self' is an effect rather than an originator of culture. In destroying 'the self' conceived as a thinking sub-ject passively mirroring an objective world from a contemplative standpoint, post-structuralist theory has difficulty in conceiving of any location for 'the self' other than as an effect of culture. By focusing on human activity and its distinct modes, rather than thinking as such, Arendt is able to explore alternative locations for 'the self' to those of the purely intellectual standpoint and that of an organism reacting to an environment that is set over and against it.

Arendt's third mode of human activity is that of 'action', a category she deploys to vindicate her belief in human freedom (see Canovan, 1974, p. 58; Coulter, 2002, pp. 198–203). 'Action' involves initiating change in a social situation to bring about something new in the web of social relationships that constitute it. The consequences of 'action' for the agent and those effected by them, where they will lead, cannot be entirely foreseen in advance. 'Action' therefore becomes a matter of continuous negotiation with others through the construction in process of 'tran-sient accounts' as it unfolds in the process. The full story of 'action' can only be pieced together after the event.

Since for Arendt 'action' is inextricably linked to communication with others considered as equals, it occurs in public rather than private space, which she regards as the realm of freedom. In this sense it is intrinsically 'political', and is not to be confused with the political organisations human beings establish for the pur-pose of perpetuating their natural biological needs. The sphere of 'action' tran-scends the hierarchical or sovereign relation between governments and their subjects (Canovan, 1974, p. 68).

In the activity of 'labour', human beings are bound by biological necessities and therefore do not engage in them freely. Even in the activity of 'work' their freedom is restricted by the object it aims to create. It is only in 'action' – an activity that changes a human situation by initiating something new – that human beings expe-rience unconstrained freedom. This is because in 'action', in exercising agency to effect change, human beings reveal their unique individuality to themselves and others. This is not 'a self' that they are aware of prior to acting. Human beings learn who they are from their 'actions' in the human world (see Canovan, 1974, p. 59). From an Arendtian perspective 'the self' is located in its 'actions' and the experience of agency which accompanies them.

Since for Arendt 'action' is always carried out in the company of others conceived as free and equal individuals it possesses the twin qualities of *plurality* and *natality*. In 'action' the agent takes into account the unique points of view that others hold towards the situation in question. This is not the same as acting on the basis of a negotiated consensus. In 'action' the agent reveals his or her own distinctive view of the situation, but it is developed in communication with others and accommodates or 'invoices' (my term) their own distinctive outlooks. It is in this sense that Arendt regards 'action' as plural. The more an agent accommodates the plural voices of others, the more his or her activity constitutes 'action'. The concept of *natality* as a quality of action is used by Arendt to contrast 'action' with mere role governed behaviour. In 'action' conditions are created that enable the agent and others to reveal their individuality and uniqueness by starting something new and, in doing so, to transcend what is merely required of them in their roles in life. If 'action' has an aim, it is to enlarge the space in which human beings can relate to each other as unique individuals in the situation. Such an aim is not the intention to produce an outcome or result, but a value built into the process of action itself.

In articulating these distinctive modes of human activities Arendt perhaps achieves what post-structuralist theory fails to; namely, an alternative social location to the 'Cogito' for the existence of 'the self', other than as a mere effect of culture. For Arendt 'the self' only exists in 'action'. However, one might argue that the possibility of 'action' in her sense of the term is what Foucault alludes to when he talks about *resistance* and the *struggle of power*, and indeed what Derrida (1995) is attempting to articulate when exploring the possibility of an *ethics of deconstruction* in his later work (see Belsey, 2000, p. 90). The fact that we live in a culturally differentiated world does not exonerate us, Derrida argues, from the responsibility to acknowledge this in the way we live. Such an acknowledgement may leave no certain foundations for living, but it does leave what he calls 'messianicity', not the hope of realising some utopean or fixed vision of the future but of a different future (see Belsey, p. 91). Within such a post-modern 'acknowledgement' of the possibility of *new beginnings* for human beings lies the 'seeds' of an Arendtian view of 'action' and 'the self' as agent.

I am struck by the parallels between Arendt's account of action and my own account of 'educational action research'. Interestingly Coulter (2002, pp. 189–206), drawing on Arendt's categories, finds few examples of 'action' research reported in his review of papers published in the Educational Action Research Journal compared with 'labour' and 'work' research.

I have always stressed the importance of viewing 'education' as an activity directed by process values rather than objectives which refer to extrinsic outcomes of the activity. Also I have attempted to locate action research in the context of teachers attempts to effect changes in the conditions governing life in classrooms and schools for themselves and their students. Again, in researching educational practice to effect change I have argued that teachers and their collaborators should gather multiple perspectives on the situation in question from their colleagues, students and even parents in the form of *triangulation data*. Finally, the value Arendt places on 'action' in particular human situations, as the context in which human beings realise their freedom and dignity, makes her sceptical about the value of sociological theory couched in the form of generalisable representations of events. She views such 'representations' as potential devices for social control and centralising power within the state. I have argued, consistently with Arendt's position, that action researchers may use such 'representations' as resources to inform their understanding of particular aspects of the situation they face as agents of change, but they should not treat them as 'law-like' generalisations which offer firm prescriptions for what to do. They need to be integrated into a more personal holistic understanding of the situation forged by the agents of change themselves in the course of 'action'. We may refer to such understanding as a *theory of the situation*.

It is to the articulation of such a conception of 'theory', one that is largely hidden from the post-structuralist thinker's gaze, that I shall now turn in the next section. In doing so, I will draw heavily on John Macmurray's 'The Self as Agent' (1957). His standpoint on the location of 'the self' in action is remarkably consistent with Arendt's philosophy of action.

Theorising from the standpoint of action

In this section, I will argue that action research need not exclude the development of a theoretical representation of action, albeit a highly particularised one. One can provide a meaningful account of action research as a process of theorising about a practical situation. This will involve challenging the assumptions that the term 'theory' exclusively refers to generalisable representations of events, which can only be produced under conditions that are dissociated from the intentions of agents to effect change in practical situations. In challenging these assumptions, I hope to demonstrate that improving the quality of action in such situations involves the development of theory. I have elsewhere tended to use the term 'situational understanding' (see Elliott, 1993) to demarcate the theoretical outcomes of action research from theory construed as generalisable representations of events and occurrences.

My account of action research includes rather than excludes theoretical activity as an aspect of the practical. In doing so it dissolves the dualism between theory and practice. Few have articulated the position I shall argue for better than Macmurray. I will begin with the following extract from 'The Self as Agent':

> Action – involves knowledge as its negative aspect. The carrying out of a practical intention therefore involves a development of knowledge – or if you will, a continuous modification in the representation of the Other – as its negative aspect. This indeed is the primary source of that knowledge which comes unsought with the growth of experience.
>
> (p. 179)

Here the use of the term 'negative' to refer to an aspect of action should not be construed as an undesirable characteristic to be excluded from action. For Macmurray, "Practical activity includes theoretical activity, of necessity in its constitution" (p. 180). The latter therefore is secondary to the primacy of practical activity and derivative from it. It is in this sense that it constitutes the negative aspect of action. This in no way implies that knowledge is simply instrumental to action that can be defined independently of it. Macmurray defines 'action' as "a unity of movement and knowledge" (p. 128). Therefore, he argues, "Knowledge is that in my action which makes it an action and not a blind activity" (p. 129).

Donald Schon's idea of 'reflection-in-action' echoes Macmurray's account of *knowledge in action*, although his influential book 'The Reflective Practitioner' (1983) makes no reference to Macmurray's work. However, Macmurray's account of the growth of 'knowledge-in-action' as depicted above does not in itself add up to an account of action research. What is missing is any reference to the intention to seek knowledge of a situation through systematic and self-conscious inquiry (which bears some resemblances to Schon's idea of 'reflection-on-action').

Since this intention must be viewed as the negative aspect of a broader practical intention to change a situation, it would imply that the action undertaken to effect change was developed systematically and self-consciously. Action research may be viewed as *a systematic form of action* in which the theoretical intention to 'modify the representation of the Other', to use Macmurray's terms, arises as the negative aspect of a positive intention to systematically and self-consciously bring about some change in 'the Other', understood as a practical situation for an agent. From this perspective, it is inappropriate to treat educational action research as merely a minor subdiscipline within a broader domain of educational research. It implies a radical reconceptualisation of the domain itself.

Such a position would assert the primacy of the practical and embrace the proposition "I act therefore I am." This implies, as Macmurray argues in 'The Self as Agent', that the self exists only as an agent in a practical situation, who acts with the intention of changing it in some respect. Can we talk sensibly about theorising from the standpoint of practice as opposed to the intellectual standpoint of the 'Cogito'? Like Macmurray (p. 85) I believe we can. Indeed the idea of action research embraces this belief (see Elliott and Adelman, 1996).

To reflect about the world from the purely intellectual standpoint of the 'Cogito' excludes any reference to the self as an agent in action intent on changing the world, since this standpoint presumes that the self is the substance of a mind that thinks about the world independently of any action to change it. Macmurray succinctly summarises the ideal of this intellectual mode of reflection, one which still shapes our educational system in the west and what counts as research in the academy.

> a pure activity of thought which is cool, passionless and completely disinterested, seeking truth for its own sake, with no eye to the practical advantage for the seeker or for anyone else.
>
> (p. 192)

It is impossible for the knowledge produced by this type of reflection to make any direct link with the experience of those who want to effect change in the world. Any link to the action context must be indirectly determined by agents. Macmurray (pp. 192–193) argues that since the intellectual mode of reflection suppresses any feelings the observer of a situation may have towards it, and abstracts features in it which make no reference to the practical valuations of participants as they seek to effect change in it, the knowledge produced can have no practical value in itself other than as a means to an end. From the practical standpoint the knowledge yielded by the intellectual standpoint can only have instrumental significance at best. It is always knowledge of the World-as-means and takes the form of generalised representations of facts about the world in the form of "formulae which express the recurrent patterns of continuance in experience" (p. 198). If Macmurray is correct, then we cannot argue that the Knowledge generated from the intellectual standpoint in the academy is useless knowledge if agents can find a use for it in deciding on the means they will adopt to realise their intentions. However, if one accepts the post-modern critique that the intellectual standpoint masks a will to power and that the 'knowledge' it produces invariably serves the interests of those who wish to coerce and control the activities of others, then one might question its usefulness to ethical agents like teachers who wish to effect change in ways which respect the agency of their students. See, for example my analysis of the control values that shape much of what counts as 'school effectiveness' research (Elliott, 1996).

Macmurray contrasts the intellectual mode of reflection with the emotional mode. In the latter mode, although reflection involves a suspension of action it adopts the standpoint of the agent and proceeds "as though we were in action" (p. 86). In emotional reflection, adopting the practical standpoint does not exclude the theoretical. Since it is this mode of theoretical reflection which lies at the heart of the action research process (see Dadds, 1995), let me now summarise Macmurray's account of it (pp. 198–202).

1   When reflection proceeds as though we were in action it does not abstract from the agent's feelings about the situation. Action is motivated by a feeling of dissatisfaction with a situation and terminated when the agent feels satisfied that the situation has been improved. Reflection involves understanding what makes the situation an unsatisfactory one for the agent, discriminating the possibilities of action in it, and selecting one of these possibilities for realisation in action. Valuation is integral to this mode of reflection. There is a unity of understanding the situation and the valuation of it (see also O'Hanlon, 2002). As Macmurray puts it, "The world is known primarily as a system of possibilities of action" (p. 191). Valuation and Knowledge are the positive and negative aspects of forming and sustaining an intention to change a situation from an unsatisfactory to a satisfactory state. Without them action would be impossible, and in some situations they require a prolonged period when action is suspended for the sake of reflection about the situation from the standpoint of the agent.

2   Emotional reflection seeks to determine a situation as an end in itself. In constructing a representation of a possibility for realisation in action, it expresses a valuation of what is represented as something to be enjoyed for its own sake and not for the sake of accomplishing some further objective. Such a representation will constitute an image of a particular situation yet to be realised. Emotional reflection therefore moves towards a greater particularisation of the representation of the possibility of action (see, for examples in the context of teacher-based action research, Elliott and MacDonald, 1975). This contrasts with the intellectual mode of reflection which seeks generalisable representations of the events and occurrences it selects for attention. It constructs knowledge scientifically. Emotional reflection constructs knowledge aesthetically. Both are activities of knowing and forms of research. Within the intellectual mode of reflection 'theory' refers to generalisable representations of the world while within the emotional mode it refers to a representation of a possibility for realisation in action within a particular situation. However, this does not rule out the discernment of similarities as well as differences through a comparison of cases. Such discernment will take the form of general insights into the problems of effecting change in relation to a practice such as teaching. Action research does not rule out the development of overlapping theories that yield shared insights into the possibilities for action (see, e.g., Ebbutt and Elliott, 1985, Somekh, 2006, pp. 27–28).

Concluding remarks

Action research resolves the theory-practice problem by theorising from the standpoint of the agent in a situation s(he) feels to be unsatisfactory. It need not simply involve the agent who wants to effect the change. Educational researchers in the academy can collaborate with an educational agent by adopting his/her practical standpoint as though they were in the action context. Educational action research need not be exclusively practitioner research. The fact that it is so often construed as such by educational researchers, suggests that they are viewing it as a low level, non-theoretical activity from an intellectual standpoint.

As an emotional mode of systematic reflection, educational action research constitutes an art rather than a science and constructs knowledge aesthetically in unity with the activity of valuation. However, this does not make it any less theoretical.

So how can one explain the resistance in the academy to educational action research? I can only conclude that it is a resistance to educational change effected by teachers. The widespread involvement of teachers as active agents in changing educational situations would reduce the power exerted by academic researchers – perhaps on behalf of the centralising power of the state – over what is to count as knowledge about their practice. This is because theoretical knowledge from the standpoint of educational action is meaningless and valueless if it cannot be validated in action as knowledge of the aims of education, conceived as possibilities for action in a particular situation.

In discussing Arendt's distinction between 'Action' and 'Making', Joseph Dunne (1993, pp. 89–90) highlights her concern about the extent to which the products of 'making' in the sphere of science and technology were increasingly deployed as standards of technocratic efficiency to shape human behaviour. Through her eyes, he points out, the passive adaptation of citizens to the products of science and technology leads to an increasing intolerance of 'action'. This, in my experience, is precisely what is happening with respect to the teaching profession. Governments hold teachers and other public service professionals accountable in terms of 'quality assurance' systems that equate 'standards' with 'value-for-money'. It is the task of educational researchers to 'make' knowledge, in the form of 'generalisable representations' that can be deployed as means-ends rules, to maximise the performativity of teachers in delivering 'value-for-money'. In embracing this task, with national research assessment exercises providing incentives for doing so, mainstream educational researchers will tend to be intolerant of too much 'action' in teaching, and of a form of research which supports it. In this context, action research constitutes a reverse discourse that offers teachers an alternative future.

References

Arendt, H. (1958) *The Human Condition*, University of Chicago Press: Chicago.

Belsey, C. (2000) *Post Structuralism: a very short introduction*, Oxford University Press: Oxford.

Canavan, M. (1974) The Political Thought of Hannah Anendt, Harcourt Brace: New York.

Coulter, D. (2002) Defining Action in Action Research, *Educational Action Research*, Vol. 10, No. 2.

Dadds, M. (1995) *Passionate Enquiry and School Development: a story about teacher action research*, Falmer Press: London.

Derrida, J. (1995) *The Gift of Death*, University of Chicago Press: Chicago.

Descartes, R. (1968) *Discourse on Method*, Penguin Books: London.

Dunne, J. (1993) *Back to the Rough Ground: practical judgement and the lure of technique*, University of Notre Dame Press: Notre Dame, Indiana.

Ebbutt, D. and Elliott, J. (1985) *Issues in Teaching for Understanding*, Longmans: York.

Elliott, J. (1991) *Action Research for Educational Change*, Open University Press: Milton Keynes (published in Spain by Morata: Madrid).

Elliott, J. (1993) Professional Education and the Idea of a Practical Educational Science, in Elliott, J. (Ed.) *Reconstructing Teacher Education*, Falmer Press: London.

Elliott, J. (1996) School Effectiveness Research and its Critics: Alternative Visions of Schooling, *The Cambridge Journal of Education*, Vol. 26, No. 2.

Elliott, J. and Adelman, C. (1996) Reflecting Where the Action Is: an account of the Ford Teaching Project, in O'Hanlon, C. (Ed.) *Professional Development through Action Research in Educational Settings*, Falmer Press: London (originally published in 1973 in *Education for Teaching*).

Elliott, J. and MacDonald, B. (1975) *People in Classrooms*, CARE Occasional Publications No 1, Centre for Applied Research in Education, University of East Anglia: Norwich UK.

Elliott, J., Maclure, M., and Sarland, C. (1996) *Teachers as Researchers in the Context of Award Bearing Courses and Research Degrees*, UK Economic & Social Research Council End of Award Report No R000235294.

Foucault, M. (1979a) *Discipline and Punish*, Penguin Books: London.

Foucault, M. (1979b) *The History of Sexuality*, Vol. 1, Allen Lane: London.

Hargreaves, D. (1997) In Defence of Research for Evidence-based Teaching: a rejoinder to Martin Hammersley, *British Educational Research Journal*, Vol. 23, No. 1.

Macmurray, J. (1957) *The Self as Agent*, Faber & Faber: London.

O'Hanlon, C. (2002) Reflection and Action in Research: is there a moral responsibility to act? *Theory and Practice in Action Research: some international perspectives*, Symposium Books: Oxford.

Saussure, F. de (1974) *A Course in Linguistics*, (transl.) Wade Baskin, Fontana Books.

Schon, D. (1983) *The Reflective Practitioner: how professionals think in action*, Temple Smith: London.

Somekh, B. (2006) *Action Research: a methodology for change and development*, Maidenhead: Open University Press.

Stronach, I. and MacLure, M. (1997) *Educational Research Undone: the post-modern embrace*, Open University Press: Buckingham & Philadelphia.

INDEX